2—

Celebrations on the Bayou

Invitations to Dine in Cotton Country Style

Junior League of Monroe, Inc.

Since 1930 the members of the Junior League of Monroe, Inc. have been improving the quality of life in this community through their volunteer efforts. They have provided the manpower and financial aid to implement programs concerning the elderly, child advocacy, historical preservation, substance abuse, domestic violence, public education, and the arts.

The proceeds from the sale of **Celebrations on the Bayou** will be returned to the community through the League's support of these and other volunteer projects to build a better tomorrow.

Additional copies of **Celebrations on the Bayou** may be obtained by writing or calling:

Celebrations on the Bayou
Cotton Bayou Publications
The Junior League of Monroe, Inc.
P.O. Box 7138
Monroe, Louisiana 71211
(318) 322-3863

Corporate Sponsors
The Emy-Lou Biedenharn Foundation
and
Super 1 Foods

First Edition, First Printing 15,000 copies, November 1989
Copyright 1989
The Junior League of Monroe, Inc.
Monroe, Louisiana 71201

All rights reserved
ISBN 0-9602364-1-4
Library of Congress Card Catalog 89-86012

Wimmer Brothers
Memphis   Dallas
USA

Forword

French, Spanish, African, Native American...Louisiana life has been influenced throughout the centuries by many cultures. The result is that Louisiana has a rhythm all its own. To the south, hot jazz notes reverberate as ageless musicians keep alive the music born out of bondage. To the west, the smaller towns echo with the zydeco refrains of the *Fais-do-do* on Saturday night. To the north, the guitars and banjos search for music as the *Hayride* explodes over the airwaves. And, to the east, a farmer pauses atop a stately Indian mound and listens for the ghosts in the wind.

In Louisiana, life itself is a celebration — of hope, of family, of faith, and of love for the land. Nowhere else are you likely to find more natural beauty, more abundant food, or more hospitable folk. Louisiana's people are a carefree, happy lot who make friends easily and for life. Evidence of their conviviality is their fondness for "getting together" — often on the spur of the moment — to celebrate virtually any occasion.

Celebrations on the Bayou is our attempt to capture some of that spirit and share it with you. In the tradition of our first cookbook, *the Cotton Country collection*, we have assembled the finest recipes indicative of Louisiana's varied cuisine. We've gone one step further this time, however, and suggested menus and parties based on our own particular style of entertaining.

We invite you to join us for 30 "celebrations" --- a glittering *Mardi Gras Buffet*, a whimsical *Cotton Pickin' Picnic*, or even A *Scare Affair*...*If You Dare!* Slow down and experience the hospitality of the South today just as our ancestors experienced it during that earlier, quieter time.

Come look into our homes. There you will find our hearts.

Joie de vivre!

Georgiann Potts

Table of Contents

Whenever the name of a recipe appears in bold type, the recipe is included elsewhere in the book. Consult the index for page numbers.

Whenever an * appears in the list of ingredients in a recipe, there is additional information about the ingredient at the end of the recipe.

Whenever an * appears in a menu, the recipe is not included in *Celebrations on the Bayou*.

The Committee

Cyndy Perry, Chairman

Judy Edmondson, Finance

Martha Jane Upshaw, Sustaining Advisor

Design and Development

Charlotte Breard   Pam Miller   Amy Norris

Production

Brenda Bonin   Kay Dixon   Gretchen Ezernack

Carolyn Perry   Susan Tarver   Kathy Traweek

Lynda Gavioli, Marketing Research Chairman

Beverly Banks, Testing Co-ordinator

Georgiann Potts, Copy Editor/Contributor

Design

Wesson and Associates

Bruce Wesson

Beth Seward

Photography

Peerless Photography

Mark Matthews

Food Stylist

Kay Wright

Cookbook Consultant

Sheryn Jones

Copy Consultant

Ivanette Dennis

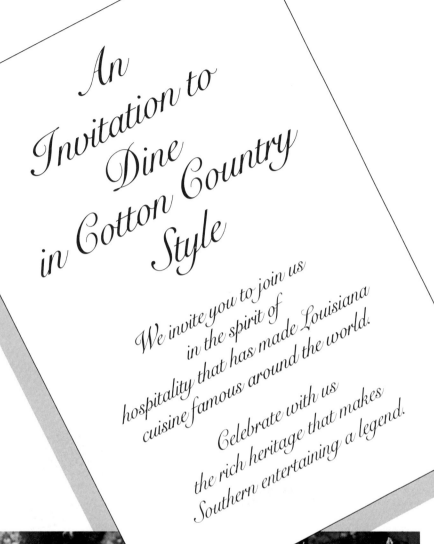

An Invitation to Dine in Cotton Country Style

We invite you to join us in the spirit of hospitality that has made Louisiana cuisine famous around the world.

Celebrate with us the rich heritage that makes Southern entertaining a legend.

Here's To A Good Year

A Cup Of Kindness. . .That Old Team Spirit. . .Auld Lang Syne. . .

New Year's Day — a time for both looking forward and thinking back. On this day we should also pause to celebrate our present with favorite friends, without worrying too much about resolutions either not yet made or already broken. Crackling fires, football games, and hearty fare should mark this day. Traditional favorites, cabbage and black-eyed peas, are laced with piquant spices and eaten for good luck. Spirits soar in the assurance that the New Year will be even better than the old.

Spicy Black-Eyed Pea Dip

Hot Turnip Green Dip
Miniature Mexican Cornbread Muffins

Turkey Jambalaya
Good Luck Cabbage Slaw
Parmesan Garlic Bread

Apple Dapple Cake
Chocolate Sheet Cake
Cinnamon Coffee

Monterey Vineyards Classic Red
Monterey Vineyards Classic White

Menu for 10

A Tapestry Of
Venetian Treasures

Favorite ''Finds''. . .Tuscan Treasures. . .Bon Voyage. . .

What better way to celebrate a trip — either one about to be taken, or the memory of one already enjoyed — than to plan a dinner that reflects that journey? Favored treasures from travels afar are splendid sources for inspiration. This exquisite collection of Venetian glass serves as the perfect backdrop for a classic Italian dinner. *Arriverderchi!*

Giant Ravioli with Cheese Sauce Rossi

Melon and Proscuitto*

Chicken Saltimbocca
Greens Roman Style
Broiled Tomatoes Basil
Braided Italian Bread

Lemon-Orange Cups with Cardinal Raspberry Sauce

With the Giant Ravioli
Orvieto

With the Chicken Saltimbocca
Valpolicella or Bardolino

Menu for 6

Take A
Slow Boat To China

Chopsticks . . . Incense . . . Jade Dragons . . .

Sounds of firecrackers popping incessantly and gigantic paper dragons moving snake-like through the streets set the tone for this extravaganza. Whether you are "officially" welcoming the Year of the Tiger or simply looking for an excuse to give a glittering dinner party, this Chinese New Year celebration is just the affair. Although the preparations are time-consuming, the result is well worth the effort. Why not invite a good friend to co-host so that you can share both the tasks and the anticipation of this stunning event? Then gather your favorite friends and enjoy a slow-paced evening that reflects the ambiance of the Orient. Why, even the venerable Charlie Chan would feel comfortable here!

Walnut Chicken Strips

Hot and Sour Soup

Pot Stickers

Shanghai Red-Cooked Chicken
Ginger and Green Onion Lo Mein

Dry Sautéed Shrimp

Mu Shu Pork

Oriental Oranges

Tsing Tau Beer
Hot Tea

Menu for 12

Mardi Gras Buffet

Me Oh My . . .Crawfish Pie. . .Throw Me Somethin' Mister!. . .

Carnival is a season of feast and frolic — spicy food, elaborate costumes, and parades with royalty. Once famous only in New Orleans, this festival is finding an eager following in the Northern region of Louisiana and beyond. Our Mardi Gras Buffet featuring typical Creole foods adapts perfectly whether for dinner to honor the King and Queen before the Ball or to restore high spirits to costumed Revelers following a parade. So join the merriment, and remember: *Laisse-Bon Temps Rouille!* (Let the Good Times Roll!)

Avocado Mold

Crawfish Etouffee Pie
Mardi Gras Salad
French Bread

White Chocolate Cloud
Café Brûlot

— Heavy Beer —
St. Pauli Girl Dark

— French Wine —
Côtes-du-Rhône

Menu for 8

17

New Beginnings

Silver Spoons. . .Rosebuds. . .Blessings And Feasts. . .

What happier celebration can there be than one which marks life's beginning? Whether the expected child is the first or the fourth, family and friends gather to rejoice with the mother-to-be. A wicker baby carriage overflowing with gifts. . .a table set with the finest linen. . .the doll-like quality of heirloom christening gowns. . .these are the elements that create the perfect setting for this glorious celebration of a new beginning.

Olive Cheese Turnovers

Bloody Marys

Southwest Chili Strata

Minted Fruit Baskets

Ham and Asparagus Roll-Ups

Mocha Ice Cream Cups

Amaretto Coffee*

Domaine St. George Chardonnay

Menu for 8

A Plantation Easter

Baskets... Bonnets... Bunnies...

At Eastertime spring bursts forth with colorful bouquets of nature's most spectacular creations. Azaleas and dogwood blend with tulips, daffodils, and jonquils in the shadows of ancient oak trees. Children revel in the early morning egg hunts punctuating the air with their delighted squeals. Fresh spring lamb with all the trimmings is the perfect choice to mark this celebration of winter's end.

Hot Shrimp Puffs

Roast Leg of Lamb with Mint Gravy
Fresh Julienne Carrots*
Brussels Sprouts with Walnuts
Man-Pleasing Potatoes
Creole Rice Pilaf
Old-Fashioned Buttermilk Biscuits

Kiwi Fruit Collage
Carrot Cake Supreme

Châteauneuf-du-Pape

Menu for 8

Afternoon Delight

White Gloves. . .Pearls And Petals. . .Demitasse. . .

When the azaleas bloom, thoughts turn to a delightful afternoon tea. Whether to announce an engagement or simply to initiate the rites of spring, friends gather together in celebration. An arbour of silk roses transforms a tea table into a "basket" holding the spectacular *Chilled Raspberry Soup, Strawberry Iced Brie,* and fresh vegetable bouquet.

Chilled Raspberry Soup

Avocado Bacon Sandwiches
Cucumber Sandwiches with Dill
Shrimp Delight Spread on Bread Rounds

Crabmeat Ravigoté in Tart Shells

Vegetable Bouquet of
Steamed Asparagus Spears and Snow Peas*
Celery and Carrot Sticks*
Cauliflower and Broccoli Flowerets*
served with
Lemon Anchovy Dip
Dilly Dip

Roquefort Cheese Ball with Green Apple Slices
Strawberry Iced Brie

Hummingbird Cake   *Tiny Meringues*
Orange Walnut Cake   *Chocolate Mocha Filling*
                                          Lemon Filling

Spring Punch
Beringer White Zinfandel

Menu for 80

Welcome
To The Neighborhood

New House. . . New Friends. . . New Life. . .

Welcome to Louisiana where neighborhoods still exit and people go out of their way for each other! The frenzy of moving is eased by Southern hospitality at its best. Gather the neighbors and make new friends. The best of Louisiana's seafood bounty is offered in a combination of lump crabmeat, shrimp, and pasta. What better way to greet newcomers than to surprise them with a glass of wine, an unexpected meal, and the chance to establish new bonds?

Pesto Bread Rounds

Seafood Manicotti
Salvatore's Italian Salad
French Bread

Chocolate Strawberry Cheesecake

French Macon Village

Menu for 12

Wedding Celebration

Something Old...Something New...Something Just For Two...

If home really *is* where the heart is, then what better place could there be to exchange the vows of a lifetime? The final round of parties begins with the Bridesmaids' Luncheon, that traditional time of tears and laughter when lifelong friends remember. Then comes the Rehearsal Dinner, with its toasts and conviviality. And finally, the wedding itself...an aura of innocence and a celebration of love. This is, and always will be, the romance of the South.

Bridesmaid Luncheon

Cold Zucchini Soup

Shrimp and Artichoke Orleans
Fresh Steamed Asparagus*
Baked Tomatoes with Pesto
French Rolls*

Summer Sorbets
Ginger Jumbles

French White Burgundy

Menu for 8

Wedding

Dinky's Peppered Beef
Crusty Rolls*

Avocado Party Shrimp

Cheese Doubergé
Party Pâté

Raw Vegetable Platters*
Creamy Buttermilk Dressing

Chef Han's Poached Salmon

Crawfish "Tout Etouffee"
Toast Points

— Tea Sandwiches —
Smoked Chicken Salad
Sliced Louisiana-Style Country Ham
Minted Apricot Spread

Fruit and Cheese Trays*

Wedding Cake*   Bishop's Punch
Groom's Cake   Champagne

Rehearsal Dinner

Shrimp Pâté with Basil Butter
Toast Points
New Orleans Oysters
Cajun Catfish Bits

Breard's Outdoor Rib-Eyes
Dressed New Potatoes
Vegetables and Herbs Julienne

Pralines 'n Cream Crepes

Robert Mondavi White Table Wine
Robert Mondavi Red Table Wine

Menu for 20

For Love Of Liberty

Family Fun...Flags...Fireworks...

A rootin' tootin' celebration in the grandest Southern style! From bicycles, scooters, and skates, to baby's red wagon, each parade marcher keeps his own time to the local band's version of ''Stars and Stripes Forever.'' The parade disperses to family picnics featuring a new twist on the favorite barbeque — catfish straight from the bayou waters — with the freshest mid-summer vegetables. As evening comes, the community gathers on the river levee to view the fireworks finale. God bless America!

Domangue's Grilled Fish

Cajun Fried Fish

Tartar Sauce

New Potato Salad

Country-Style Okra and Tomatoes

Corn on the Cob with Basil Butter

Garlic French Bread*

Coca-Cola Cake

Ruston Peach Ice Cream

Coca-Cola

Assorted Beer

Menu for 12

Shrimp Night

Start Early . . . Move On . . . Everyone Cooks! . . .

One of the most endearing of Southern traditions is the progressive supper where each course is prepared and served at a different house. Just a truck ride away from coastal waters, fresh Gulf shrimp provide the centerpiece for this perfect menu for just such an occasion. Temptation to linger over *Shrimp and Corn Gumbo* must be avoided for each course features mouth-watering delicacies served in a special setting!

D'Arbonne Smoked Shrimp or Riverboat Marinated Shrimp

Louisiana Shrimp and Corn Gumbo
Pita Triangles

Shrimp DeSiard
Mixed Green Salad* with Tarragon Vinaigrette
New Orleans French Bread*

Brandy Alexander Pie

Assorted Beer
Simi Chardonnay

Menu for 8

A Brunch
In The Country

Icy Bloody Marys. . . Hot Jazz. . . Fun "Way Down Yonder!". . .

Nestled on the bayou bank beside a cozy Creole cottage, the brunch table awaits guests eager to enjoy a midday repast. Recipes which evoke the flavors of New Orleans are served in the leisurely style of the Old South. Stroll among the trees sipping long, cool drinks while remembering — for the moment — that earlier time, that slower pace.

Pistachios*

Champagne Fleur dé Lis

Bloody Marys

Veal Benedict or Louisiana-Style Country Ham

Cheese Grits

Creole Cream Cheese with Minted Fresh Fruit

Banana Fritters

Praline Cream Puffs

Menu for 12

Lazy Summer Supper

Casual . . .Colorful . . .Carefree . . .

After the heat of a summer's day, friends gather outdoors for an impromptu early evening supper. Taking advantage of the lingering daylight, the host lays plans for a challenging round of croquet. A sampler of summer vegetables compliments the quickly-grilled chicken satisfying warm-weather appetites. An array of freshly-picked flowers from the garden adorns the dinner table, and the crisp white wine enhances the meal and the mood.

Avondale Vegetable Spread

Mesquite Grilled Chicken with New Potato Skewers
Tomato and Pesto Salad
Cajun Squash
Peasant Bread

Louisiana Blue-Ribbon Peach Cake

Italian Pinot Grigio or Glen Ellen Chardonnay

Menu for 8

A Little Romance

Champagne. . .Candlelight. . .Cherished Moments. . .

A quiet evening on the balcony at sunset — soft music, cool breezes, lingering conversation — a night just for two. The food has been lovingly prepared in anticipation of the moment. Perhaps this most private of celebrations is to mark a special event — an anniversary, a promotion, a long-awaited purchase, or simply "found" time suddenly free to spend together. In true Southern style, the interlude is relaxed and nourishing to both body and spirit. These are the times of which memories are made!

Scallops and Bacon Broil

Veal Milanese
Fettucine with Sun-Dried Tomatoes
Roast Asparagus

Chantilly Creme with Strawberries

With the Veal Milanese
— French Chardonnay —
Meursault or Puligny Montrachet

With the Chantilly Creme
— Champagne —
Veuve Clicquot

Menu for 2

A Taste Of
Old Mexico

Sangria. . .Sombreros. . .Strolling Guitarists. . .

The vibrant colors and spicy flavors of Old Mexico and the zest of Southern cooking team to create a feast of unique Mexican fare. A kaleidoscope of decorations — terra-cotta, cacti, and colorful peppers — set the mood for this poolside fiesta. Collectively these entrées create a sumptuous spread; individually each entrée is a meal unto itself. The caramelized dessert is reminiscent of a Mexican flan but is a long-time favorite from Southern kitchens. *Bueno Appetito!*

Frozen Margaritas

Queso Flamedo

Crab Toastadas

Chicken Enchiladas

Grilled Flank Steaks with Sautéed Red Onions

Pico de Gallo

Sangria Blanca

Caramel Delight

Menu for 12

Oysters And Wine
On The Deck

A Wine Tasting . . . With An Oyster Twist! . . . Louisiana Luscious . . .

With "The Oyster" starring at this wine tasting celebration, friends share in the food preparation and bring their favorite Chardonnay. A variety of the finest oyster dishes compliment the California wines. The fresh fruit dressing is a perfect palate cleanser to enjoy before surrendering to the temptation of the sumptuous *White Chocolate Cake.* Wonderful menu . . . delightful setting . . . pleasant dreams!

Smoked Oyster Rounds

Grilled Oysters á la Mr. B

Oyster Tarts
Don Juan Oysters
Oysters Rockefeller Casserole

Fresh Fruit*
Delectable Fruit Dressing

White Chocolate Cake
Demitasse Coffee*

— California Chardonnay —
Saintsbury
Groth
Burgess

Menu for 12

Cotton Pickin' Picnic

A Moveable Feast...A Sophisticated Tailgate...Unabashed Class...

Where cotton is still "King," a contemporary twist on a classic theme is a midday feast for a gentleman planter. Would Scarlet have ever served Rhett in a cotton field? Probably not, but if she had, here's her menu. Not the usual wicker basket fare, but then this isn't the usual picnic. So go with the whim, polish the silver, and head for the field!

Creamy Potato Leek Soup

Pita Bread Pockets*
Fajita Chicken Filler
Marinated Beef Salad
Chef Salad Stuffing

Assorted Mustards*
Zorba's Greek Olives
Squash Pickles
Pickled Okra*
Stilton Cheese and Green Grapes*
Cheddar Cheese and Apples*
Assorted Nuts*

Applelicious Bread
Carrot Nut Bread
Harvest Loaf

Assorted Beer
Light Italian Frascati Wine

Menu for a Crowd

Harvest Dinner

Falling Leaves . . . First Frost . . . Fruitful Bounty . . .

Fall is harvest time in the South, a time to gather in the crops that have been so carefully nurtured during the year. It is a time of completion when man sees his labors rewarded. What better way to celebrate the successful harvest than with a juicy, rare leg of lamb grilled to perfection and laced with rosemary sprigs? The best Cabernet Sauvignon California has to offer is the finishing touch to an elegant yet carefree, cool-weather dinner.

Barbecued Pecans

Squash Bisque

Butterfly Leg of Lamb
Salad with Baked Brie on French Bread
Vegetable Tien

Elegant Apple Tart

Cabernet Sauvignon

Menu for 10

The Lure
Of The Wild

Tradition . . . Comaraderie Of The Hunt . . . Sportsman's Paradise . . .

The tradition of fathers hunting with sons and then grandsons may be traced back for generations in Louisiana. But the celebration doesn't end with the kill. A true "Hunt Celebration" includes proudly serving the evidence of the successful hunt to friends and family. Our four-course feast prepared by the master of the house features a trio of Louisiana's most desirable wild game.

Feta Cheese Triangles

Hunter's Choice Duck Gumbo

Grilled Venison Backstrap
Grilled Quail with Mustard Butter
Roasted Zucchini
Elegant Eggplant Bake
Camouflage Carrots
Sweet Pototo Rolls

Pecan Fudge Pie

French Burgundy or California Zinfandel

Menu for 10

A Scare Affair...
If You Dare!

"Ghoulies...Ghosties...Things That Go Bump In The Night..."

In Louisiana, Halloween is for everyone. Clad in elaborate costumes, young and old alike gather for traditional Halloween trampings. While our featured food is for kids, beware of what might appear! The Princess Bride downs *Spooky Soup* while the pirate Jean LaFitte escapes with the prized treasure *Peanut Butter Pumpkin Balls*. As Matilde stirs her *Witches' Brew Punch*, Dracula munches on *Scaramel Crunches*. Ooooooooooo "Deliver us!"

Spooky Soup
"Pumpkin Face" Cheese Puffs

Ghost Cookies
Peanut Butter Pumpkin Balls
Scaramel Crunch

Witches' Brew Punch

Menu for 30

Pilgrim's Progress

Pumpkins . . . Pilgrims . . . Plenty . . .

The celebration of Thanksgiving is a uniquely American holiday that emphasizes family, home, and harvest. In Louisiana, families gather for a bountiful dinner featuring the traditional turkey and dressing enhanced by spicy Louisiana specialities. No need to improve on tradition here.

Pumpkin Soup

Nutty Cranberry Mold
Marie Louise's Turkey and Gravy
Down Home Cornbread Dressing
Southern Sweet Potato Ring
Spicy Louisiana Spinach
Petits' Pois and Pearl Onions*
Asphodel Bread

Chocolate Pecan Pie
Apple Cream Pie

Nouveau Beaujolais

Menu for 12

Objects Of
Art And Champagne

Matisse, Mozart, Monet . . . Symphonic Harmonies . . . Impressionism . . .

Always a gala affair, a buffet honoring patrons of the arts is a celebration of man's response to beauty. This versatile menu — featuring a variety of native Louisiana masterpieces — offers a blend of cuisines which are themselves works of art. Whether your celebration is an elegant cocktail buffet at the museum for opening night or a post-event dinner in your home, the result will be the same. A toast to the Arts!

Italian Stuffed Mushrooms

Crabmeat Toast Rounds

Marinated Shrimp and Tortellini

Spanakopita

Salmon-Stuffed Cherry Tomatoes

Herbed Cheese Balls

Artichoke, Mushroom, Caper Marinade

Amaretto Sabayon with Strawberries,
Bananas and Raspberries

Toffee Almond Squares

Priscilla Cookies

French White Rhone Wine
— California Sparkling Wine —
Chandon
— French Champagne —
Moet et Chandon

Menu for 40

Christmas Memories

Ho Ho Ho...Cinnamon-Laced Cake For Santa...Sunrise Surprise...

Natural garlands of lush magnolias and other evergreens, a crackling fire, and the traditional reading of a *Cajun Night Before Christmas* — this is a Southern Christmas. There may not be snow, but there is excitement for all Louisiana children from one to one hundred! Whether gathered for an intimate brunch to exchange special gifts, or helping the younger children prepare refreshments for their very own party, everyone enjoys this magical season...So, please, Santa! Don't be late!

Christmas Morning Brunch

Magnolias

Ambrosia
Cheesy Sausage Crepes
Cinnamon Coffee Cake Ring
Coffee

Menu for 8

Christmas Cocktails

Wild Duck Pâté

Brie en Phyllo

Grilled Pork Tenderloin
Tangy Pork Sauce
Rolls

Crabmeat Celebré
Toast Points

Trout Burre Blanc

Lemon Tarts
Cottonland Cheesecakes
Turtle Candy

Menu for 60

Children's Christmas Party

Fruit Fondue* with Orange Sauce
Reindeer Noses
Open-Faced Ham and Cheese
Sandwiches*
Gingerbread Muffins
Cookie Monster Delight
Christmas Sugar Cookies
Red and Green Popcorn*
Rudolph Punch
Hot Chocolate*

Menu for 50

Desserts

A Southern tradition for generations, the invitation to drop over for dessert is one that is eagerly accepted. And why not, when the desserts are as lovely as these? Confections that delight the eye as well as please the palate draw rave reviews. As Shakespeare wrote, ``All's well that ends well.''

Appetizers and Beverages

THE BAYOUS OF LOUISIANA

Before the advent of highways and telephones, the waterways of Louisiana served as the major means of communication and transportation for her people. The mighty Mississippi River was joined by other smaller rivers to form the main thoroughfares, while the sleepy bayous were the "quiet streets" connecting man with "civilization." At one time the 120-mile Bayou Lafourche was called "the longest village street in the world." Even today, with modern highways and satellite communications systems linking all parts of the world, boating down the bayou is still a unique and favorite way of "visiting" your neighbor in Louisiana.

An aura of mystery and romance haunts the bayous of Louisiana. Some of them, such as Black Bayou, are dark, swampy, mossy streams lined with cypress and oak that trail whispy streamers of Spanish moss. They teem with an abundance of wildlife from bass, bream, and perch to nutria, turtles, ducks, alligators, snakes, frogs, snowy egrets, blue herons and countless other birds nesting in the marshland. The twilight songs of the cicadas and frogs joined by the cries of the birds as they fly among the towering trees is an eerie concert that makes traveling bayous such as the Black an unsettling experience.

Not all of Louisiana's bayous are as dark and mysterious as the Black, however. Others, such as Bayou DeSiard here in Monroe, are broad expanses of water that teem with tamer wildlife and provide recreation for North Louisianians. Beautiful homes line both banks while fishing piers and boating docks stretch out across the waters. These slow-moving waters are disturbed by the rapid waves of ski boats as well as the gentler circles made by paddlers easing into the inlets for one last cast before nightfall. Families picnic along the banks celebrating every occasion imaginable. Children learn to fish and to swim at an early age, and when they are older can be found playing hooky down on the bayou skiing. When the humidity is at its highest, there is no better escape than a quick dip. While cicadas, frogs, and birds also sing their twilight songs along Bayou DeSiard, the effect here is hypnotic and soothing.

Barbecued Pecans

2 Tablespoons butter or
   margarine
¼ cup Worcestershire sauce
1 Tablespoon ketchup
2 dashes hot pepper sauce
4 cups pecan halves
Salt

In a large saucepan, melt butter. Add Worcestershire, ketchup, hot pepper sauce, and stir in pecans. Spoon into a *glass* baking dish, spreading evenly. Toast at 400 degrees for 20 minutes, stirring frequently. **Watch carefully for they will easily burn.** Turn out on a paper towel and sprinkle with salt.

Apache Cheese Bread

1 9-inch Apache* loaf of bread
16 ounces sharp Cheddar
   cheese, grated
1 8-ounce package cream cheese,
   softened
1 8-ounce carton sour cream
½ cup minced green onions
1 teaspoon Worcestershire sauce
2 4½-ounce cans green chilies,
   chopped
1 cup chopped ham

Cut the top off the bread, reserving top, and scoop out the inside. Combine remaining ingredients and mix well. This will be a very stiff mixture. Fill the bread with the cheese mixture, replace the top, and place on a cookie sheet. Bake in a 350 degree oven for 1 hour and 10 minutes. Serve with tortilla chips or tear and dip with the bread.
*Any hard round loaf of bread may be used.

Use this cheese dip to start your Fiesta.

Brie en Phyllo

12 sheets of phyllo pastry
1 pound sweet butter, melted
1 whole Brie, not fully ripe,
   about 5 pounds

Butter baking sheet large enough to hold the Brie. Lay 5 sheets of phyllo on a baking sheet, brushing melted butter on each layer. Set Brie on top of the phyllo and fold the edges of the phyllo up around the cheese. Cover top of cheese with 6 sheets of phyllo, brushing melted butter on each layer. Tuck ends of pastry under the cheese. Fold last sheet of phyllo in a 1-inch wide strip. Brush it with butter and cut into leaf shapes. Decorate top of Brie with phyllo leaves and again brush with butter. Bake for 20-30 minutes or until golden brown. Let stand for at least 30 minutes before serving.
20 servings

Phyllo dough usually comes in a 1 pound package, containing 24 or more sheets, and is found in the freezer section of most large supermarkets. Let phyllo defrost in refrigerator for at least 2 days. When ready to work with dough, be sure it is completely defrosted. Unwrap the dough, unroll it, and cover immediately with towel. Let sit 15 minutes. Moist phyllo is easier to handle. Have a damp cloth handy to moisten if necessary.

Strawberry Iced Brie

Wheel of fresh Brie cheese
Strawberry Neufchâtel cheese*
Fresh strawberries
Ginger snaps

Ice top and sides of fresh Brie cheese with softened strawberry Neufchâtel cheese. Decorate with fresh strawberries and greenery. Serve with ginger snaps.
*Cream cheese puréed with sweetened strawberries may be substituted for Neufchâtel cheese.

A spectacular presentation.

Cheese Doberge

2 8-ounce packages cream cheese, softened
2 Tablespoons finely chopped green onion tops
2 Tablespoons anchovy paste
1-2 teaspoons fresh dill*
Few drops lemon juice
Dash of hot pepper sauce
5-6 slices deli Swiss cheese, cut ¼-inch thick and 4 x 6 inch pieces

In bowl of food processor, combine cream cheese, green onion, anchovy paste, dill, lemon juice, and hot pepper sauce, and process until smooth. "Ice" the Swiss cheese as you would a cake. Spread the cream cheese mixture between layers of Swiss cheese, then cover top and sides. Cover tightly with **wax paper** and refrigerate until creamed cheese mixture is hardened. Preparing 24 hours before serving enhances flavor. Garnish with finely chopped dill weed and serve with cracked wheat crackers.
*If fresh dill is not available, dill weed may be substituted.
25 servings

For a nice change, add a can of drained chopped shrimp to the cream cheese mixture, reserving some of the chopped shrimp for garnish.

Herbed Cheese Balls

2 8-ounce packages cream cheese
4 ounces Bleu cheese
2 Tablespoons chopped parsley
2 Tablespoons chopped chives
½ cup chopped walnuts

Herb mixture:
¼ cup finely chopped parsley
¼ cup finely chopped chives

Allow the cheeses to come to room temperature. Place the cheeses in bowl of food processor and blend well. Add parsley, chives, and walnuts, blending well again. Form into 1-inch balls. A melon baller works well for this. Chill. Combine the parsley and chives. Roll the balls in the herb mixture. Refrigerate until serving time. Serve with baguette French bread rounds.
Makes 5 dozen.

This cheese mixture could be served in a crock with assorted crackers.

Feta Cheese Triangles

1 pound phyllo pastry
1 pound Feta cheese, crumbled
2 eggs, slightly beaten
1 cup freshly grated Parmesan
   cheese
2 Tablespoons chopped parsley
1 cup butter, melted

Prepare Béchamel and allow to cool. Thaw phyllo pastry 15 minutes before using and cover with a damp cloth. To the Béchamel sauce, add the Feta cheese, eggs, Parmesan cheese, parsley, and 3 Tablespoons butter, and mix well. Cut phyllo sheets into long strips, 3-inches wide and brush with melted butter. Place 1 teaspoon of the cheese mixture at the bottom of each strip and fold the corner up to form a triangle. Continue folding as you would a flag. Repeat for remaining strips and until all the filling is used. To serve, place triangles on a cookie sheet, brush with remaining butter, and bake in a 375 degree oven for 15-20 minutes until golden brown. Serve at once. Triangles may be frozen before baking by placing in a single layer on sheets of foil. When frozen, transfer to a sealed container. Bake as usual.
Makes 6½ dozen

Béchamel Sauce

2 Tablespoons butter
2 Tablespoons flour
1 cup milk
Salt
Black pepper
Dash of nutmeg

In a saucepan, melt butter, add flour, and stir until smooth. Gradually add the milk, stirring constantly as it thickens. Season with salt, pepper, and nutmeg. Allow to cool completely.
Makes about 1 cup

Prepare these triangles when you have a free afternoon. Pop them out of the freezer for a terrific hors d'oeuvre.

Nutsnacker

1¼ cup whole natural almonds
4 ounces cream cheese, softened
1 cup Cheddar cheese, shredded
½ cup mayonnaise
5 slices crisp bacon, crumbled
½ cup slivered unblanched
   almonds, roasted and chopped
1 Tablespoon chopped green
   onions
½ teaspoon horseradish, optional
¼ teaspoon salt
⅛ teaspoon pepper

Spread whole almonds in a single layer in a shallow pan. Bake in 300 degree oven for 15 minutes, stirring often, until almonds just begin to turn color. Reserve for garnish. Combine cream cheese, mayonnaise, and Cheddar cheese, mixing well. Add bacon, ½ cup chopped almonds, green onions, horseradish, salt, and pepper. Blend well. Cover and chill overnight. Form cheese mixture into the shape of a pinecone on a serving platter. Beginning at the narrow end, press whole almonds at a slight angle into the cheese mixture in rows. Continue overlapping rows until all the cheese is covered. Garnish at the top with parsley sprigs.
Makes 1½ cups

This makes a nice holiday gift, surrounded by crackers, and with a spreader tied into the ribbons.

Olive Cheese Turnovers

Olive Cheese Filling:
1½ cups grated sharp Cheddar
  cheese
1 4½-ounce can chopped ripe
  olives, drained
½ cup mayonnaise
2 dashes cayenne

Pastry:
3 cups sifted flour
1 teaspoon salt
⅛ teaspoon cayenne
6 ounces freshly grated
  Parmesan cheese
1 cup butter, room temperature
½ cup water

1 egg white, beaten with 1
  teaspoon water

Combine cheese, olives, mayonnaise, and cayenne, and set aside. Sift together flour, salt, and pepper. Stir in Parmesan cheese. Add butter and cut in as for pastry. Add water to make a stiff dough. This pastry may be mixed in a food processor. Roll dough very thinly about ⅛-inch and cut into 2½-3 inch circles. Place a slight teaspoon of filling on half of circle, moisten edges with water, fold over filling, and press edges together with a fork. Prick the top with a fork. At this point the turnovers may be frozen.* For a prettier finished turnover, brush with egg white. Bake on ungreased baking sheet in 400 degree oven 10 minutes or until golden brown. Serve hot.
*Bake frozen turnovers for 20-30 minutes.
Makes 6 dozen

The olive cheese filling makes an easy delicious sandwich spread.

"Pumpkin Face" Cheese Puffs

1 8-ounce package cream cheese,
  softened
2 teaspoons grated onion
2 Tablespoons dried chopped
  chives
½ teaspoon cayenne, optional
¼ cup grated Parmesan cheese
¾ cup grated Cheddar cheese
½ cup mayonnaise
1 small loaf bread, white or
  wheat

Combine all ingredients except bread and mix well. Cut bread into pumpkin shapes with a cookie cutter. Spread each slice with cheese mixture. These may be frozen at this point. Bake fresh or frozen at 350 degrees for 15 minutes.
Makes 36 3-inch pumpkins

For cocktails, cut bread into 2-inch rounds. Makes 100 puffs.

Everyone, young and old, will love these puffs. Perfect to keep in the freezer for a quick nibble.

Roquefort Cheese Ball

4 ounces cream cheese, at room
temperature
4 ounces Bleu cheese, at room
temperature
¼ cup butter
2 Tablespoons chopped fresh
chives
Coarsely ground pecans*

In bowl of food processor, combine cheeses, butter, and chives, and blend together well. Remove to a small bowl, cover, and refrigerate until firm enough to form a ball. Cover the cheese ball with pecans. Serve with fresh green apple or pear slices, warmed French bread, or crackers.

*Toasted sesame seeds may be used in place of pecans.

This cheese ball is great to take along on a picnic. To add zip to a grilled hamburger or chicken breast, roll cheese into a log-shape and cover with sesame seeds. Slice and place on top of meat. This makes an excellent and unique sandwich.

Surprise Cheese Ball

1 pound mild Cheddar cheese,
grated
1 8-ounce package cream cheese
6 ounces Velveeta cheese
·1 cup cooked mashed sweet
potatoes
1 teaspoon Worcestershire sauce
1 teaspoon garlic powder
1 cup finely chopped pecans

Let all cheeses come to room temperature. Combine cheeses, sweet potatoes, Worcestershire, and garlic powder, and mix until smooth. Divide in half and shape into two balls. Roll in pecans. Cover and chill 24 hours. To serve, let come to room temperature and spread on wheat thins.

Your guests will marvel over this cheese ball. The surprise? Sweet potatoes!

Cheese Straws

2 cups grated New York Extra-
Sharp Cheddar Cheese
2 sticks butter
2⅔ cups sifted flour
¼ teaspoon cayenne
½ teaspoon salt

Preheat oven to 275 degrees. In food processor using steel blade, cream together 1 cup cheese and 1 stick butter. Add 1⅓ cups flour, ⅛ teaspoon cayenne, and ¼ teaspoon salt. Process until ball forms around blade. Remove from processor, form into ball, and refrigerate 1 hour. Repeat same procedure with the other half of ingredients. Put dough in pastry gun and form into straws. Bake on ungreased cookie sheets for 20-25 minutes or until crispy.
Makes 4 dozen

For a spicier cheese straw, add another ¼ teaspoon cayenne.

Appetizers

Bayou DeSiard Cheese Logs

Filling:
1 pound mild Cheddar cheese,
 finely grated
6 Tablespoons Miracle Whip
1 4-ounce jar chopped pimento
 with juice
2 Tablespoons finely chopped
 fresh parsley
1 scant Tablespoon finely grated
 fresh white onion and juice
¾ teaspoon garlic powder
¼ teaspoon cayenne
¼ teaspoon salt

28 slices white bread

Combine the filling ingredients and mix well. Cover and chill overnight. Allow cheese to come to room temperature to spread. Trim crust from 3 sides of bread and lightly spread 2 Tablespoons cheese mixture on the bread. Beginning with the crusted edge, roll up tightly, and place on a foil-lined baking sheet. Spread about 1 teaspoon of mixture on top of each cheese log. Fill and spread remaining logs. At this point the cheese logs may be frozen. Bake in a preheated 400 degree oven until brown, about 8 minutes. Serve warm.
Makes 28 logs

Minted Apricot Spread

1 3-ounce package cream cheese,
 softened
1 17-ounce can apricots, drained
 and chopped
1 Tablespoon honey
1 Tablespoon chopped mint

Beat cream cheese until smooth and fluffy. Stir in remaining ingredients. Serve on white or whole wheat bread.
Makes 2½ dozen tea sandwiches

If fresh mint is not in season, substitute ¼ cup chopped pecans to make a delightfully delicious spread.

Swiss Artichokes and Crab

2 14-ounce cans whole artichoke
 hearts
2 cups mayonnaise
Parsley flakes
Hot pepper sauce
Lemon juice
White pepper
Salt
Lemon pepper
1 pound fresh crabmeat
3 cups grated Swiss cheese

Chop artichoke hearts and allow to drain in a colander. Season mayonnaise to taste with parsley flakes, hot pepper sauce, lemon juice, white pepper, salt, and lemon pepper. Add crabmeat, cheese, and artichokes, and mix well. Adjust seasonings. Place in a lightly greased 11-inch quiche dish or 2-quart baking dish. Bake at 350 degrees until cheese melts and it is lightly browned around the edges. Serve warm with toast points.
12 servings

Artichoke, Mushroom, Caper Marinade

2 pounds small fresh
   mushrooms, cleaned
2 14-ounce cans artichoke
   hearts, drained and quartered
1 3.25-ounce jar capers,
   drained

Marinade:
1 cup tarragon vinegar
½ cup vegetable oil
1 teaspoon minced garlic
2 Tablespoons Worcestershire
   sauce
½ cup Catalina French Dressing
⅓ cup Pickapeppa
½ cup sugar dissolved in ½ cup
   hot water
1 teaspoon salt
1 Tablespoon curry powder
2 Tablespoons lemon juice

In a large container, combine whole mushrooms, artichokes, and capers. In another bowl, combine the marinade ingredients and whisk until blended. Gently toss the marinade with the vegetables. Refrigerate. Drain well before serving. This is especially pretty on a big shallow platter with a bed of red-tip lettuce leaves and garnished with red bell pepper rings.

Best prepared one day ahead of time. Beautiful! Good! Different! This is also good as a salad with grilled meats. Everyone will want the recipe!

Avocado Mold

1 envelope unflavored gelatin
¼ cup cold water
1 cup mashed avocado, about
   2-3 ripe
1 Tablespoon lemon juice
1 .6-ounce package Italian
   dressing mix
1 pint sour cream
3 Tablespoons chopped parsley
¼ teaspoon hot pepper sauce
2 tomatoes, chopped
1 cucumber, chopped
1 4-ounce can chopped black
   olives
1 bunch green onions, chopped

Dissolve gelatin thoroughly in water. Mix together the avocado, lemon juice, Italian dressing, sour cream, parsley, and hot pepper sauce. Stir into the gelatin. Pour into well-greased 1½-quart ring mold. Refrigerate until firm. Unmold and fill center and top of mold with chopped vegetables. Serve with crackers.
Makes 4 cups

Men love this mold.

Zesty Guacamole

½ cup chopped purple onion
1 8-ounce package cream cheese, softened
1 10-ounce can Rotel tomatoes
7 avocados, medium size
1 Tablespoon lemon juice
1 teaspoon lemon pepper
Few dashes hot pepper sauce
Salt
Black pepper

Chop onion in food processor. Add cream cheese and process until smooth. Add Rotel tomatoes and process quickly. Pour mixture into a bowl. Chop 6 avocados, one at a time, in processor. Add to mixture. Cut the last avocado into chunks and add to the mixture. Add lemon juice, lemon pepper, then season to taste with hot pepper sauce, salt, and pepper. Serve with **Crab Tostadas** or tortilla chips.
Makes 4 cups

Avocado Bacon Sandwiches

8 slices bacon, preferably smoked
¼ cup lemon juice
¼ cup water
1 ripe avocado
½ cup **Mayonnaise**
1 Tablespoon butter
½ teaspoon Worcestershire sauce
Hot pepper sauce to taste
24 slices thin white bread, crust removed

Fry bacon over medium-low heat until golden brown, drain, and chop finely. Mix lemon juice and water together in a small bowl. Halve, peel, and thinly slice avocado, dip into lemon juice mixture, and drain well. In a bowl, combine mayonnaise, butter, Worcestershire, and hot pepper sauce. To assemble the open-faced sandwich, cut bread slices in half, lightly coat one side of each slice of bread with mayonnaise mixture, top with avocado slice, and sprinkle with bacon bits.
Makes 4 dozen

Cucumber Sandwiches with Dill

1 8-ounce package cream cheese, softened
1 .6-ounce package Italian dressing mix
2 teaspoons milk
1 large cucumber
1 loaf Pepperidge Farm Party Rye Bread
Dill weed

Combine cream cheese, dressing mix, and milk. Set aside for at least 30 minutes to allow flavors to blend. Slice cucumbers very thin. Cut bread into 1½-inch rounds. Spread cream cheese mixture onto bread slices, top with a cucumber slice, and sprinkle with dill weed. Refrigerate. These may be made ahead if covered carefully.
Makes 3 dozen

Dilly Dip

2 cups sour cream
2 cups mayonnaise
3 Tablespoons dill weed*
3 Tablespoons dried, minced
  onions
2 Tablespoons Beau Monde
  seasoning
2 Tablespoons parsley, flakes or
  fresh

Mix all ingredients together the day before serving. Cover and refrigerate. Serve with chilled raw or steamed vegetables. This is excellent with all types of raw vegetables such as celery, carrots, broccoli, or cauliflower.
*Six Tablespoons fresh dill may be substituted for dill weed.
Makes 4 cups

For the Ladies Tea, **Afternoon Delight,** *serve dill dip in a hollowed out red pepper for color. Arrange fresh steamed asparagus on a tray with the red peppers.*

Lemon Anchovy Dip

2 egg yolks
3-4 Tablespoons Dijon mustard
1 2-ounce can anchovies,
  undrained
Juice of 1 lemon
1 shallot, chopped
1 cup vegetable oil
¼ cup sour cream
Salt
Black pepper

Combine egg yolks, mustard, anchovies, lemon juice, and shallot in food processor and mix until smooth. With machine on, slowly add oil. Pour into bowl and stir in sour cream by hand. Season with salt and pepper. Cover and refrigerate.

Serve in bowl surrounded by snow peas in a circular pattern. Garnish with capers. Also good with cucumbers, blanched asparagus, and green beans.

Olive Relish Dip

1 12-ounce jar chili peppers,
  drained, seeded, and finely
  chopped
½ cup pimento stuffed olives,
  drained and finely chopped
1 4½-ounce can chopped black
  olives, drained
4 green onions with tops, finely
  chopped
3 medium tomatoes, finely
  chopped
1 jalapeño, seeded and finely
  chopped, optional
¼ cup oil
2 Tablespoons vinegar

Combine chili peppers, stuffed olives, black olives, green onions, tomatoes, and jalapeño, and mix well. Combine oil and vinegar and stir into vegetables. Chill overnight. Serve with tortilla chips.
Makes 4½ cups

Ole!

Mushrooms Burgundy

Sauce:
4 sticks butter
1 quart Gallo Hearty Burgundy
1½ Tablespoons Worcestershire
    sauce
1 teaspoon dill seed
1 teaspoon black pepper
1 teaspoon garlic
2 cups boiling water
4 beef bouillon cubes
4 chicken bouillon cubes

4 pounds mushrooms, cleaned

In a stockpot, melt butter, then combine remaining sauce ingredients. Add mushrooms. Bring to slow boil on medium heat. Reduce heat, cover, and cook 3-5 hours. Remove cover and cook an additional 3-5 hours until liquid barely covers mushrooms. Let cool to room temperature. At this point do not stir. Pour into container. Reheat to serve. Freezes beautifully.
12 servings

This is an excellent accompaniment to grilled or roasted meats. For cocktails for 100, triple the recipe and serve in a chafing dish.

Italian Stuffed Mushrooms

30 small mushrooms
Olive oil
12 ounces lean bacon
2 small onions, finely minced
2 stalks celery, finely minced
2 green onions, finely minced
½ cup bread crumbs
Garlic salt
Salt
Black pepper
Grated Parmesan cheese

Pull stems from mushrooms and scoop out centers. Chop stems and centers to a fine consistency. Wipe mushroom caps with a damp cloth. Lightly rub each mushroom inside and out with olive oil. Fry bacon over medium-low heat until golden brown, drain, and reserve 1-2 Tablespoons bacon drippings in skillet. Tear bacon into small pieces and set aside. Sauté onion, celery, and green onions in reserved drippings until vegetables are clear, about 10 minutes. Drain well. Add chopped stems and enough bread crumbs to make a moist stuffing. Season well with garlic salt, salt, and pepper. Fill each cap generously with stuffing, top with bacon piece, and dredge in cheese. Arrange caps in a lightly oiled baking dish. Bake at 325 degrees for 10-15 minutes, or until cheese is golden. Serve hot.

Pesto Bread Rounds

3 dozen French bread rounds,
    ¼-inch thick
½ pint PESTO SAUCE
½ pint sun-dried tomatoes
2 cups grated whole milk
    Mozzarella

Toast French bread rounds. Spread each with thin layer of pesto sauce. Top with thinly sliced tomatoes in "X" shape. Cover with cheese and broil until cheese melts. These may be made ahead and frozen.
Makes 3 dozen

Cilantro may be added to tomatoes for an unusual flavor.

Salmon-Stuffed Cherry Tomatoes

11 ounces cream cheese, softened
½ cup coarsely chopped smoked
   salmon*, firmly packed
2 pints cherry tomatoes

Beat cheese. Add salmon and mix well. Fill tomatoes using a pastry bag or spoon. Garnish with fresh dill and capers.
*This is best when a good quality smoked salmon is used.
Makes 4 dozen

"Tomato Hints": Remove the seed and pulp from the non-stem end of the tomatoes with a melon baller. Put the tomatoes cut side down on a paper towel to drain. This may be done the day before if the tomatoes are kept in the refrigerator. Stand them on the stem end and fill using a pastry bag or baby spoon. There are approximately 25 cherry tomatoes in 1 pint.

Spanakopita "Spinach Pie"

1 bunch green onions, chopped
½ cup olive oil
2 10-ounce boxes frozen chopped
   spinach
½ cup chopped parsley
Salt to taste
Black pepper to taste
2 eggs, slightly beaten
1-1½ cups Feta cheese,
   crumbled*
¼ cup freshly grated Parmesan
   or Romano cheese
¼ cup cooked rice
1 pound phyllo
1 stick butter, melted
1 egg, beaten

Sauté onion in oil until tender. Remove from heat, add spinach, parsley, salt, pepper, eggs, cheeses, and rice. Mix well. Place one sheet of phyllo on bottom of greased 9 x 13 baking dish and brush with melted butter. Repeat until 9-10 sheets have been used, brushing each with butter. Add spinach filling and cover with 10 sheets of phyllo, each sheet individually brushed with butter. Butter top sheet. With a very sharp knife, cut through *only* top layers of phyllo, in square or diamond shaped pieces. Beat egg and brush on top. Bake in 350 degree oven for 30-40 minutes or until golden brown. Do not overcook. Allow pie to cool completely before cutting into 1-inch squares. It's a bit messy, and it requires a very sharp, heavy knife, and some patience. You will be adequately rewarded for your pains. May be reheated in microwave.
*Make no substitutions.

The beauty of this dish is that it is wonderful at room temperature. It can be an elegant snack, an hors d'oeuvres, a starter, or a side dish. Work gently but quickly with the phyllo.

Hot Turnip Green Dip

½ cup finely chopped onion
½ cup finely chopped celery
2 Tablespoons butter
1 3-ounce can sliced mushrooms,
   drained
1 10-ounce package frozen
   chopped turnip greens
¼ teaspoon grated lemon rind
1 10¾-ounce can cream of
   mushroom soup
1 6-ounce package garlic cheese
   spread
1 teaspoon Worcestershire sauce
5 drops hot pepper sauce

Sauté the onion and celery in butter until tender. Stir in mushrooms and set aside. Cook turnip greens according to package directions and drain well. Combine drained turnip greens and lemon rind in the bowl of a food processor, and process until smooth. In the top of a double boiler, combine sautéed vegetables, puréed turnip greens, soup, cheese, Worcestershire, and hot pepper sauce, stirring frequently until mixture is well blended and heated. Serve hot with miniature **Mexican Corn Bread Muffins.**
Makes 6 cups

Avondale Vegetable Spread

10 ounces cream cheese, softened
1 8-ounce carton low fat cottage
   cheese
2 teaspoons packaged Ranch
   salad dressing mix
1 Tablespoon Worcestershire
   sauce
1 medium green pepper,
   chopped
1 small sweet onion, chopped
2 Tablespoons sliced black olives
2 small fresh tomatoes, peeled,
   chopped, and slightly drained
1-2 Tablespoons cauliflower, cut
   into tiny flowerets
1-2 Tablespoons corn relish,
   drained, optional

Garnish:
1 Avocado
Lemon juice

Combine cheeses, dressing mix, and Worcestershire, and spread in pie pan or 8-inch serving dish. Add vegetables in circular manner, alternating colors. Just before serving, garnish with sliced avocado which has been marinated in lemon juice. Serve with unsalted crackers.
12 servings

For a more casual dip, combine and toss vegetables then spread over cheese mixture.

Spicy Black-Eyed Pea Dip

½ bell pepper, finely chopped
2 stalks celery, finely chopped
1 large onion, finely chopped
1 teaspoon black pepper
1½ teaspoons hot pepper sauce,
  to taste
½ cup ketchup
1 teaspoon salt
3 chicken bouillon cubes
¼ teaspoon nutmeg
½ teaspoon cinnamon
2 15-ounce cans black-eyed peas
1 15-ounce can Rotel tomatoes
1 clove garlic, pressed
1 teaspoon sugar
½ cup bacon drippings
3 Tablespoons flour

In a medium saucepan, combine bell pepper, celery, onion, black pepper, hot pepper sauce, ketchup, salt, bouillon cubes, nutmeg, and cinnamon. Over low heat, cook and stir until boiling and the cubes have dissolved completely. Add peas, tomatoes, garlic, and sugar, and simmer 30 minutes. Combine bacon drippings with flour and stir into peas. Cook 10 minutes more. Adjust seasonings. Stir well and serve hot with large corn chips.
Makes 4½ cups

This is a unique and delicious way to insure good luck for the coming year by eating black-eyed peas on New Year's Day.

Queso Flameado

Chorizo:
2 pounds pork shoulder
2 large onions
8 cloves garlic, minced
½ cup red wine vinegar
¼ cup Tequila
¼ cup chili powder
1 teaspoon cinnamon
1½ teaspoons ground cumin seed
1 teaspoon corriander
1 Tablespoon salt
1 teaspoon cayenne
1 teaspoon red pepper flakes

Queso Flameado:
1 to 2 4-ounce cans chopped
  green chilies
Whole milk Mozzarella cheese
Tortilla chips

Chorizo ``Mexican Sausage'':
Cut meat into chunks leaving the fat on. Either chop coarsely in the food processor or have your butcher grind it. In the food processor, chop the onions, add remaining ingredients, and blend well. Then knead together with the pork. This is best when allowed to marinate overnight.

Queso Flameado:
In a skillet, brown chorizo into small chunks. Drain. Place in a shallow baking dish. Top with chilies, large slices of cheese, then run under the broiler until bubbly. Serve warm with tortilla chips.
20 servings

Spiked Meatballs

Meatballs:
1 pound ground beef
¾ cup seasoned bread crumbs
1 Tablespoon Parmesan cheese
2 eggs, well beaten
2 Tablespoons finely chopped
    onions
2 Tablespoons finely chopped
    shallots
1 Tablespoon ketchup
6 drops hot pepper sauce
½ teaspoon horseradish
½ teaspoon MSG
½ teaspoon salt
¼ teaspoon black pepper
Butter

Sauce:
½ cup ketchup
¼ cup chili sauce
¼ cup cider vinegar
½ cup brown sugar
2 Tablespoons finely chopped
    onions
1 Tablespoon Worcestershire
    sauce
1 teaspoon MSG
Dash of hot pepper sauce
½ teaspoon dry mustard
9 drops Angostura Bitters
1 teaspoon salt
¼ teaspoon black pepper

Combine the ingredients for the meatballs and mix well. Shape meatballs about ¾-inch in diameter and brown in butter. In a large saucepan, combine the sauce ingredients and simmer for 5 minutes. Add meat balls to the sauce and simmer another 10 minutes. Serve in a chafing dish.
Makes 4 dozen

Dinky's Peppered Beef

5 to 6 pounds boneless eye of
   round, ribeye. or beef roast
½ cup coarse ground black
   pepper or cracked black
   pepper
⅓ cup poppy seeds

Marinade sauce:
4 Tablespoons ketchup
½ teaspoon garlic powder
½ teaspoon onion powder
1 teaspoon paprika
1 cup soy sauce
¾ cup vinegar

First Day:
Trim fat from meat and lay on a flat surface. Combine pepper and poppy seeds and rub into meat with palm of your hand. Completely cover roast using all the pepper mix. Place roast in a shallow baking dish. Combine marinade ingredients and carefully pour over the roast. Cover and refrigerate for 24 hours.

Second Day:
Remove meat from marinade and place on heavy aluminum foil. Pour marinade juice into a bowl and spoon pepper that has settled at the bottom of the dish back over roast. Close foil using sandwich wrap fold. Before making final fold, spoon 8-10 Tablespoons of marinade into foil and close tightly. Place in pan and bake in 300 degree oven for 2½-3 hours. Check after 2½ hours. Do not over cook or the roast will crumble when sliced. When done, remove roast from foil and juices to cool. Reserve juice.

Third Day:
Slice roast. For nice slices, return to butcher where roast was purchased and have sliced. Pour reserved juices over meat. Refrigerate and let stand for at least one day before serving. The longer meat remains in juices the better the flavor. Will keep for several weeks in refrigerator.

A *favorite in our city for years.*

Walnut Chicken Strips

3 chicken breast halves
¼ cup cornstarch
2 teaspoons salt
¼ teaspoon MSG, optional
1 teaspoon sugar
1½ Tablespoons sherry
2 egg whites
2 cups very finely chopped
   walnuts
Oil

Skin and debone chicken breasts. Spread breasts on a cutting board, and with a sharp knife, slice across breast to cut 3 thin layers. Take these layers and slice into 1½-inch strips. There will be quite a few strips. Combine cornstarch, salt, MSG, and sugar. Mixing with a wire whisk, add sherry and egg whites. Dip chicken pieces in the batter, coat with the nuts, and deep fry in oil until brown. Serve immediately.
10 servings

Appetizers

Scallops and Bacon Broil

1 *dozen fresh scallops**
12 *sliced water chestnuts*
6 *strips bacon, cut in half*

Preheat broiler. Wrap a scallop and a sliced water chestnut in each bacon half. Repeat using all the scallops. Broil 4 inches from heat until bacon is crisp.
*Smoked oysters may be used instead of scallops.
2 servings

Eggplant & Pepper Caviar

3 *red bell peppers**
1 *1-pound eggplant*
1 *clove garlic, minced*
½ *tomato, peeled, seeded, and finely chopped*
¼ *cup olive oil*
2 *Tablespoons red wine vinegar*
1-2 *Tablespoons chopped fresh parsley*
2 *teaspoons fresh lemon juice*
½ *teaspoon salt*
Freshly ground black pepper
Lettuce leaves
Chopped green onions

Roast bell peppers according to **Roasted Pepper** recipe then seed and finely chop. Broil eggplants four inches from heat source, turning frequently, until soft and charred. When cool enough to handle, remove skin. Mash pulp in a bowl. Add remaining ingredients and mix well. Adjust seasonings. Refrigerate at least 3 hours. To serve, line platter with lettuce leaves and spoon eggplant mixture evenly over top. Sprinkle with green onion.
*Four green peppers may be used.
Makes 2 cups

KAJMAK "Feta and Cream Cheese Spread"
Used by Yugoslavians as Americans use butter

2 *ounces Feta cheese*
½ *teaspoon salt*
½ *cup water*
1½ *sticks unsalted butter, room temperature*
4 *ounces cream cheese, room temperature*

Drain Feta cheese. Place in bowl of salted water. Let stand 30 minutes. Drain well and pat dry. Combine Feta cheese, butter, and cream cheese in processor or blender and mix just until smooth. Over processing will make butter too soft and texture cannot be corrected. Transfer cheese to crock or bowl. Cover and refrigerate. To serve, bring to room temperature. Arrange tomato wedges over top and decorate with lettuce leaves.
Makes 1¾ cups

To enjoy, spread Kajmak on any good dark bread slices and top with eggplant caviar. Wonderful.

Caviar Ring

6 hard boiled eggs
2 Tablespoons water
2 Tablespoons lemon juice
1 envelope unflavored gelatin
1 cup mayonnaise
2 Tablespoons grated onion
1 teaspoon Worcestershire sauce
Salt
Black pepper
2 2-ounce jars black lump fish
    or caviar

Grate or chop eggs until very fine. In top of a double boiler, combine water, lemon juice, and gelatin, stirring to dissolve gelatin. Add eggs, mixing well. Add mayonnaise, onion, and Worcestershire. Season well with salt and pepper and mix well. Gently fold in caviar. Pour into greased 1-quart mold. Refrigerate 24 hours. To serve, unmold and garnish with lemon slices, parsley, and additional caviar if desired. Serve with toast points.

Beautiful.

Crabmeat Celebré

8-12 ounces cream cheese,
    softened
1½ cups ketchup
3 Tablespoons horseradish
1 Tablespoon lemon juice
2-3 teaspoons Worcestershire
    sauce
Salt
Black pepper
1 pound white lump crabmeat
Fresh parsley, chopped

Spread cream cheese on large shallow platter. To prepare the red sauce, combine ketchup, horseradish, lemon juice, and Worcestershire. Season well with salt and pepper. Spread red sauce on top of cream cheese, sprinkle on the crabmeat, and garnish lightly with the parsley. Serve with unsalted saltine crackers.

Crabmeat Toast Rounds

1 pound crabmeat
2 green onions, chopped
1 cup grated Cheddar cheese
6 Tablespoons mayonnaise
Creole seasoning
1½ loaves bread, cut into
    1½-inch rounds*

Combine crabmeat, onions, cheese, and mayonnaise, and mix well. Place 1 Tablespoon on each bread round. Bake in 450 degree oven for 8 minutes.
*May use English muffins that have been quartered.
Makes 5 dozen

A quick and delicious appetizer.

Appetizers

Fried Crab Claws

2 eggs
½ cup milk
Cajun seasoning
1 pound fresh, peeled crab
   claws, approximately 60
Cornmeal
Peanut Oil

Heat oil to 350 degrees. In a bowl, whip eggs and milk with a pinch of Cajun seasoning. Bathe claws in mixture and coat with cornmeal. Fry until golden brown. Serve with tartar sauce or cocktail sauce.
6 servings

Grilled Oysters á la Mr. B

32 oyster shells
1 stick butter
¼ cup extra virgin olive oil
3 pods garlic, minced
¼ cup lemon juice
Black pepper
32 oysters
Creole seasoning
Parmesan or Romano cheese or
   mixture of both

Before using oyster shells, scrub them well and wash in dishwasher. In a saucepan, melt butter. Add olive oil, garlic, lemon juice, and pepper, and simmer. Prepare grill and place shells on grill for 10-15 minutes to heat. Place 2 teaspoons of sauce in each shell and heat for 5 minutes. Place oyster in shell and sprinkle with Creole seasoning and cheese. Grill with the lid on, until the cheese melts and the oysters begins to curl, approximately 5 minutes. Garnish with parsley or lemon curls. Fresh basil is especially good as a garnish as it imparts a bit of aroma to the oysters.
8 servings

A Louisiana favorite!

Smoked Oyster Rounds

2 1½-pound loaves white bread
Butter
1 8-ounce package cream cheese
⅓ cup milk
¼ cup minced onion
¼ teaspoon Worcestershire sauce
1 clove garlic, minced
¼ teaspoon Creole seasoning
1 3¾-ounce tin smoked oysters,
   drained and chopped

Cut bread into 1½-inch rounds, spread butter on one side, and toast. Whip cream cheese, milk, onion, Worcestershire, garlic, and Creole seasoning together in food processor. Fold in oysters. Butter the untoasted side of the bread rounds and top with a heaping spoonful of the oyster mixture. Bake at 350 degrees for 15 minutes until lightly browned and puffed.
Makes 6 dozen

Quick and easy!

Oyster Tarts

1 quart oysters
3 Tablespoons bacon drippings
3 Tablespoons flour
1 cup finely chopped green
   onions
½ bunch parsley, minced, about
   1 cup
Salt
Black pepper
Hot pepper sauce
4 dozen **Basic Tart Shells**,
   baked

Drain and chop oysters, reserving the oyster liquid in case the mixture is too dry. Oysters emit so much liquid when they are cooked that you seldom need to add any liquid. It is important that they be well-drained beforehand.

In a heavy saucepan, make a medium brown roux by combining drippings and flour, stirring constantly. Add green onions and sauté for 5 minutes. Add parsley and sauté another minute. Add oysters and season with salt, pepper, and a few dashes of hot pepper sauce. Simmer slowly for 15 minutes. Add mixture to tart shells just prior to serving to prevent their becoming soggy. Heat in 400 degree oven for 15 minutes or until bubbly and browned.
Makes 4 dozen

To make an oyster pie, line a 9-inch pie shell with sliced artichoke bottoms, fill with the oyster mixture, and bake until bubbly and browned.

Smoked Salmon Spread

1 8-ounce package cream cheese,
   softened
¼ cup whipping cream
1 green onion, thinly sliced
1 teaspoon fresh lemon juice
Dash of hot pepper sauce
4 ounces smoked salmon, gently
   shredded

Blend cheese and whipping cream in food processor. Add green onion, lemon juice, and hot pepper sauce. Remove to a mixing bowl. Gently fold in smoked salmon. Do not overmix. Refrigerate overnight. Serve with toast points, black bread, or bagels.
Makes 1¾ cups

Hot Shrimp Puffs

1 8-ounce package cream cheese,
   softened
2 teaspoons grated onions
½ cup **Mayonnaise**
2 Tablespoons chopped chives
¼ teaspoon cayenne
¼ cup freshly grated Parmesan
   cheese
1 cup boiled shrimp, chopped*
1 small loaf white bread
Dill weed for garnish

Combine first seven ingredients and blend. Cut bread into 1½-inch rounds and spread each with cheese mixture. Bake in 350 degree oven for 15 minutes, longer for crispier puffs. The bread may be cut and spread with mixture, then frozen. Bake when ready to use. Garnish with dill weed.
*Fresh or canned shrimp may be used.
Makes 2½ dozen

Omit shrimp for a cheese puff which is equally as good.

D'Arbonne Smoked Shrimp

2 *pounds large shrimp*
1 *stick butter*
3 *Tablespoons Worcestershire*
sauce
¼ *cup lemon juice*
2 *teaspoons garlic powder*
1 *teaspoon salt*
1 *teaspoon black pepper*
1 *gallon zip lock bag*
French bread

Peel shrimp, leaving tails on. Rinse shrimp in hot water, drain, and place in zip lock bag. Heat butter, Worcestershire, lemon juice, garlic, and seasonings, and pour hot mixture over shrimp. Freeze early in day or overnight. When ready to serve, heat grill with hickory chips until very smokey. Remove zip lock bag and place block of frozen shrimp in uncovered pan on grill. Close lid and smoke, stirring occasionally. Start testing for doneness in 20 minutes or when butter begins to bubble. Serve with plenty of French bread to dip in pan drippings. The dip is as good as the shrimp! Reheats well in microwave.
4 servings

Dry Sautéed Shrimp

1½ *pounds large shrimp,*
uncooked and unpeeled
8 *large scallions*
3 *Tablespoons peanut oil*
1 *teaspoon salt*
2 *Tablespoons dark soy sauce*
5 *Tablespoons chicken stock*
1 *Tablespoon Szechlean*
peppercorns, optional*
¼ *teaspoon sesame oil*

Wash shrimp and drain well. Cut scallions into 2-inch pieces, discarding green tops, and set aside. In a wok, mix the oil and salt, and heat until sizzling. Using long chopsticks or tongs, place ½ of the shrimp flat in the wok. Fry 2-3 minutes on each side until shells are brown. Remove from wok and set aside. Cook the remainder of the shrimp. When shells are brown, put all shrimp into wok and add dark soy sauce, chicken stock, scallions, and peppercorns. Stir well over high heat until all ingredients are very hot and well blended. Add sesame oil and toss. Serve at once.
*Available in oriental markets.

Riverboat Marinated Shrimp

½ *cup olive oil*
¼ *cup soy sauce*
½ *cup white wine*
2 *Tablespoons lemon juice*
2 *Tablespoons Italian seasoning*
½ *teaspoon ground ginger*
½ *teaspoon garlic salt*
3 *Tablespoons capers*
2 *good dashes hot pepper sauce*
2 *pounds large shrimp, cooked*
and peeled

Mix first nine ingredients and pour over shrimp. Refrigerate for at least 24 hours, stirring constantly. For better results, marinate 48 hours.

So easy and so good!

Shrimp Delight Spread

1 pound peeled shrimp
1 8-ounce package cream cheese,
    softened
¼ cup mayonnaise
2 teaspoons finely chopped
    green onions
2 teaspoons dried parsley
½ teaspoon Worcestershire sauce
¼ teaspoon lemon juice
⅛ teaspoon hot pepper sauce
Dash of paprika
Dash of garlic powder
Salt
Black pepper

Boil shrimp in well-seasoned water. Drain and cool. Coarsely grind shrimp and set aside. Add remaining ingredients in bowl of food processor and process until smooth. Add cream cheese mixture to shrimp and mix well. This may be used for sandwiches or spread on bread rounds. For an excellent salad, coarsely chop the shrimp and all ingredients.
Makes about 1½ cups

For tea sandwiches, serve spread open-faced on 1½-inch bread rounds, topped with a whole small shrimp, and garnished with a dill sprig. This spread will make 6 dozen tea sandwiches.

Avocado Party Shrimp

10 pounds large shrimp
2 cups sliced celery
2 6-ounce jars whole
    mushrooms, drained
½ cup chopped green onions

Avocado Dressing:
2 large ripe avocados, mashed
1 cup lemon juice
½ cup vegetable oil
2 pods garlic, crushed
1 teaspoon red pepper flakes
¼ cup horseradish
¼ cup Creole mustard
2 Tablespoons Worcestershire
    sauce
½-1 cup reserved shrimp liquor

Topping:
1 cup seasoned salad olives
    and/or ripe olives
Red and green bell pepper slices
Fresh basil leaves for garnish

Boil shrimp in well-seasoned water. Drain, reserving 1 cup liquid for dressing. Cool and peel shrimp. In a large bowl, combine shrimp, celery, mushrooms, and onions. Combine dressing ingredients and toss well with shrimp mixture. Chill. Serve on large platter or scalloped shell on bed of colorful lettuce. Top shrimp with red and green pepper rings and mounds of olives. Garnish with basil leaves.
30 servings

A beautiful combination. Stand back and watch it disappear.

Marinated Shrimp and Tortellini

1¼ cups olive oil
½ cup vinegar
⅔ cup ketchup
1 Tablespoon Dijon mustard
1 Tablespoon lemon juice
5 teaspoons horseradish
5 cloves garlic, minced
1 teaspoon hot pepper sauce
1 teaspoon salt
1 teaspoon black pepper

½ cup chopped celery
3 pounds medium shrimp,
   cooked and peeled
1 pound cheese-filled tortellini,
   cooked and drained

Combine the marinade ingredients and whisk until blended. In a large bowl, combine the celery, shrimp, and tortellini and gently toss with the marinade. Refrigerate for at least 24 hours.

Serve this in a clear glass bowl or shell. It makes a delicious first course or a beautiful hors d'oeuvre.

Shrimp Pâté with Basil Mayonnaise

1 pound shrimp, boiled and
   peeled*
⅔ cup dry white wine
1 egg, beaten
1 Tablespoon instant minced
   onion
½ teaspoon thyme
¼ teaspoon salt
⅛ teaspoon black pepper
6 Tablespoons butter, softened

Grind shrimp in food processor or blender turning on and off to make sure all shrimp are finely ground. Add wine, egg, onion, thyme, salt, and pepper, and mix well. Add butter, mixing well. Pour into a lightly greased 2-cup mold or baking dish. Bake in 350 degree oven for 50 minutes. Chill. To serve, unmold, and serve with toast points and Basil Mayonnaise on the side.
*The secret of this recipe is to boil the shrimp in well-seasoned water.

A zesty and light shrimp mold.

Basil Mayonnaise

1 recipe **Mayonnaise**
2 Tablespoons fresh chopped
   basil

Combine mayonnaise and basil and mix well.

Party Pâté

1 14½-ounce can beef broth
1 package unflavored gelatin
½ cup finely chopped onion
3 dashes hot pepper sauce
¼-½ cup sherry
1 8-ounce package cream cheese,
   softened
1 8-ounce package
   Braunschweiger

Heat ½ cup broth in a saucepan. Add gelatin and stir until dissolved. In another saucepan, heat remaining broth with onion, hot pepper sauce, and sherry. Add to dissolved mixture. Pour ½ mixture into a greased 1-quart mold. Chill to set. Combine cream cheese and Braunschweiger in food processor and blend well. Add to remaining broth mixture and mix well. Pour on top of set mold. Refrigerate. Serve with French bread rounds.

Herbs may be arranged in a design in the gelatin after it is slightly thickened. A beautiful effect when served.

Wild Duck Pâté

Gelatin topping:
1 package gelatin
2 cups beef bouillon
2 Tablespoons Worcestershire
   sauce
1½ Tablespoons lemon juice
2 dashes hot pepper sauce

Ducks:
8 Mallard ducks
Salt
Black pepper
Creole seasoning
2 onions, chopped
3 stalks celery, chopped
2 bell peppers, chopped
Red wine
Water

Pâté:
¾ cup reserved duck liquor
3 envelopes gelatin
9 hard boiled eggs, grated
2 small onions, grated
3 stalks celery, finely chopped
2¾ cups mayonnaise

Gelatin topping:
Sprinkle gelatin over ¼ cup bouillon and let stand 5 minutes. In the top of a double boiler over hot water, dissolve the gelatin. Add remaining bouillon, Worcestershire, lemon juice, and hot pepper sauce. Spray a 3-quart mold with cooking spray, add bouillon mixture, and chill until set.

Ducks:
Season ducks with salt, pepper, and Creole seasoning, and rub into skin. Put ducks in roasting pan and cover with onion, celery, and bell pepper. Put a combination of red wine and water in roaster to almost cover the ducks. Cover and bake at 350 degrees for about 2 hours until the ducks are tender. Skin, debone ducks, and put meat in bowl of food processor and process until fine. Strain and reserve ¾ cup duck liquor.

Pâté:
Sprinkle gelatin over ¼ cup reserved duck liquor and let stand 5 minutes. In top of a double boiler over hot water, dissolve gelatin. Add remaining duck liquor and set aside. In a large bowl, combine egg, onion, celery, mayonnaise, and gelatin mixture. Add duck meat and mix well. Pour over congealed bouillon and chill several hours or overnight to set.
50-60 servings

This is especially good with any variety of dark bread.

Beverages

Café Brûlot

2 sticks cinnamon
8 whole cloves
Peel of one lemon
1½ Tablespoons sugar
3 ounces brandy
24 ounces strong, black, hot
 coffee

In a Brûlot bowl or saucepan, place cinnamon, cloves, lemon peel, sugar, and brandy, and heat on an open flame. When brandy is hot, but not boiling, bring the bowl to the table and ignite with match. Use a ladle to stir and pour the liquid around in the bowl for 2 minutes. Pour hot coffee into flaming brandy and then ladle coffee mixture into demitasse cups.
Makes 6 4-ounce servings

Cinnamon Coffee

To brew cinnamon coffee, add 2 teaspoons cinnamon to coffee grounds. Brew "pot" of coffee as usual. Add 2 teaspoons vanilla to pot of brewed coffee. Serve.

Company Coffee

¼ cup non-dairy creamer
¼ cup sugar
¼ teaspoon cinnamon
32 ounces hot coffee

Mix together and serve hot.
Makes 8 4-ounce servings.

Mocha Coffee

4 rounded Tablespoons instant
 coffee
6 Tablespoons chocolate syrup
3 cups boiling water
1 quart sweet milk
½ gallon vanilla ice cream

Stir the coffee, chocolate, and water together and refrigerate. This may be done days ahead of time. To serve, mix the chocolate and milk together in a punch bowl. Spoon in the ice cream.
25 servings

Wonderful for a morning coffee on a hot summer day.

Mint Tea

6 *cups hot water*
5 *regular size tea bags*
6 *sprigs of mint, about 3-4*
   inches each
2 *cups sugar*
¾ *cup lemon juice*
2½ *cups pineapple juice*
1 *liter ginger ale, chilled*

Boil water, tea, and mint for 5 minutes. Remove mint and squeeze tea bags before removing from water. Add sugar, lemon juice, and pineapple juice to tea. Chill. Before serving, add ginger ale and serve over ice.
Makes 3½ quarts

Cool and refreshing

Bishop's Punch

2 *46-ounce cans pineapple juice*
3 *6-ounce cans frozen lemonade*
2 *quarts white grape juice*
2 *quarts ginger ale*
Ivy Ice Ring

Combine first three ingredients in a punch bowl. When ready to serve, add ginger ale and float ivy ice ring.
Makes 5 quarts

Ivy Ice Ring:
Place cleaned ivy vine face down in bottom of ring mold. Add enough water to just cover ivy and freeze. When frozen, fill remainder of mold with water and freeze again.

Pink Perfection Punch

½ *cup sugar*
1½ *cups water*
2 *cups cranberry juice*
1 *cup pineapple juice*
½ *cup orange juice*
3 *cups ginger ale*

In a saucepan, boil sugar and water until sugar dissolves. Cool. Stir in cranberry, pineapple, and orange juices. Chill. Just before serving, add ginger ale.
Makes 2 quarts

Serve this in a champagne flute for a mock pink champagne.

Spring Punch

1 *46-ounce can pineapple juice*
1 *64-ounce jar apple juice*
1 *2-liter bottle Sprite*

Chill juices and Sprite. When ready to serve, combine and serve in punch bowl. This is also beautiful served in crystal pitchers. This may be frozen and served as a slush punch.
Makes 4½ quarts

For the Ladies Tea, **Afternoon Delight,** *double this recipe.*

Rudolph Punch

1 12-ounce can frozen orange
   juice concentrate
1 12-ounce can frozen lemonade
   concentrate
1 quart cold water
1 46-ounce can pineapple juice,
   chilled
1 46-ounce can Hawaiian
   Punch, chilled
1 2-quart jar cranberry juice,
   chilled
1 liter bottle ginger ale, chilled
Ice Ring

Put orange juice and lemonade in punch bowl and mix with water.
Stir in pineapple juice, Hawaiian Punch, cranberry juice, and ginger
ale. Float ice ring fruit side up.
Makes 7½ quarts

Ice Ring:

1 16-ounce jar maraschino
   cherries*, drained
1 8-ounce bottle lemon juice
Water

In a 6-6½ cup ring mold, arrange cherries in an attractive design.
Pour water into mold to partially cover fruit. Freeze. When frozen,
add lemon juice and water to fill mold ¾ full. Freeze. At serving
time, unmold and float, fruit side up, in punch bowl. *Any fruit
combinations may be used but children like cherries the best!

Witches' Brew Punch

2 12-ounce cans frozen orange
   juice concentrate, undiluted
1½ cups unsweetened pineapple
   juice
1 liter ginger ale
Fruit cubes

Mix orange juice, pineapple juice, and ginger ale. To serve Witches'
Brew Punch, place dry ice in a large container, gumbo pot, wash tub,
cast iron pot, etc. In a separate container, add punch and fruit cubes.
Place container on top of dry ice. Smoke will rise around the punch.
Makes 1½ quarts

Fruit Cubes:

Mandarin orange sections
Maraschino cherries
Green grapes

Using standard ice cube trays, fill with water and drop a fruit chunk
into each section. Freeze until solid.

For a summer cooler, fill a tall glass with honeydew melon balls. Pour in
icy cold punch.

Brandy Freeze

½ gallon vanilla ice cream
6-7 ½ ounces brandy
3-4 ½ ounces Creme de Cocoa
Nutmeg

In food processor, blend all ingredients until smooth. Ingredients may be divided into thirds to process. May be made before serving and kept in freezer. Serve in brandy snifters or wine glasses with a dash of nutmeg.
Makes 16 6-ounce servings

As a variation, use Amaretto in place of brandy and Creme de Cocoa.

Champagne Fleur dé Lis

1 12-ounce can frozen pink lemonade
1 6-ounce can frozen limeade
1 6-ounce can frozen tangerine juice
1 bottle champagne, chilled
Mint

Thaw and mix juices. Do not add water. Chill. To serve from punch bowl, pour in chilled juices and add champagne. Serve in punch cups or champagne glasses. To serve from a pitcher, add chilled juices to the pitcher. When ready to serve, pour glass ½ to ⅔ full of juice, then top with champagne. This may be served over ice and garnished with a sprig of mint.
Makes 2 quarts

Magnolias

3¼ cups orange juice, chilled
1 fifth champagne, chilled
⅓ cup Grand Marnier

When ready to serve, mix juice and champagne. Pour into individual glasses, drizzle 2 teaspoons Grand Marnier over juice, and garnish with an orange slice or mint sprig.
8 servings

Frozen Margaritas

Fresh lime
Salt
1 6-ounce can frozen limeade concentrate, undiluted
4 ounces Tequila
1½ ounces Triple Sec
Crushed ice

Rub rim of cocktail glasses with wedge of lime. Place salt in a saucer and spin rim of glass in the salt, if desired. Set prepared glasses aside. Combine limeade, Tequila, and Triple Sec in the container of an electric blender. Blend well. Add crushed ice to fill blender ¾ full, blending well, then pour into prepared glasses. Garnish with a slice of lime. These may be made ahead of time and placed in the freezer in a sealed container. Stir before serving.
6 servings

For the **Gourmet Mexican Dinner,** *have plenty on hand to serve with the* **Queso Flamedo.**

Bloody Marys
''By the Glass''

2 parts V-8 juice to 1 part
   vodka
Lemon juice
Salt
Black pepper
Hot pepper sauce

Combine V-8 juice and vodka. Season to taste with remaining ingredients. Serve over ice and garnish with a celery stick.

''For a Crowd''

2 46-ounce cans V-8 juice
¾ cup Worcestershire sauce
¾ cup lemon juice
3 Tablespoons salt
1 Tablespoon black pepper
10 dashes hot pepper sauce
½ gallon vodka

Combine ingredients several days in advance and refrigerate, stirring at least once a day. Garnish with celery stalks.
Makes 5 quarts

Sangria Blanca

1 fifth bottle chilled dry white
   wine, 3½ cups
½ cup Cointreau*
⅓ cup sugar
1 10-ounce bottle club soda,
   chilled
1 unpeeled orange, sliced
1 unpeeled lemon, sliced
2 unpeeled limes, cut into
   wedges
4 fresh pineapple sticks
1 unpeeled green apple, cut into
   wedges
Small bunches of green grapes

In a clear glass pitcher, combine wine, Cointreau, and sugar until well blended. Chill. When ready to serve, stir in ice cubes and club soda. Garnish pitcher with pieces of fruit.
*Any orange liqueur may be used.
Makes 1 quart

For the **Gourmet Mexican Dinner** have plenty of extra wine and club soda chilled. This light cool drink is a palate pleaser with spicy Mexican fare.

Soups and Salads

THE EMY-LOU BIEDENHARN FOUNDATION
ELsong Gardens, Biedenharn Home, and Bible Research Center

Located in the historical section of ''Old North Monroe'' is a remarkable complex known locally as the Biedenharn Estate. This complex includes the stately Biedenharn family home, ELsong Gardens, and the Bible Research Center and Museum. Every year thousands of visitors enjoy strolling through the award-winning ELsong Gardens, visiting the Biedenharn home, and studying the amazing collections at the Bible Research Center and Museum.

Roses, hydrangea, azaleas, and camellias accent the clipped boxwood hedges, ferns, and ivy to form the backdrop for ELsong Gardens. Seasonal beds of pansies, tulips, caladiums, and other colorful plants nestle against oriental magnolia trees. Fountains brought from Europe add their waterfalls to the scene while laser-activated music greets the guests as they walk through the various walled gardens.

This marriage of music and nature would not have been possible had it not been for the remarkable dream and unrelenting energy of Emy-Lou Biedenharn. The beginnings of World War II halted Miss Biedenharn's successful European career as a concert contralto; she returned to Monroe in 1939 with a desire to bring to Louisiana the beautiful gardens and musical events which she had so enjoyed during her European tours.

Miss Emy-Lou was the daughter of Joseph A. Biedenharn, a prominent Monroe businessman. Mr. Biedenharn was the first bottler of Coca-Cola and an early investor in Delta Airlines, the international carrier that began as a crop-dusting venture in the cotton fields surrounding Monroe. He supported his daughter's plans and declared that the proposed gardens be called ''ELsong,'' for Miss Emy-Lou's ''newest'' song.

And what a song they became! Recently the gardens have been extensively renovated and named to the Smithsonian Institute's list of ''Notable Gardens of Louisiana.'' ELsong Gardens also received the Landscape Architects' 1987 Professional Design and Construction Award.

Set in the gardens as their centerpiece is the gracious Biedenharn home. With its Waterford crystal chandeliers, a silver collection dating from the 1700's, and unusual artistic accessories, this home depicts the lifestyle of an accomplished family who had great enthusiasm for life.

There was also a deeply religious side to Emy-Lou Biedenharn that was reflected when she opened The Bible Research Center and Museum, adjoining the Biedenharn Home and ELsong Gardens, in 1971. Miss Emy-Lou made certain that every feature had distinctive Biblical significance. Many artifacts and rare books were imported from the Holy Land and Europe. The large, priceless collections of rare Bibles, coins, musical instruments, and antique furnishings illustrate the importance of the Bible in American life. Typical of the emphasis on Biblical symbolism are the Carrara marble columns placed an arm span apart to represent Samson's story and the three rooms of custom-woven carpet installed in one piece to honor the seamless robe worn by Christ.

Miss Emy-Lou's legacy, as captured in the ELsong Gardens and the Bible Research Center and Museum, and reflected in her family home, is a celebration of all that she held dear — nature, the Bible, and home. All who visit the grounds become a part of Miss Emy-Lou's ''vision.''

Chilled Raspberry Soup

1½ Tablespoons unflavored
   gelatin
⅓ cup cold water
¾ cup boiling water
3 10-ounce packages frozen
   raspberries, thawed
3½ cups sour cream
1⅓ cups pineapple juice
1⅓ cups Half and Half
1⅓ cups dry sherry
⅓ cup Grenadine
2 Tablespoons lemon juice

Soak gelatin in cold water for 5 minutes. Add boiling water and stir until gelatin is dissolved. Set aside. Purée raspberries in food processor or blender. Combine all ingredients in a glass bowl and cover. Refrigerate overnight. Serve chilled and garnish with mint sprigs and raspberries.
Makes 3 quarts

For the Ladies Tea, **Afternoon Delight,** serve this soup from a crystal punch bowl into demitasse cups. A visually appealing soup—as well as tasty.

Rodeo Roundup Soup

This recipe won the state 4-H contest at Louisiana State University. The wine gives a different but good taste. Can be made in less than 30 minutes.

1 pound ground beef
½ pound hot sausage
1 small onion, chopped
2 pounds block Velveeta, cubed
2 10-ounce cans Rotel tomatoes,
   undrained and coarsely
   chopped
1 cup dry white wine
1 teaspoon jalapeño, optional

Brown beef, sausage, and onion. Drain excess fat. Combine remaining ingredients with meat mixture. Heat to melt cheese and serve.
Makes 2 quarts

Spooky Soup

1 recipe **Mom's Chicken
   Soup**
1½ cups fine egg noodles
1 medium carrot, shredded

To Mom's Chicken Soup add noodles and carrots. Heat to boiling. Reduce heat and simmer until noodles are tender, 10-15 minutes. Serve warm to ghosts and goblins!

Mom's Chicken Soup

1 2-3 pound fryer chicken
12 cups water
1 teaspoon salt
1 teaspoon celery salt
½ teaspoon black pepper
1 chicken bouillon cube
1 beef bouillon cube
1 carrot
1 onion
1 bay leaf

Place chicken in soup pot and cover with water. Add remaining ingredients and bring to a boil. Reduce heat, cover, and simmer for 1½ hours or until chicken is tender. Remove chicken, carrot, onion, and bay leaf from broth. Allow chicken to cool, remove meat from bones, cut into bite-size pieces, and return meat to chicken broth. To skim off the chicken fat, either refrigerate for several hours and skim it off with a spoon, or place lettuce leaves on top of the soup to absorb the fat.
Makes 2 quarts

Serve over rice, sprinkle with Parmesan cheese and grated nutmeg to chase away the winter chills.

Tortellini Soup

1 recipe **Mom's Chicken Soup**

Tortellini:
¼ pound proscuitto
1 cup grated Parmesan cheese
1 egg, beaten
¼ teaspoon nutmeg
Black pepper to taste
1 recipe **Basic Pasta**

Garnish:
Freshly grated Parmesan cheese
Freshly grated nutmeg

Cook Mom's Chicken Soup according to directions. Debone chicken and reserve broth.

Tortellini:
Place chicken and proscuitto in bowl of food processor and process until fine. Add Parmesan cheese, egg, nutmeg, and pepper. This filling makes enough for two recipes of pasta. Freeze the remainder for use at another time. Prepare Basic Pasta recipe and roll into thin strips. Cut out 2-inch rounds with a cookie cutter and put a teaspoon of filling in the center of each. Brush the edges of the dough with water, fold over to form a semi-circle, and press down the edges to seal firmly. Bend the shapes, seam out, to form a circle and press the ends firmly together, moistening them with water. Let dry 2-3 hours. At this point the tortellini may be frozen. Place in a single layer on a baking sheet and freeze. Store in ziplock bags when frozen. This makes 7 dozen tortellini.

To cook the tortellini, bring a large pan of salted water to a boil. A few bouillon cubes may be added to this water. Add tortellini and cook 4 minutes or until pasta is "al dente." Remove tortellini and drain. To serve soup, heat reserved broth and add tortellini, allowing 4-5 tortellini per person. Ladle into soup bowls and sprinkle with cheese and nutmeg.
8 main dish servings or 12 side dish servings

Children love to "help" make tortellini. Keep plenty in the freezer — they will ask for it! The tortellini is also good tossed with **Cheese Sauce Rossi** *or butter.*

Hunter's Choice Duck Gumbo

First Day:
2 large ducks
Salt
Black pepper
Oil
1 onion, quartered
2 stalks celery
¼ green bell pepper
1½ quarts boiling water

Second Day:
4 cups chicken broth, preferably
   hen stock
¾ cup oil
¾ cup plus 2 Tablespoons flour
1 medium onion, finely chopped
4-5 green onions, finely chopped
¼ green bell pepper, finely
   chopped
¼ red bell pepper, finely
   chopped
3 stalks celery, finely chopped
8-10 sprigs parsley, finely
   chopped
¼ lemon, peel included, finely
   chopped by hand
1 pound peeled raw small
   shrimp
2 teaspoons Creole seasoning
2 teaspoons salt
1 teaspoon black pepper
Cayenne
Filé

First Day:
Season ducks with salt and pepper. In a medium-sized stock pot, brown ducks in a small amount of oil. Drain and discard oil. Stuff ¼ onion and ½ stalk celery into each duck. Chop bell pepper, remaining onion, and celery, and place over ducks in pot. Pour water over ducks and vegetables. Simmer over low heat until ducks are tender. Cool and refrigerate overnight.

Second Day:
Skim hardened fat from ducks and stock. Debone ducks being careful to discard "BB's". Cut duck meat into chunks. Heat stock diluting with chicken or hen stock. In a skillet, make a roux with oil and flour, stirring constantly, and brown to a rich caramel color. Heat chopped vegetables until warm and add to roux. Stir and add roux mixture to boiling stock. Stir and simmer 20 minutes. Add shrimp, duck meat, Creole seasoning, salt, and pepper. Season with cayenne, if desired. Simmer until shrimp are done and gumbo is heated thoroughly. Adjust seasonings. Serve over rice and add file', if desired.
8 servings

Soups

Crab Bisque

2 Tablespoons butter
1 onion, minced
1 Tablespoon flour
1 10¾-ounce can condensed
  tomato soup
2 pints Half and Half
1 pound fresh lump crabmeat
1 teaspoon salt
½ teaspoon white pepper
¼ cup sherry

In a heavy saucepan, melt butter and sauté onion until tender. Stir in flour, add tomato soup, and gradually stir in Half and Half. Cook 10 minutes. Add crabmeat, salt, and pepper. Heat through, but do not boil. Add sherry and serve at once.
Makes 1½ quarts

Add a garlic salad and French bread for a light combination straight from New Orleans.

Back Bay Seafood Gumbo

5 Tablespoons bacon drippings
6 Tablespoons flour
2 onions, chopped
1½ cups chopped celery
2 cloves garlic, minced
1 28-ounce can tomatoes,
  chopped
1 8-ounce can tomato sauce
6 cups water
1 Tablespoon salt
1 teaspoon black pepper
1 Tablespoon parsley flakes
2 teaspoons Creole seasoning, or
  to taste
10 drops hot pepper sauce
1 pound package frozen cut
  okra
3 pounds raw medium shrimp,
  peeled
1 pound crabmeat
4 gumbo crabs, optional
1 pint oysters, optional
3 Tablespoons Worcestershire
  sauce

Make a roux by combining bacon drippings and flour, stirring constantly for 30 minutes or until very dark. Add onion, celery, garlic, and sauté 5 minutes. Add tomatoes, tomato sauce, water, and seasonings and simmer 1 hour. Add okra and cook over low heat for 1 hour. Add shrimp, crabmeat, crabs, and oysters and cook 20 minutes. Add Worcestershire and stir well. Serve over rice.
10 servings

Oyster Stew

1 quart milk
1½ teaspoons salt
Paprika
Cayenne to taste
1 Tablespoon Worcestershire
  sauce
1 stick butter
2½ pints oysters, drained and
  cut up, reserving liquid

In a double boiler over boiling water, combine milk, seasonings and Worcestershire. Cook for about 10 minutes. In a skillet, melt butter, add oysters and cook until oysters curl. Add oyster liquor to oysters, stirring well. Add this mixture to milk. Cook for about 15 minutes. Serve warm.
Makes 2 quarts

Serve with **Baked Brie on French Bread**

Louisiana Shrimp and Corn Gumbo

5 Tablespoons olive oil
5 Tablespoons flour
2 onions, finely chopped
1 green bell pepper, finely
  chopped
4 shallots, chopped
2 Tablespoons fresh minced
  parsley
Salt to taste
Black pepper to taste
⅛ teaspoon cayenne
1 teaspoon Cajun vegetable
  seasoning
3 dashes hot pepper sauce
3 dashes Worcestershire sauce
1 Tablespoon basil
1 pound can undrained
  tomatoes, chopped
1 pound frozen corn
3 cups chicken broth
2 pounds small or medium
  shrimp, peeled

In a Dutch oven over medium heat, make a dark roux with olive oil and flour, stirring constantly. When brown, add onions, bell pepper, shallots, and parsley. Sauté on low for 10 minutes. Add salt, pepper, cayenne, hot pepper sauce, Worcestershire, and basil. Simmer 5 more minutes. Add tomatoes, corn, and broth. Cover and simmer over low heat for 1-1½ hours, adding shrimp during the last 15-20 minutes of cooking time.
Makes 2½ quarts

This soup may be prepared ahead of time and slowly warmed to serving temperature.

Seafood Andouille Gumbo

Seafood Stock:

1½-2 pounds medium shrimp, unpeeled

7-8 cups water

Gumbo:

1 cup oil

1 cup flour

1 large red bell pepper, finely chopped

2 medium onions, chopped

3 stalks celery, finely chopped

4-6 cloves garlic, minced

1 Tablespoon salt

3 bay leaves

6-10 dashes hot pepper sauce

1 Tablespoon Worcestershire sauce

½ teaspoon white pepper

½ teaspoon black pepper

½ teaspoon cayenne

½ teaspoon thyme

½ teaspoon oregano

½ teaspoon basil

1½ pounds smoked andouille sausage, sliced ¼-inch thick

15 medium oysters, in liquor, optional

½ cup chopped green onions

Peel shrimp and set aside. In a soup pot, add water and shrimp shells and bring to a boil. Cover and simmer for 20-30 minutes. Strain stock through a colander and put 5½ cups in your favorite gumbo pot, discarding the shells. In a cast iron pot, add oil, slowly add flour, and whisk constantly over medium-low heat until the roux achieves a dark nutty color, about 30 minutes. Take no shortcuts! Add bell pepper, onion, and celery to roux and saute' for 4 minutes. Add garlic and seasonings, and saute' 2 more minutes. Slowly spoon roux and vegetable mixture into stock, bring to a boil, then reduce heat and simmer for 30 minutes. Add sausage, return to a boil, then reduce heat and simmer another 30-45 minutes. Add shrimp, oysters, and green onions. Return to a boil and cook until seafood is done, stirring occasionally. Serve over rice.

Makes about 3 quarts

Cream of Broccoli Soup

3 Tablespoons butter or
  margarine
1 small onion, peeled and
  minced
3 Tablespoons flour
1 teaspoons Morton Nature's
  Seasoning
½ teaspoon Greek seasoning
⅛ teaspoon black pepper
1 pint Half and Half
1⅓ cups chicken broth
½ teaspoon lemon juice
1 10-ounce package frozen
  chopped broccoli, thawed
2-4 Tablespoons grated cheese,
  optional

In a medium saucepan, melt butter then sauté onions until soft, but not brown. Add flour and seasonings and cook slowly, stirring constantly, for 2-3 minutes. Gradually add cream and chicken broth, stirring constantly. Cook slowly until thickened and smooth. Add lemon juice, broccoli, and cheese, cooking slowly and stirring frequently for several minutes to blend flavors. Serve garnished with parsley and croutons. This recipe easily doubles.
4-6 servings

Delicious! Men love this soup.

Acadian Cheese Soup

¼ cup margarine
½ cup diced onion
½ cup diced celery
½ cup diced carrot
¼ cup flour
1½ Tablespoons cornstarch
4 cups milk
3 10-ounce cans chicken broth
⅛ teaspoon baking soda
1 pound American cheese, cubed
1 Tablespoon dried parsley
2 teaspoons salt
1 teaspoon white pepper
½ teaspoon cayenne
Paprika

In a saucepan, melt margarine, add vegetables, and sauté until tender. Stir in flour and cornstarch and cook until bubbly. Gradually add milk and chicken broth, stirring to make a smooth sauce. Add soda and cheese, stirring until cheese is melted. Add parsley and seasonings and simmer at least 30 minutes. Simmer longer if thicker soup is desired. Taste and adjust seasonings. Garnish with a dash of paprika.
Makes about 2 quarts.

Excellent with large homemade croutons.

Soups

Hot and Sour Soup

¼ cup dried black mushrooms
1 cup boiling water
1 Tablespoon cloud ears, 1 large
    ear
10 tiger lily buds
½ pound lean pork
½ cup canned bamboo shoots
1 teaspoon cornstarch
½ teaspoon salt
2 Tablespoons corn oil
6 cups chicken stock
2 Tablespoons soy sauce
½ teaspoon freshly ground black
    pepper
3 Tablespoons cider vinegar
1 Tablespoon cornstarch
    dissolved in 1 Tablespoon
    water
1 Tablespoon sesame oil
2 green onions, minced
Sesame seeds
Black pepper

Put mushrooms in boiling water to soak for 30 minutes. Repeat with cloud ears and lily buds. Discard liquid. Cut off tough mushroom stems and julienne. Cut off any tough spots and coarsely chop cloud ears. Cut lily buds in halves or thirds. Cut pork and bamboo shoots into julienne strips. Mix pork with 1 teaspoon cornstarch and salt. Sauté in oil until gray and remove. Bring chicken stock to boil. Add pork, mushrooms, cloud ears, tiger lily buds, and bamboo shoots. Reduce heat to simmer and cook 5 minutes, stirring occasionally. Add soy sauce, black pepper, and vinegar. (Soup may be frozen at this point. Reheat to moderate to finish.) Add cornstarch dissolved in water and continue stirring for 3-4 minutes. Turn off heat and add sesame oil. To serve, present warmed bowls of the soup and garnishes of green onions, sesame seed, and black pepper.
Makes 1½ quarts

Onion Soup

3 Tablespoons butter
1 Tablespoon olive oil
4 large yellow onions, thinly
    sliced
1 teaspoon salt
½ teaspoon sugar
3 Tablespoons flour
2½ cups beef broth
2½ cups chicken broth
½ cup water
½ cup Vermouth
Individual rounds of French
    bread
Grated Swiss cheese

In an iron pot, melt butter, and add olive oil and onions. Cover and cook slowly for 15 minutes. Uncover pot and add salt and sugar. Cook and stir until onions are golden brown, about 30-40 minutes. Sprinkle flour over onions and stir for several minutes. Add broths, water, and Vermouth. Simmer soup partly covered for 30-40 minutes. Skim any remaining oil from top of soup. To serve, ladle soup into bowls. Float bread rounds and sprinkle with grated cheese.
6 servings

Creamy Potato Leek Soup

8 cups rich chicken broth
4 medium potatoes, peeled and diced
6 celery stalks, cut into pieces
3 leeks cut into 1-inch pieces*
Salt
Black pepper
2 Tablespoons butter, optional

Garnish:
1 cup sour cream
Chopped chives

In a saucepan over medium-high heat, combine broth, potatoes, celery, and leeks. Gradually bring to a boil. Reduce heat and cook until vegetables are tender. In a food processor or blender, purée vegetables in batches with some liquid. Return purée to saucepan, blending well. Taste and adjust seasonings. Simmer over medium heat. For a richer soup, add butter and stir until it is melted. Ladle into bowls and serve with a dollop of sour cream and a sprinkle of chives.
*May substitute 9 green onions.
Makes 2 quarts

This soup is also a tasty treat served at room temperature.

Tortilla Soup

2 Tablespoons vegetable oil
1 green bell pepper, sliced
1 onion, sliced
2 cloves garlic, minced
1·4-ounce can chopped green chilies
6 cups chicken broth
2-3 cups chopped cooked chicken
1 10¾-ounce can tomato soup
1 14½-ounce can stewed tomatoes
2 cups frozen whole kernel corn
2-3 teaspoons Worcestershire sauce
1 teaspoon cumin powder
1 teaspoon chili powder
Salt
Black pepper
Hot pepper sauce
5 tortillas, cut into bite size pieces*
1 cup grated Monterey Jack cheese

In a Dutch oven, heat oil. Add bell pepper, onion, garlic, and chilies, and sauté until tender. Add broth, chicken, soup, tomatoes, corn, Worcestershire, cumin, and chili powder. Season to taste with salt, pepper, and hot pepper sauce. Simmer for about 3 hours. To serve, place tortilla pieces in soup bowl, ladle in soup and top with two Tablespoons cheese. Garnish with avocado or lime slices, if desired.
*May use corn chips.
8 servings

Soups

Pumpkin Soup

6 Tablespoons butter or
   margarine
1 medium onion, finely chopped
½ cup flour
6 cups chicken broth
2 16-ounce cans pumpkin
2 teaspoons lemon juice
¼ teaspoon apple pie spice or
   cinnamon
⅛ teaspoon nutmeg
¼ teaspoon black pepper
Salt to taste
4 cups Half and Half

In a large saucepan, melt butter, add onion, and sauté until tender. Stir in flour, then add broth, pumpkin, lemon juice, and seasonings. Cover and cook 15 minutes to blend flavors, stirring occasionally. Add Half and Half and cook until heated. Do not boil. Serve hot or refrigerate to serve as a cold soup. Garnish with either chopped parsley, sour cream, or lemon slices.
Makes 3½ quarts

Squash Bisque

2 medium onions, chopped
2 Tablespoons butter
1 quart chicken broth
4 cups sliced squash
¾ cup sliced carrots
2 medium potatoes, diced
1 teaspoon salt
1 teaspoon thyme
2-4 teaspoons Worcestershire
   sauce
1 16-ounce carton Half and
   Half

In a saucepan, sauté onions in butter. Add chicken broth, squash, carrots, potatoes, salt, and thyme, and cook only until vegetables are tender. Cool. Purée in food processor. Return to saucepan and add Worcestershire and Half and Half. Heat on *low* and serve. High heat will make the soup curdle.
Makes 2 quarts

This soup is delicious cold, too!

Cold Zucchini Soup

1½ pounds zucchini, peeled and
   sliced
⅔ cups chopped yellow onion
¼ cup chopped green bell
   pepper
5 cups chicken broth
1 cup sour cream
½ teaspoon dill weed
Salt
Hot pepper sauce

In a 3-quart covered saucepan over medium heat, cook zucchini, onion, and green pepper in chicken broth for 30 minutes or until vegetables are soft. Cool. Put in blender and purée until smooth. Add sour cream and dill weed. Stir well to blend. Season to taste with salt and hot pepper sauce. Chill until very cold, 6-8 hours. Garnish with a sprinkle of dill weed. This also is good served warm.
Makes 1½ quarts

Vegetable Chowder

½ cup chopped onion
1 clove garlic, minced
1 cup sliced celery
¾ cup sliced carrots
1 cup cubed potatoes
3½ cups chicken stock
1 10-ounce package frozen
   chopped broccoli, thawed
¼ cup butter or margarine
¼ cup flour
2 cups milk
1 Tablespoon dry mustard
¼ teaspoon white pepper
⅛ teaspoon paprika
2 teaspoons diced jalapeño
2 cups shredded Cheddar cheese
Sherry

In a Dutch oven, combine onion, garlic, celery, carrots, potatoes, and chicken stock. Bring to a boil, cover and reduce heat. Simmer 15-20 minutes or until potatoes are tender. Stir in broccoli and remove from heat. Meanwhile, in a heavy saucepan over low heat, melt butter and add flour, stirring until smooth. Cook 1 minute, stirring constantly. Gradually add milk, cook over low heat and stir constantly until mixture is thick and bubbly. Stir in mustard, pepper, paprika, jalapeño, and cheese. Cook until cheese melts, stirring constantly. Gradually stir cheese mixture into vegetable mixture. Cook over medium heat, stirring constantly, until chowder is heated thoroughly. Ladle into bowls and drizzle sherry over the chowder, if desired. This may be made ahead of time but reheat carefully.
4-6 servings

Creole Cream Cheese Mold with Minted Fresh Fruit

4 cups plus 1 Tablespoon
   whipping cream
1½ cups sugar
3 envelopes unflavored gelatin
1½ cups sour cream
1½ teaspoons vanilla

Marinade:
1½ cups sugar
1 cup water
7-8 sprigs of mint
1-1½ cups light rum
3 lemons juiced

Fruit:
6 cups fresh fruit: peaches,
   blueberries, oranges, grapes,
   strawberries, or melons.

Mold:
In a saucepan, combine cream, sugar, and gelatin, and heat gently until gelatin is thoroughly dissolved. Cool until just slightly thickened. Fold in sour cream with vanilla. Whisk until the mixture is velvety smooth. Pour into a greased 8-cup metal mold. Chill. It takes 2 hours to congeal. Unmold on a serving platter and surround with marinated fruit. Garnish with fresh mint.

Marinade:
Boil water and sugar for 2 minutes. Add mint. Cool then remove mint. Add rum and lemon juice, mixing well.

Fruit:
Slice an attractive assortment of seasonal fruits. Soak the fruit in the prepared marinade for several hours or overnight.
12-14 servings

Beautiful!

Salads

Apricot-Pineapple Piquant Molded Salad

1 17-ounce can apricot halves
1 8-ounce can pineapple tidbits
¼ cup vinegar
1 teaspoon whole cloves
2 sticks cinnamon
1 3-ounce package orange Jello

Drain apricots and pineapple, reserving juices. Add vinegar, cloves, and cinnamon to juices and enough water to make 2 cups. Bring to a boil, add fruit, and simmer 3 minutes. Strain to remove fruit, discarding cloves and cinnamon sticks. Add Jello to juice. Chill until "jelly-like." Add apricots and pineapple, and pour into eight 4-ounce individual molds or a 1-quart mold. Chill until set.
8 servings

Delicious for a luncheon or buffet supper. The "one" molded salad that men like! May also be served on a cranberry slice — very colorful and a nice garnish for a platter of ham or turkey.

Nutty Cranberry Mold

1 15¼-ounce can crushed pineapple
2 3-ounce packages raspberry Jello
1 cup cold water
1 16-ounce can whole berry cranberry sauce
½ cup chopped pecans

Drain pineapple and reserve liquid. Add water to reserved liquid to make 1 cup liquid. Heat to boiling, add Jello and stir to dissolve. Add cold water. Place in 2-quart mold and chill until partially set. Fold in pineapple, cranberry sauce, and pecans. Chill until firm.
10-12 servings

A festive holiday accompaniment.

Ambrosia

5-6 cups peeled, sectioned oranges, approximately 6 large oranges
1 8½-ounce can crushed pineapple, drained
½-¾ cup chopped pecans
1 6-ounce jar maraschino cherries, drained and halved
½ cup frozen Baker's coconut
1 teaspoon sugar, optional

Combine all ingredients and toss gently. Chill. Drain before serving.
8 servings

Frosty Fruit Salad

3 bananas, sliced
4 Tablespoons lemon juice
1½ cups sugar
2 15¼-ounce cans crushed
    pineapple, drained
1 6-ounce jar maraschino
    cherries, drained and chopped
1 cup chopped pecans
½ pint sour cream
1 12-ounce carton Cool Whip
1 16½-ounce can bing cherries,
    drained and halved

Combine bananas, lemon juice, and sugar. Add remaining ingredients and mix well. Pour into a 9 x 13 pan or 30 muffin tins. Freeze for 1½ hours or overnight.
Makes 2½ dozen

Kiwi Collage

4 cantaloupes
6 kiwi, peeled and sliced
1 pint fresh blueberries, washed

Halve the cantaloupes and remove seeds. Decorate edges in zigzag fashion. Fill 8 cantaloupe cups with sliced kiwi and blueberries. Garnish with fresh mint.
8 servings

Minted Fruit Baskets

1 pint strawberries
3 kiwi
1 medium cantaloupe
1 medium honeydew melon
½ cup fresh orange juice
¼ cup fresh lemon juice
2-3 Tablespoons sugar
2-3 teaspoons chopped fresh
    mint
12 6-inch flour tortillas*

Wash and hull strawberries. Peel kiwi and slice thinly, reserving a few slices for garnish. Cut melons into cubes or use melon baller. Mix all fruits. Combine juices, sugar, and mint. Pour over fruits and toss gently. Chill 2-3 hours. Fry tortillas in tortilla basket. Cool and fill with fruit that has been drained well. Garnish with mint leaves, reserved kiwi slices, or fresh flowers.
*For a party of 8, fry extra baskets to allow for breakage and "nibbling."
8 servings

Salads

Dilled Chicken Salad

8 chicken breast halves, cooked,
  deboned, and cubed
1 cup chopped celery
3 hard cooked eggs, chopped
½ cup slivered almonds, optional
1 3-ounce package cream cheese,
  softened
½ cup mayonnaise
½ cup sour cream
1½ teaspoons dill weed
1 teaspoon dry mustard
¼ teaspoon salt
⅛ teaspoon black pepper

In a large bowl, mix chicken, celery, egg, and almonds. In another bowl, whisk together cream cheese, mayonnaise, sour cream, dill weed, mustard, salt, and pepper. Combine the two mixtures and mix well. Chill. This is best if made the day before serving.
6-8 servings

This is a wonderfully creamy salad zipped with dill. It makes a beautiful salad plate with fresh vegetables and fruits of the season.

Grilled Chicken and Rotini Salad

16 ounces Rotini pasta
1 bunch broccoli, cut into
  flowerets
1 bunch green onions, chopped
3-4 carrots, thinly sliced
4-6 grilled chicken breasts,
  cubed
1 8-ounce bottle Martinque
  Poppy Seed Dressing
Cavender's Greek Seasoning
Garlic powder
Coarse ground black pepper

Cook pasta according to package directions. Drain. Combine pasta, broccoli, green onions, carrots, and chicken. Toss with poppy seed dressing. Season to taste. Refrigerate. Before serving, toss salad and adjust seasonings. This pasta salad is best when made a day ahead.
12-14 servings

This is also delicious as a vegetable pasta salad. Simply omit the chicken.

Smoked Chicken Salad

6 boneless chicken breast halves,
  smoked
⅔ cup mayonnaise
¼ cup minced celery
2 Tablespoons minced green
  onions
1 teaspoon Creole seasoning
Dash black pepper

Finely chop chicken and blend with mayonnaise. Add celery, green onions, Creole seasoning, and pepper. Additional mayonnaise may be added to reach desired consistency. Refrigerate several hours or overnight.
Makes 2⅔ cups filling or spread for 4½ dozen tea sandwiches.

Stuff in an avocado for a quick light lunch.

Chinese Chicken Salad

As with all Chinese food, a little bit of planning makes for an enjoyable meal. Plan to start a day ahead of time. This is a bit of work, but this marvelous salad makes an outstanding presentation and is delicious!

3 Tablespoons hoisin sauce
1 Tablespoon soy sauce
¼ teaspoon garlic salt
¼ teaspoon salt
Black pepper to taste
3 pound fryer, cut in half
3 green onions, cut into 1-inch lengths
1¼ cups Chinese pea pods
½ large head iceberg lettuce, thinly sliced
2 green onions, tops and bottoms, thinly sliced
¼ cup cilantro, cut into 1-inch sections
1 7-ounce can baby corn, cut into ½-inch round sections
1 6-ounce package rice sticks
Peanuts

Hoisin Dressing:
4 Tablespoons hoisin sauce
4 Tablespoons lemon juice
3 Tablespoons safflower or salad oil
3 Tablespoons olive oil
2 Tablespoons sesame oil
4 teaspoons sugar

Combine the hoisin sauce, soy sauce, garlic salt, salt, and pepper and rub all over the chicken. In a roasting pan, place the chicken skin-side up, tucking the green onions under it. Roast in a 350 degree oven for 1 hour or until tender. When chicken is still slightly warm, remove the skin and any fat and cut into tiny thin slivers. Pull the meat from the bones, and shred with your fingers into long thin shreds. Return the chicken to the baking pan and toss in the drippings with your hands until all the chicken is coated well. Refrigerate.

The following may also be prepared a day ahead: Blanch pea pods for a few seconds, run under cold water, then slice lengthwise into 2 strips. Prepare remaining vegetables, seal tightly, and refrigerate.

Prior to assembling, fry rice sticks according to package directions. To assemble, place the lettuce on a large platter. Top with chicken, green onions, and cilantro. Arrange the pea pods, decoratively around the outside edge and the corn around an inside border. Pour the dressing over all or serve in a bowl on the side.

If the platter is large enough, make a ring of rice sticks on the very outside edge, or serve in a separate bowl to be sprinkled on the salad as a garnish. A third bowl of chopped peanuts to add a salty crunch is the "piece de resistance" for this marvelous salad.
8 servings

Hoisin Dressing:
Combine all ingredients and whisk until the sugar is dissolved.
Makes 1 cup

This is perfect for lunch accompanied with peeled, slices of orange and kiwi.

Salads

Marinated Beef Salad

2½-3 pounds grilled or broiled
    beef steak, 3-4 cups*
½ red or green bell pepper
½ purple onion, sliced
1 green onion, sliced
⅔ cup garlic dressing
¼ cup fresh chopped parsley
Sliced orange rings

Cut steak and pepper into julienne strips. In a mixing bowl, combine beef, pepper, onion, and green onion. Toss with dressing. Add parsley and orange rings and toss again. Cover and refrigerate. Serve at room temperature in pita pockets.
*Rare beef steak is preferred.
16 servings

Garlic Dressing

1 egg yolk
⅓ cup red wine vinegar
½ teaspoon salt
2 garlic cloves, minced
Salt to taste
Black pepper to taste
1 cup olive oil

In the bowl of a food processor with a steel blade in place, combine the egg yolks, vinegar, salt, and garlic. Process on and off. With the motor running, slowly add oil through the feeder tube. Process on and off again. Transfer to a jar and store in refrigerator.
Makes 1½ cups

Crab Tostadas

1 pound white crabmeat
Juice of 2-3 limes
2 Tablespoons peanut or corn oil
½ teaspoon salt
3-4 dashes hot pepper sauce
1-2 Tablespoons chopped parsley
12-16 corn tortillas*
Oil
Shredded lettuce
1 recipe **Zesty Guacamole**
3 tomatoes, chopped and
    seasoned with salt and pepper
1 4½-ounce can sliced black
    olives
1 4-ounce can chopped green
    chili peppers

Garnish:
Sour cream
Radish
Red onion, thinly sliced

Check the crabmeat for shells. Combine the lime juice, oil, salt, and hot pepper sauce, then toss with the crabmeat and parsley. Fry tortillas using a tortilla basket in hot oil until crisp.
*Be sure to fry extra to allow for breakage. To serve, place tortilla baskets on a large platter and layer each basket with lettuce, Zesty Guacamole, tomatoes, crab, olives, and chili peppers. Top with a dollop of sour cream. Garnish with a radish and red onion, if desired.
12 servings

Crabmeat Ravigoté

1 pound lump crabmeat
2 green onions, minced
2-3 stalks celery, chopped
1 Tablespoon capers, optional
¼ cup **Best Vinaigrette Dressing**
¼ cup mayonnaise
1 teaspoon Creole seasoning

Blend crabmeat with remaining ingredients, being careful not to break up crabmeat. Chill. Serve on bed of lettuce surrounded by sliced avocados and tomatoes. Sprinkle top of crabmeat mixture with small amount of cayenne. Doubles easily.
4 servings

For the Ladies Tea Party, **Afternoon Delight**, make 2 recipes and serve on a bed of lettuce with **Basic Tart Shells** on the side.

Salad with Baked Brie on French Bread

½ cup vinaigrette dressing
4 small heads Bibb lettuce
Coarse ground black pepper
Sprinkles of chopped fresh parsley

Arrange lettuce leaves on salad plates. Sprinkle with vinaigrette, ground pepper, and parsley. Serve with Baked Brie on French Bread.
8-10 servings

Vinaigrette Dressing

2 Tablespoons vinegar, red wine, or vinegar with garlic
½ teaspoon salt
1 teaspoon freshly ground black pepper
6 Tablespoons extra virgin olive oil
Pinch of sugar, optional

Mix vinegar, salt, and pepper together. Gradually add the oil, whisking until the mixture thickens. Add sugar, if desired. Taste and adjust seasonings.
Makes ½ cup

Baked Brie on French Bread

1 loaf baguette French bread
Dijon mustard
Butter
½ pound Brie cheese, rind removed

Slice French bread into ½-inch slices. Spread lightly with Dijon mustard and butter. Cover with thin slices of Brie. Broil under preheated broiler for 2 minutes or until cheese is bubbly. Allow 2 slices of bread per person.

Broccoli Salad

2 large bunches fresh broccoli
1 cup sliced, stuffed green olives
8 green onions, chopped,
    including tops
5 hard-boiled eggs, chopped
1 pound bacon, fried and
    crumbled
Grated Cheddar cheese, optional
Chopped purple onion, optional

Clean broccoli and cut flowerets into bite size pieces. If the broccoli is really fresh, you can cut up part of the stems. Drain well in colander. To prepare salad, combine salad ingredients and toss with dressing. Cover and refrigerate, stirring occasionally. This will keep for 3 days.
8 servings

Dressing:
1 cup mayonnaise
¾ cup grated Parmesan cheese
1 8-ounce bottle Italian dressing
2 Tablespoons finely chopped
    ripe olives, optional

Combine dressing ingredients and mix well. Chill.
Makes about 2¾ cups

Crisp and cool.

Good Luck Cabbage Slaw

1 large head green cabbage,
    sliced
½ head purple cabbage, chopped
1 small white onion, chopped
1 bunch green onions, chopped
1 small green bell pepper,
    chopped
1½ cups mayonnaise
⅓ cup yellow mustard
1 Tablespoon wine vinegar
1 Tablespoon lemon juice
1 Tablespoon sugar
1½ teaspoons garlic powder
1 Tablespoon black pepper
Salt to taste

In a large bowl, combine cabbage, onions, and bell pepper. In another bowl, whisk together remaining ingredients. Toss with cabbage. This is best if made the day before.
10 servings

The best coleslaw. A crisp cool salad for a hot summer day — A spicy salad to chase away a winter chill.

Chef Salad Stuffing

Salad fixings:
½-¾ head of lettuce, shredded
¼ pound ham, cut into thin strips
¼ pound chicken or turkey, cut into thin strips
¼ pound Monterey Jack cheese, cut into thin strips
1 4½-ounce can black olives, sliced
2 tomatoes, chopped
2 ribs celery, chopped
2 green onions, thinly sliced
½ green bell pepper, chopped
8 slices bacon, fried crisp and crumbled

2 avocados, chopped
1 recipe **Mayonnaise**
Salt
Black pepper
Lemon pepper
Whole wheat pita pockets
Alfalfa sprouts

Prepare salad fixings ahead of time. To serve, toss salad fixings, avocado, and mayonnaise as desired. Season with salt, pepper, and lemon pepper and toss again. Serve in pita pockets and garnish with sprouts, if desired.
20 servings

This salad stuffing can vary with your favorite ingredients.

Zesty Corn Salad

5 cups or 24 ounces frozen whole kernel corn, thawed
1 small cucumber, diced and peeled
2 small tomatoes, chopped
2 Tablespoons diced onion, optional
¼ cup plain yogurt
2 Tablespoons mayonnaise
1 Tablespoon vinegar
½ teaspoon salt
¼ teaspoon dry mustard
¼ teaspoon celery seed

Combine vegetables. Blend together remaining ingredients and add to vegetable mixture. Toss to coat and chill.
8-10 servings

This is an easy, colorful, make-ahead salad that will be a great addition to any summer fare.

Salads

Country Club Salad

6-8 cups mixed salad greens
3 green onions, chopped
3 cups chunked, smoked turkey
  or chicken
3 avocados, chopped
4 ounces Bleu cheese, crumbled
6 strips smoked bacon, cooked
  and crumbled
Coarse black pepper
Croutons
Best Vinaigrette Dressing

Combine greens, green onions, turkey, avocados, Bleu cheese, bacon, and pepper. Toss with croutons and Best Vinaigrette dressing and serve.
8 servings

Croutons:
Slice French bread ½-inch thick. Paint bread with garlic butter, then cut bread into cubes. Toast in 425 degree oven until lightly brown.

Fiesta Salad

1 large head lettuce, torn
1 pint cherry tomatoes, halved
1 purple onion, sliced and
  separated into rings
1 green bell pepper, sliced into
  strips
1 15-ounce can Ranch style
  beans, drained
2 avocados, peeled and cubed
1 11-ounce bag corn chips,
  crushed
1 cup grated Cheddar cheese
1 8-ounce bottle Catalina
  French Dressing

Combine lettuce, tomatoes, onion, bell pepper, beans, avocados, corn chips, and cheese. Toss with dressing.
10 servings

Excellent with hot tamales or chili. The sweet taste of the dressing cuts the spiciness of Mexican food. A very pretty and colorful salad.

Tomato and Pesto Salad

4 fresh tomatoes
8 ounces whole milk Mozzarella
  cheese
½ cup **Pesto Sauce,** room
  temperature
Extra virgin olive oil, to taste
Salt
Freshly ground black pepper

Slice each tomato into 4 slices. Slice cheese to place on tomatoes. Place cheese over each tomato. Top cheese with a heaping teaspoon of pesto sauce. Arrange tomatoes in a circle on a platter, overlapping slightly. Lightly drizzle olive oil over all and salt and pepper to taste. Serve at room temperature. Garnish with fresh basil leaves, if available.
8 servings

Mardi Gras Salad

Mardi Gras Dressing:
2 teaspoons chopped onion, or 2
   teaspoons onion juice
½ cup cider vinegar
¼ cup sugar
1 teaspoon dry mustard
1 teaspoon salt
⅔ cup oil

Mardi Gras Salad:
1 head lettuce, shredded
1 10-ounce bag spinach leaves,
   stemmed and shredded
10 slices bacon, fried and
   crumbled
1 red onion, slivered
1½ cups Mandarin orange
   sections
1 8-ounce package mushrooms,
   sliced

Put onion, cider vinegar, sugar, dry mustard, and salt in blender. Start on low speed and slowly add oil. Dressing can be made ahead of time and refrigerated in blender container. Mix and toss salad ingredients. Briefly blend dressing before tossing and serving salad. 8-10 servings

For a ''Main Meal Salad'' add 1 cup small curd cottage cheese.

Cajun Potato Salad

2 cups fresh small shrimp,
   peeled*
2-3 Tablespoons lemon juice
1 clove garlic
4 cups cubed, cooked potatoes,
   about 4 medium potatoes
½ cup diced celery
½ cup chopped green onion
½ cup sour cream
½ cup mayonnaise
1 teaspoon salt
1 teaspoon dry mustard
¼ teaspoon dried leaf tarragon,
   crushed
½ teaspoon cayenne

Boil shrimp until pink, 3-5 minutes. Drain. In a small bowl, mix shrimp with lemon juice. Chill. Rub the inside of a large salad bowl with cut side of garlic clove. Discard garlic. Combine potatoes, celery, and onion in the large salad bowl. Add shrimp. In a small bowl, combine remaining ingredients and mix well. Add to potato mixture, stirring gently. Refrigerate several hours, preferably overnight. Taste and adjust salt and cayenne.
*May use 2 cups chopped shrimp.
8 servings

A Louisiana picnic favorite.

Salads

New Potato Salad

2 pounds whole new potatoes, about 20 new potatoes
3 cups water
1 teaspoon salt
1 pound fresh green beans, steamed and cut in half
1 pound fresh mushrooms, sliced
4 green onions, chopped
½ teaspoon salt
1 teaspoon coarse black pepper
½ teaspoon Creole seasoning
2 Tablespoons chopped parsley
2 teaspoons dill weed, optional
1-1½ cups **Creamy Buttermilk Dressing**

In a baking dish cover potatoes with water and add salt. Bake in 350 degree oven for 1 hour and 15 minutes or until potatoes are tender. Drain. When cool, slice in half. Cooking the potatoes this way makes the skin stay perfect when slicing and makes a prettier salad. Place the vegetables in a very large bowl. Combine the seasonings and spices. Gently toss the vegetables, seasonings, and dressing. Chill for at least one hour. Serve cold. Garnish with fresh dill or sliced dill pickle.
12-14 servings

A salad with a fresh, light approach.

Spicy Tomato Aspic

1 quart tomato juice
2 cloves garlic, pressed
½ teaspoon dry mustard
1½ teaspoons salt
2½ teaspoons sugar
5 Tablespoons lemon juice
1 teaspoon paprika
1 bay leaf
⅛ teaspoon cayenne
3 Tablespoons unflavored gelatin
¾ cup bouillon
1 8-ounce package cream cheese, softened
3 Tablespoons grated onion
½ teaspoon hot pepper sauce

In a saucepan, bring tomato juice and all seasonings to a boil. Continue cooking for 3 minutes. Remove from heat and discard bay leaf. Soften gelatin in bouillon. Add gelatin mixture to tomato juice and stir to dissolve. Pour into 1½-quart mold and refrigerate. Combine cream cheese, grated onion, and hot pepper sauce. Roll into 1-inch balls. Chill. When aspic becomes slightly firm, arrange cheese balls in the mold. When all is firm, unmold and serve on a bed of lettuce garnished with fresh rosemary or bay leaves.
10 servings

Best Vinaigrette Dressing

½ cup olive oil
½ cup vegetable oil
⅓ cup wine vinegar
2-3 cloves garlic
1 teaspoon Dijon mustard
1 teaspoon salt
1 teaspoon coarse ground black
   pepper

Place all ingredients in food processor or blender and blend until creamy and garlic is shredded, about 60 seconds. Keeps well in refrigerator.
Makes 1½ cups

A *superb basic vinaigrette.*

Creamy Buttermilk Dressing

1 pint buttermilk
1 pint Hellmann's mayonnaise
½ teaspoon garlic powder
1 teaspoon onion powder
2½ Tablespoons dry parsley
   flakes
1 teaspoon salt
½ teaspoon MSG
½ teaspoon black pepper

Combine all ingredients and mix well. Let stand in refrigerator 24 hours before serving. Serve over **New Potato Salad** or any salad.
Makes about 1 quart

Great as a dip with raw vegetables.

Dijon Dressing

½ cup olive oil
½ cup plain yogurt
2 rounded Tablespoons Dijon
   mustard
1-2 Tablespoons wine vinegar
Salt to taste
Black pepper to taste

Blend all ingredients in food processor. Pour in jar. Chill well.
Makes 1 cup

Serve as a dressing over fresh lump crabmeat or shrimp on a bed of lettuce. The Dijon mustard enhances the seafood flavor.

Delectable Fresh Fruit Dressing

2 eggs
¼ cup sugar
¼ cup pineapple juice
¼ cup lemon juice
⅛ teaspoon salt
½ cup whipping cream, whipped
½ teaspoon grated lemon rind

Beat eggs and stir in sugar, juices, and salt. Cook until thickened. Cool. Fold in cream and rind. This is much better if it is made on the day it is to be served.
Makes 1 cup

This is fluffy, tangy-sweet, and delicious with seasonal fresh fruit for an hors d'oeuvre, salad, or dessert.

Salads

Salvatore's Italian Salad Dressing

½ cup olive oil
2 Tablespoons minced onion
1 Tablespoon freshly grated
   Parmesan cheese
1 teaspoon salt
¾ teaspoon Worcestershire sauce
¾ teaspoon dry mustard
¾ teaspoon basil
¾ teaspoon oregano
¾ teaspoon sugar
¾ teaspoon black pepper
¼ cup red wine vinegar
1 Tablespoon lemon juice

In a blender or food processor, blend the first 10 ingredients for 30 seconds. Add the vinegar and lemon juice and blend for 30 seconds. Chill. Serve with mixed salad greens, hearts of palm, tomatoes, and avocado.
Makes 1 cup

This is very strong, flavorful, and delicious!

Spicy Sour Cream Dressing

2 cups mayonnaise
2 8-ounce cartons sour cream
1 can anchovy fillets, drained
   and minced
1 Tablespoon lemon juice
1 handful chopped fresh parsley
1 handful chopped green onions
¼ teaspoon garlic powder
Hot pepper sauce to taste

Combine all ingredients and mix well. Chill. Dressing will keep well in refrigerator two weeks.
Makes 1 quart

Serve with mixed greens and crunchy vegetables. Garnish with whole peppercorns.

Tarragon Vinaigrette

2 Tablespoons tarragon vinegar
2 Tablespoons lemon juice
1 teaspoon Dijon mustard
1 teaspoon salt
1 teaspoon black pepper
1 cup olive oil

Combine first six ingredients in food processor. Process 30 seconds. With motor running, slowly add oil in a steady stream. Adjust seasonings. Blend.
Makes about 1¼ cups

Exceptionally good with mixed greens of Romaine, iceberg, spinach, and watercress.

Breads

MARDI GRAS: TWIN CITY STYLE

Mardi Gras was first celebrated on the land mass that was in time to be called Louisiana in 1699. The French explorer Iberville and his men, homesick and lonely, found themselves camped near a stream on Shrove Tuesday. Recalling their French customs, they celebrated this last day before the onset of Lent by resting and feasting. In honor of the event, Iberville named the stream *Bayou de Mardi Gras*.

From that humble beginning, Mardi Gras has become a statewide celebration, cheerfully mixing the pagan with the religious for the most spectacular Carnival this side of Rio! The official colors of green, gold, and purple adorn everything from the massive floats rolling past to the faces in the crowds shouting "Throw me somethin', Mister!" And thrown something they are, as riders toss out doubloons (colored coins imprinted with logos and themes), multi-colored beads, golden coconuts, and other prizes to the parade-watchers.

In the rural areas, masked men ride horseback from farm to farm gathering ingredients for a gigantic gumbo and jambalaya...a chicken from this house, a sausage from that one, rice from still another. All of these are put together in great iron pots on the town square to simmer slowly into the evening while the people dance and hold contests in celebration. In the cities, the celebrations take on a more elaborate form. As early as 1743 New Orleanians were holding formal balls to mark the Carnival season, a tradition that is continued today. In 1837 a group of young men formed the "Mystic Krewe of Comus," a secret society dedicated to Carnival. The "Krewe" held a fantasy parade of beautifully decorated carriages for the city that year. Soon other Krewes were formed, and Carnival celebrations were intensified. Today, a far more elaborate Comus parade still rolls on Fat Tuesday and brings joy to millions.

In 1984, the Twin Cities of Monroe and West Monroe (known as such because they are located on opposite sides of the Ouachita River and are linked by bridges and a common heritage) began a formal celebration of Carnival with the founding of the Krewe of Janus. Krewe members work all year preparing for the holiday. Crowds of onlookers line the streets of both cities in anticipation of the annual Mardi Gras parade. Here, as elsewhere, trinkets are thrown by masked revelers from spectacular floats. Later, a masked ball is held honoring the royal court of Janus. This glittering spectacle of beaded gowns, plumed collars, and regal crowns is not to be missed!

Applelicious Bread

4 cups baking apples, diced and
   peeled
1 cup finely chopped pecans
2 cups sugar
3 cups flour
2 teaspoons soda
¼ teaspoon salt
¼ teaspoon allspice
¼ teaspoon nutmeg
1 teaspoon cinnamon
2 sticks margarine, melted
2 eggs, slightly beaten
2 teaspoons vanilla

Preheat oven to 325 degrees. In a large bowl, combine apples, pecans, and sugar and stir well. Add flour, soda, salt, spices, and margarine to apple mixture. Combine eggs with vanilla, then add to batter. Mix well. Pour into two 9 x 5 x 3 greased loaf pans. Bake for 1 hour or until done.
Makes 2 loaves

Sour Cream Banana Bread

½ cup butter
1 cup sugar
2 eggs, beaten
1½ cups flour
1 teaspoon baking soda
½ teaspoon salt
1 cup mashed bananas, about 3
   bananas
½ cup sour cream
1 teaspoon vanilla
½ cup chopped pecans

Cream butter and sugar, add eggs, and mix well. Sift flour, soda, and salt and combine with the butter mixture. Add bananas, sour cream, and vanilla, and stir well. Add nuts. Pour into greased 9 x 5 x 3 loaf pan or several smaller loaf pans. Bake in 350 degree oven for 1 hour.
Makes 1 loaf

Breads

Banana Fritters

This batter is much like a simple pancake batter but has an elastic consistency that allows it to stick to the fruit when it is deep fried. The banana must be perfectly dry for it to adhere. The batter must be made at least two hours ahead but preferably overnight. This resting period allows it to ferment with the beer.

Batter:
1⅓ cups flour
1 teaspoon salt
1 Tablespoon butter, melted
2 Tablespoons sugar
2 eggs, separated
¾ cup beer, not including foam

To prepare batter, combine flour, salt, butter, sugar, and beaten egg yolks. Mix well and then gradually add the beer. Beat reserved egg whites until stiff. Put both batter and egg whites away in the refrigerator for the resting period.

6 large bananas
Corn oil
4 Tablespoons butter, melted
4 teaspoons sugar
2 teaspoons nutmeg
2 teaspoons cinnamon

Gently combine the batter and egg whites. Dip chunks of banana about 1-inch long into the batter. Use slightly green bananas. Deep fry in corn oil that is very hot, about 375 degrees, for 3 or 4 minutes, or until nicely browned. Drain and brush tops with butter. Combine sugar, nutmeg, and cinnamon. Sprinkle fritters with spice mixture. Serve in place of biscuits.
Makes about 3½ dozen

Carrot Nut Bread

1 cup vegetable oil
1½ cups sugar
3 eggs
1 teaspoon vanilla*
1½ cups sifted flour
1½ teaspoons baking soda
1 teaspoon cinnamon
½ teaspoon salt
½ teaspoon nutmeg
4 large carrots, grated on large
   grate
1 cup chopped pecans

Cream together the oil, sugar, eggs, and vanilla. Sift together the flour, soda, cinnamon, salt, and nutmeg, and add to the first mixture. Blend well. Fold in carrots and pecans. Pour into two greased and floured 9 x 5 x 3 loaf pans. Bake at 350 degrees for 50 minutes.
*Mexican vanilla may be used.
Makes 2 loaves

A moist, nutty bread.

Cranberry Orange Bread

½ cup sugar
3 Tablespoons butter
1 egg
1 teaspoon vanilla
Grated peel from 1 medium
   orange, about 2 Tablespoons
3 cups whole wheat flour
2 teaspoons baking powder
1 teaspoon soda
1 teaspoon salt
1 16-ounce can whole cranberry
   sauce
Juice of 1 large orange, about 8
   Tablespoons
1 cup walnuts, chopped

Cream the sugar and butter. Beat in egg. Blend in vanilla and orange peel. Combine the flour, baking powder, soda, and salt. Drain the cranberries, add the cranberry syrup to the orange juice, and reserve the cranberries. Add the juice alternately with the dry ingredients to the creamed mixture, blending well after each addition. Stir in cranberries and walnuts. Pour into a greased 9 x 5 x 3 loaf pan or several smaller greased pans. Bake in a 350 degree oven for 1 hour or until toothpick inserted comes out clean. Cool before slicing.
Makes 1 loaf

Perfect for holiday gift giving.

Harvest Loaf

½ cup margarine
1 cup sugar
2 eggs
1 cup pumpkin
1¾ cups flour
1 teaspoon soda
½ teaspoon salt
1 teaspoon cinnamon
½ teaspoon nutmeg
½ teaspoon cloves
¼ teaspoon ginger
¾ cup chocolate chips
¾ cup chopped pecans

Spice glaze:
½ cup powdered sugar
½ teaspoon cinnamon
⅛ teaspoon nutmeg
1-2 Tablespoons cream or milk

Cream margarine and sugar until fluffy. Add eggs, one at a time, mixing well after each addition. Add the pumpkin and mix well. In another bowl, sift the flour, soda, salt, and spices together. Add to the pumpkin mixture and mix well. Stir in chocolate chips and pecans. Pour into a greased 9 x 5 x 3 loaf pan and bake in 375 degree oven for 70-75 minutes or until done. While loaf is slightly warm, combine the glaze mixture and pour over the loaf.
Makes 1 loaf

This is a melt-in-your-mouth bread.

Breads

Mango Bread

2 cups flour
1¼ cups sugar
2 teaspoons soda
2 teaspoons cinnamon
½ teaspoon salt
3 eggs, beaten
¾ cup vegetable oil
2½ cups peeled, chopped
   mangos, about 3 medium
   mangos
1 teaspoon lemon juice
½ cup raisins*
½ cup chopped pecans

Preheat oven to 350 degrees. Sift together flour, sugar, soda, cinnamon, and salt. Combine eggs with vegetable oil and add to dry ingredients. Add mangos, lemon juice, raisins, and nuts. Pour into two greased 9 x 5 x 3 loaf pans. Bake for 40 minutes or until done. *Chopped dates may be substituted for raisins.

A very moist, unusual, and delicious fruit bread. Serve with the main course or as a dessert bread.

Cinnamon Coffee Cake Ring

1 package yeast
¼ cup warm water
¼ cup shortening
1 egg
1 teaspoon salt
¼ cup sugar
¾ cup lukewarm milk, scalded
   then cooled
3½ cups flour, ¼ cup more if
   needed
2 Tablespoons butter, softened
½ cup sugar
2 teaspoons cinnamon
1 cup chopped nuts

Frosting:
1 cup powdered sugar
1 Tablespoon vanilla
1 Tablespoon warm milk

In a cup dissolve yeast in warm water. In food processor or mixing bowl, cream shortening. Add egg, salt, and sugar, and mix well. Slowly add dissolved yeast. Continue mixing and slowly add the milk. Add flour, 1 cup at a time, mixing well after each addition. If a food processor is used, cover and let rise in a warm place, 85 degrees, until doubled, about 1½ hours. If a mixing bowl is used, knead dough until smooth and elastic, about 5 minutes, cover and let rise. Punch down and let rise again until doubled in bulk, about 30 minutes. Shape into coffee cake by rolling dough 9 x 15-inches. Spread with butter and sprinkle with a mixture of cinnamon and sugar. Sprinkle with chopped nuts. Roll dough tightly lengthwise and seal well by pinching edges. Place sealed edge down on a lightly greased baking sheet and shape into a ring. With scissors or sharp knife, cut ⅔ of the way through the ring at 1-inch intervals, pulling each section apart as you cut. Let rise until double, about 35-40 minutes. Bake in a 375 degree oven for 25-30 minutes. Combine frosting ingredients, mix well, and frost coffee cake while still warm.

This ring freezes well and is easily doubled.

Cinnamon Breakfast Bread

3 cups flour
¼ teaspoon soda
¾ teaspoon salt
2 sticks butter, softened
2¾ cups sugar
4 eggs
1-2 teaspoons vanilla
1 teaspoon lemon extract*
1 cup buttermilk
1 cup chopped nuts
2 Tablespoons cinnamon
2 Tablespoons sugar

Sift together the flour, soda, and salt, and set aside. Cream butter and sugar until light. Beat in eggs one at a time, then add vanilla and lemon extract. Beat on high for 2½ minutes, then lower speed and add dry ingredients alternately with the buttermilk. Fold nuts into batter. In a small bowl, mix together the cinnamon and sugar. Grease and flour a 10-inch tube pan or 4 small loaf pans. Pour half of batter into pan. Sprinkle with half of cinnamon-sugar mixture. Cover with remaining batter and top with remaining cinnamon-sugar. With a knife swirl cinnamon mixture through batter. Bake at 325 degrees for one hour and 15 minutes.
*Almond flavoring may be substituted for lemon extract.

Drizzle thin slices with honey and butter and broil. Serve with cold milk.

Honey Bran Muffins

2 cups Kellogg's All-Bran
1 cup buttermilk
1 cup raisins
1-2 bananas
1 egg
¼ cup corn oil
¼ cup honey
1 cup whole wheat flour
1 teaspoon baking soda
1 teaspoon cinnamon
¼ teaspoon nutmeg
Pinch of salt

Honey Glaze:
2 Tablespoons margarine, melted
2 Tablespoons honey

Mix bran, buttermilk, and raisins, and let stand for 10 minutes. In a bowl, mash bananas and blend in egg, corn oil, and honey. In another bowl, stir together flour, soda, cinnamon, nutmeg, and salt. Combine the three mixtures and mix well. Grease a 12-cup muffin pan and fill each cup ⅔ full. Bake in a 375 degree oven for 18-20 minutes. Do not overcook! Cool and remove muffins from pan. Mix glaze ingredients and dip tops in honey glaze.

So healthy!

Breads

Gingerbread Muffins

1 cup vegetable oil
1 cup sugar
3 eggs
1 cup molasses or cane syrup
2 teaspoons soda
2 teapoons hot water
2¼ cups flour
1 teaspoon cinnamon
1 teaspoon ginger
1 teaspoon cloves
Pinch of salt
1 cup boiling water

Cream oil and sugar. Add eggs one at a time, beating well after each addition. Blend in syrup. Combine soda and water and add to sugar mixture. Sift together flour, spices, and salt, and add to sugar mixture. Add 1 cup boiling water and mix well. Pour into greased miniature muffin pans, filling the muffin cups ¾ full. Bake in a 325 degree oven for 8-10 minutes.
Makes 8 dozen miniature muffins

For a true gingerbread, bake in 9 x 13 pan at 350 degrees for 30 minutes and cut in squares.

Gingerbread Flaps

¼ cup butter, softened
¼ cup sugar
¼ cup molasses
2 eggs, beaten
½ cup applesauce
2 cups flour
2 teaspoons baking powder
1 teaspoon soda
¼ teaspoon salt
1 teaspoon cinnamon
½ teaspoon ginger
1 cup milk

Cream butter and sugar until light and fluffy. Add molasses, mixing well. Stir in eggs and applesauce. Combine dry ingredients and add alternately with milk to creamed mixture, mixing lightly. Bake in a waffle iron. Serve with syrup that has been flavored with cinnamon or ginger. May be prepared ahead and refrigerated overnight.
Makes 8 waffles

These are great as a dessert served with a hot apple topping.

Sweet Potato Rolls

2 packages yeast
4 Tablespoons sugar
½ cup warm water, 110-115
  degrees
3 Tablespoons butter, melted
1 Tablespoon salt
3 eggs
3½-4 cups flour
½ cup mashed sweet potatoes
2 Tablespoons cream

Combine the yeast with 1 Tablespoon of sugar and the warm water. Cover and put in a warm place until the mixture doubles in bulk. Add the remaining sugar, butter, salt, and 2 eggs to the yeast mixture. Stir until well blended. Stir in the flour, 1 cup at a time, then add the sweet potatoes. Knead the dough until smooth and elastic and allow to rise, about one hour. If dough is too sticky, add a little more flour. Punch the dough down and shape into a ball. For rolls, pinch off 3 small balls of dough and place in each cup of a buttered muffin pan. Let rise again. Beat remaining egg with cream and brush on the tops of the rolls. Bake in preheated 375 degree oven for 20 minutes.
Makes 2 dozen

These are good for breakfast but are really delicious with wild game dinners.

Old-Fashioned Buttermilk Biscuits

2 cups buttermilk
2 Tablespoons sugar
1 teaspoon soda
1 cup shortening
5½ cups self-rising flour
1 package yeast
¼ cup warm water

Preheat oven to 350 degrees. Combine the buttermilk, sugar, and soda, stirring well, and set aside. In a large bowl, cut the shortening into 4 cups of the flour until it is the size of small peas. Dissolve the yeast in warm water. Add the buttermilk and yeast mixture to the flour and mix well. This will be sticky. Sprinkle 1 cup flour on a large piece of foil and pour biscuit mixture on it. Add a little more flour to the top. Pick up the sides of the dough with a flat hand and fold to middle. Continue kneading dough until it is stiff enough to turn over and no longer sticky. Roll out to 1-inch thick and cut with a biscuit cutter. Put on a pan lightly sprayed with non-stick cooking spray and bake in 400 degree oven for 25 minutes or until lightly browned.
Makes 4 dozen

Breads

Easy-Doughs-It Yeast Rolls

1 package yeast
½ cup warm water
1 egg
½ cup milk
1 Tablespoon sugar
½ stick margarine, melted
3½ cups Pioneer Biscuit Mix

Dissolve yeast in water. Mix egg, milk, sugar, and margarine together. Add yeast to egg mixture and mix well. Add biscuit mix and stir together until smooth. Pour into buttered bowl, cover with towel, and let rise until doubled in size, about 1 hour. Turn dough out onto surface floured with biscuit mix. Work biscuit mix into dough until it is elastic and not sticky. Roll out and cut with cutter. Fold each roll in half and put in greased pan with sides lightly touching. Let rise again for 30-45 minutes. Bake at 350 degrees for 15-20 minutes.
Makes 2 dozen

Perfect!

Asphodel Bread

Asphodel is a plantation home near Jackson, Louisiana. This light bread from the Asphodel kitchen is famous statewide.

5 cups Pioneer Biscuit Mix
4 Tablespoons sugar
½ teaspoon salt
2 envelopes yeast
2 cups warm milk
4 eggs
¼ teaspoon cream of tartar

Into a very large bowl sift the biscuit mix, sugar, and salt. Soften the yeast in warm milk. If the milk is too hot, it will kill the yeast. Beat eggs with the cream of tartar. Combine milk and eggs and pour into the dry ingredients. "Stir," do not use a mixer. This is a heavy, sticky mixture that must be mixed well. Set in a warm place and cover with a damp dish towel, or seal with plastic wrap. When doubled in bulk, punch down and place into two greased 9 x 5 x 3 loaf pans. Let double in size before baking in a 350 degree oven. Serve very hot! This bread freezes well. Thaw completely before reheating.
Makes 2 loaves

Burgundian Cheese Bread

2 cups milk
2 teaspoons salt
¼ teaspoon black pepper
½ cup butter
2 cups sifted flour
8 eggs
1 pound Cheddar cheese, grated
1 egg yolk, beaten with a little
   milk

Preheat oven to 375 degrees. In a large saucepan, combine milk, salt, and pepper. Add butter and heat, stirring until butter melts and the mixture is boiling. Remove from heat and add flour all at once. Cook over low heat, and beat until the mixture detaches itself from the side of the pan. Remove from heat and let cool. Beat at high speed, adding eggs one at a time. As much air as possible needs to be incorporated into the mixture to give the bread its lightness. When the dough is shiny and smooth, mix in cheese, saving ½ cup for the topping. Spray a bundt or angel food pan with non-stick cooking spray. Using a Tablespoon, scoop out dough about the size of an egg. Arrange the egg-shaped dough in the pan in an overlapping manner. Again, allow as much air in between as possible to aid in the final product. Brush with beaten egg and sprinkle with additional cheese. Bake for 45 minutes or until browned, puffed, and crusty. Do not open oven while dough is baking. Serve whole and let the guests break off pieces.

Perfect to complete a hot soup and salad luncheon.

Peasant Bread

1½ cups hot water
2 Tablespoons butter
2 Tablespoons sugar
2 teaspoons salt
1 package yeast
½ cup warm water
3 cups wheat flour
2½ cups flour
Melted butter or oil

Pour hot water into a large bowl. Stir in butter, sugar, and salt. Set aside and cool until lukewarm. Meanwhile, dissolve the yeast in warm water, let sit 5 minutes, then blend into the first mixture. Stir in the wheat flour and beat with a wooden spoon for about 1 minute. Add the flour and blend well. Turn out onto a floured board. Knead for about 10 minutes, adding more flour if necessary, until surface is satiny. Place dough in a large greased bowl, brush top with butter or oil, and cover with a slightly damp cloth. Allow to rise in a warm place, until nearly doubled in size, about 1 hour. Punch down and knead lightly, then divide dough in half. Shape each half into a round loaf, place on a lightly greased baking sheet, and press down with hands until the dough is about 1-inch thick. Cover and let rise about 45 minutes or until nearly doubled. Bake in 400 degree oven for 25-30 minutes or until crust is light brown. Freezes well.
Makes 2 loaves

Perfect with homemade jelly.

French Bread

2 packages active dry yeast
2½ cups warm water, 115
    degrees
1 Tablespoon salt
2 Tablespoons sugar
7 cups bread flour
1 egg white, beaten
Cornmeal

In large bowl, dissolve yeast in water. Stir in sugar and salt until dissolved. Add 5 cups flour and mix with wooden spoon. Add one cup flour and mix until blended. Turn out onto floured surface and knead for 10 minutes, using as much of the seventh cup of flour as needed to make dough smooth and elastic and prevent from sticking. Put dough into bowl which has been greased with butter. Turn dough in bowl to lightly coat with butter. Cover with damp cloth and let rise until doubled, about 1½ to 2 hours.
Turn out risen dough onto lightly floured surface. Punch down and knead for 2-3 minutes. Let dough rest for 15 minutes.

Cut dough into four pieces and roll each one into a rectangle, approximately 12 x 15 inches. Roll up dough from the long side as you would a jelly roll. Seal the ends. Grease 4 open-ended long bread pans with butter. Lightly sprinkle greased pans with cornmeal. Place each piece of dough in pan with seamed side down. Make four diagonal cuts in each piece of dough with a razor blade or sharp knife. Brush the top of each piece with beaten egg white. Let dough rise until doubled (no need to cover).

Preheat oven to 450 degrees. Spray tops of dough with fine mist of water. Bake 5 minutes. Open oven and spray again. Let bake another 10 minutes, then lower oven temperature to 350 degrees and bake 25 minutes. When done, remove from bread pans and let cool on wire racks. This bread freezes very well. To freeze, wrap tightly in aluminum foil. To reheat, remove from foil and bake at 350 degrees for 20 minutes.
Makes 4 baguette loaves

ENJOY!

Pita Bread Triangles

1 12-ounce package or 6 round
    loaves pita bread
1 stick butter, melted

Cut pita bread into eighths and divide top from bottom, making 16 triangles. Brush melted butter inside triangles. Toast in oven at 275 degrees for 1 hour or until light brown and crisp. Serve plain or with hors d'ouevres.
Makes 8 dozen

Sprinkle with lemon pepper for a spicy chip or with a cinnamon-sugar mixture for a sweet chip treat.

Party Bread Sticks

3-3½ cups flour
1 Tablespoon sugar
1 teaspoon salt
2 packages active dry yeast
¼ cup olive oil or salad oil
1¼ cups hot water, 120-130
 degrees
1 egg white, beaten with 1
 Tablespoon water
Coarse salt, toasted sesame seed,
 or poppy seed

In the large bowl of an electric mixer, add 1 cup of flour to the sugar, salt, and yeast, stirring to blend. Add the oil, then gradually stir in hot water and beat at medium speed for 2 minutes. Add ½ cup flour and beat at high speed for 2 minutes. Use a mixer and stir in remaining 1½-2 cups flour or use a wooden spoon to make a soft dough. Turn dough out onto a well-floured board. With well-floured hands, work the dough into a smooth ball. Shape dough into an even log or block. Use a sharp knife and cut into 20 equal pieces. Roll each piece of dough into a rope 16 inches long. Arrange 1 inch apart on oiled baking sheets or foil-covered racks. Roll to grease all sides of dough. At this point sticks may be covered tightly with clear plastic wrap and frozen until solid. Transfer to plastic bags and store in freezer up to 4 weeks. Remove sticks from freezer about 30 minutes before baking. Arrange frozen bread sticks on ungreased baking sheet or foil-covered oven rack. Cover and let stand at room temperature until fully thawed, about 15 minutes. Set thawed dough in a warm place, cover, and allow to rise until puffy, about 15 minutes. With a soft brush, paint each stick with the egg white and water. Sprinkle lightly with salt or either of the seeds. Bake in a 300 degree oven for 25-30 minutes, turning while baking until lightly brown. To recrisp already baked sticks, put into a 300 degree oven for about 5 minutes.
Makes 20 16-inch sticks

For appetizer bread sticks, divide the dough into 40 equal pieces. Roll each piece to 12 inches in length. Freeze or bake directly on cookie sheets or foil-covered racks as directed for larger sticks. Bake in a 300 degree oven for 20-25 minutes, or until golden brown.

Toast Points

1 loaf Pepperidge Farm thin
 sliced white or wheat bread
1 stick butter, melted*

Preheat oven to broil. Then reduce to 250 degrees. Cut each slice of bread into 4 squares or triangles. Brush bread slices with butter. Place on ungreased cookie sheets and bake for one hour.
*For seasoned toast points, add 1 teaspoon lemon pepper seasoning and 1 teaspoon garlic powder to butter.
Makes 7 dozen

Breads

Braided Italian Bread

3 cups warm water
2 packages yeast
4 Tablespoons sugar
10 cups unbleached white flour
4 teaspoons salt
4 eggs
3 Tablespoons oil
1 egg for glaze

Mix water, yeast, sugar, and let sit. With a wooden spoon, mix flour, salt, eggs, and oil, and add to yeast mixture. On a floured surface, knead mixture until smooth and elastic. Place dough in a large, lightly greased bowl and let rise until doubled in size, about 1½ hours. Punch down. Divide dough into three parts. Then divide each part into three sections. Roll each section into a 12-inch strand. Braid each trio, pinching ends to seal. On a lightly greased baking sheet, let rise until doubled in size, about 1 hour. Brush with slightly beaten egg. Bake at 375 degrees for 30 minutes or until browned.
Makes 3 loaves

Parmesan Break-Aparts

⅓ cup butter
2¼ cups flour
1 Tablespoon sugar, optional
2½ teaspoons baking powder
1 teaspoon salt
1 clove garlic, minced
1 cup milk
2-3 Tablespoons butter, melted
1-2 cups freshly grated
  Parmesan cheese
Parsley
Garlic salt
Paprika

Preheat oven to 450 degrees. Melt butter in a 9 x 13 baking dish. Sift flour, sugar, baking powder, and salt into a large mixing bowl. Add garlic to flour mixture. Add milk and mix in with a fork or pastry blender until mixture resembles coarse meal or clings together on a well-floured surface. Knead dough slightly then roll out into a rectangle ½-inch thick. Cut into strips 3-inches long and 6-inches wide. Place in the buttered dish and brush the bread with melted butter, sprinkle with Parmesan cheese, parsley, garlic salt, and paprika. Bake for 15 minutes or until golden brown. Serve hot.
8-12 servings

Variations: 1. Add ½ cup Cheddar cheese to mixture and omit toppings. 2. Omit garlic for dough. Sprinkle with cinnamon sugar before baking.

Parmesan Garlic Bread

1 loaf French bread
1 stick butter, melted
2 cloves garlic, pressed
¼ cup grated Parmesan cheese
1 Tablespoon minced parsley
1 teaspoon paprika

Split loaf in half lengthwise. Combine butter and garlic and completely cover cut surfaces of bread. Combine Parmesan cheese, parsley, and paprika and sprinkle over buttered bread. Bake in 350 degree oven for 5-10 minutes or until very hot. Cut into 1-inch slices.

Cornbread Cake

2 cups self-rising cornmeal
1 cup self-rising flour
½ cup sugar
½ cup vegetable oil
2 cups buttermilk
1 egg, beaten

Combine all ingredients and beat well. Pour into two greased 9 x 5 x 3 loaf pans and bake in 325 degree oven for 45 minutes or until brown.
Makes 2 loaves

For a breakfast treat, slice thin, and broil. Drizzle with honey.

Grandma's Cornbread

3 Tablespoons bacon drippings, butter, or oil
2 cups buttermilk
1 teaspoon soda
1 teaspoon salt
2 eggs
1½ cups yellow cornmeal

Preheat oven to 400 degrees. Place bacon drippings in 10-inch black iron skillet or other heavy ovenproof skillet. Put in oven. Mix buttermilk and soda, stirring well. Add salt, eggs, and cornmeal, and mix thoroughly. Pour into heated skillet, return to oven, and bake for 25 minutes. Do not overbake.
8-12 servings

This old-fashioned, non-sweet cornbread is wonderful for making dressing or just for eating with butter or molasses.

Mexican Cornbread Muffins

1 egg, beaten
⅓ cup milk
1 6-ounce package cornbread mix
1 8¾-ounce can cream-style corn
½ cup picante sauce, hot or mild
1 cup grated Cheddar cheese
1 jalapeño, chopped finely, optional

Combine egg and milk. Add cornbread mix, corn, picante sauce, cheese, and jalapeño. Mix thoroughly. Fill greased muffin pan ½ full. Bake in a 400 degree oven for 15-20 minutes. This freezes well and easily doubles or triples for a crowd.
Makes 24 miniature or 12 cornsticks

*This is a good accompaniment to **Hot Turnip Green Dip** or **Chicken Enchilada Soup.***

Breads

Hot Water Cornbread

2 cups plain white corn meal
½ cup self-rising flour
2 Tablespoons sugar
½ teaspoon salt
1½-2 cups boiling water
Oil

Combine dry ingredients, add 1½ cups boiling water and mix well. This mixture should have the consistency of a thick batter. If it is too stiff, add more water. Rinse hands with tap water, since this is a hot mixture and pat into cakes.* Fry in hot oil over medium-high heat on each side until golden brown. Serve warm with butter.

*The batter may be spooned into the hot oil but it is not authentic unless you pat it!

Spoon Bread

2½ cups whole milk
½ cup white cornmeal
1 Tablespoon butter
1 teaspoon salt
½ teaspoon baking powder
1 teaspoon sugar
3 eggs, separated

In a saucepan, heat 2 cups milk to boiling point. Add meal gradually, stirring constantly. Cook until the consistency of thick "mush." Add butter, ½ cup cold milk, salt, baking powder, and sugar. Remove from heat. Beat egg yolks until lemon colored. Add to mixture. Beat egg whites until stiff and fold into meal mixture. Put in buttered 2-quart round casserole and bake at 350 degrees for 40 minutes. Serve at once.
6 servings

This traditional southern dish is as light as a souffle. Use this in place of rice or potatoes.

Eggs, Cheese, and Pasta

NATURE'S BOUNTY

Ghosts of the antebellum South still haunt the great halls of the stately mansions that are so much a part of Louisiana's landscape. Visions of hooped skirts and thoughts of Southern chivalry fire the imaginations of romance writers as they spin their tales of that earlier time.

From the simple farmer content to raise only enough to sustain his family and share with his neighbors, to the "gentleman planter" cultivating hundreds of acres using the most advanced technology, Louisiana's natural abundance has sustained her people. Cotton, sugar cane, rice, soybeans, sweet potatoes, strawberries, peaches, and pecans number among our traditional food crops.

The bounty of Louisiana's natural resources has led to the growth of the forestry, salt mining, sulphur, seafood, and oil and gas industries. The diversity of her resources can be seen everywhere on the land and off the coast. Cotton stalks share space with oil derricks; rice gives way to crawfish during the off season. Offshore, the drilling rigs that mark Louisiana's major resource form artificial reefs that attract sea life to enhance the fishing industry.

Louisiana is rapidly becoming a world leader in aquaculture, the farming of fish and seafood. This marriage of agriculture methods and the seafood industry offers new opportunities for economic growth. Louisiana's long growing season, warm climate, and clay soil make her a perfect location for the development of high profit yields of crawfish and catfish. Experimentation is currently underway with redfish, oysters, and Malaysian prawns as well.

One day soon these staples of Louisiana's cuisine will be available all over the world because of the modern technology being developed today in our aquaculture ponds. Louisiana's future, as always, will be determined and enhanced by the innovative use and aggressive protection of her natural resources.

Cajun Eggs

8 eggs
1 cup grated Cheddar cheese
¼ cup chopped chives
¼ cup chopped onions
¼ teaspoon salt
¼ teaspoon seasoned salt
Cayenne
Black pepper
Hot pepper sauce
1 pound hot smoked link
  sausage
1 Tablespoon flour
⅓ cup milk

In a large bowl, combine eggs, cheese, chives, onions, salt, and seasoned salt. Season with cayenne, black pepper, hot pepper sauce and set aside. Cut sausage into ½-inch slices. In a cast iron skillet, pan-fry sausage. When cooked, removed sausage, then add flour, stirring constantly until roux is light brown. Stir in enough milk to make a light gravy. Add egg mixture and sausage, stirring constantly until it is the consistency of soft scrambled eggs. Serve immediately.
6 servings

This will wake you up for sure!

Southwest Chili Strata

6 slices white bread, buttered on
  one side
2 cups shredded sharp Cheddar
  cheese
2 cups shredded Monterey Jack
  cheese
2 4½-ounce cans chopped green
  chilies
6 eggs
2 cups milk
2 teaspoons salt
2 teaspoons paprika
1 teaspoon crumbled oregano
¼ teaspoon garlic powder
¼ teaspoon dry mustard
Pimento or red bell pepper rings
  for garnish

Trim crusts from bread. Arrange bread, buttered side down, in a 9 x 12 baking pan. Sprinkle cheeses evenly over bread and spread chilies evenly over cheeses. In a bowl, beat eggs with milk and seasonings until well-blended. Pour egg mixture over chilies. Cover and chill at least four hours or overnight. Bake uncovered at 325 degrees for 50-60 minutes or until lightly browned. Let stand for 10 minutes before serving. Garnish with pimento or red bell pepper rings.
8 servings

Cheesy Sausage Crêpes

16 **Cotton Country Basic Crêpes**

Filling:
1 *pound bulk sausage*
¼ *cup chopped onion*
½ *cup grated sharp Cheddar cheese*
1 *3-ounce package cream cheese, softened*
1 *4½-ounce jar sliced mushrooms, drained*
¼ *teaspoon ground thyme*
¼ *teaspoon garlic salt*
½ *cup sour cream*
¼ *cup butter, softened*

Prepare crêpes ahead of time. In a heavy skillet, cook sausage and onion, stirring to crumble the meat, until the sausage is browned. Drain well. Add cheeses, mushrooms, thyme, garlic, salt, and mix well. Fill each crêpe with 2 Tablespoons sausage mixture, roll up and place seam side down in two greased 8 x 12 baking dishes. At this point the crêpes may be refrigerated. To serve, bake covered in 350 degree oven for 25 minutes or until crêpes are hot. Combine sour cream and butter, mixing well, and spoon over crêpes. Bake uncovered 5 minutes.
8 servings

A *super Sunday supper.*

Cotton Country Basic Crêpe Batter

1 *cup cold milk.*
1 *cup cold water*
4 *eggs*
1 *teaspoon salt*
2 *cups sifted flour*
4 *Tablespoons butter, melted*

Whirl all ingredients in blender. Store in refrigerator several hours. Spray a 6 or 7-inch crêpe pan or iron skillet with non-stick cooking spray and heat until a drop of water dances. Pour scant ¼ cup batter into pan and swirl rapidly until batter covers the bottom. Immediately pour off batter that does not adhere. Cook until browned, lift edge and turn. Cook a few seconds on the other side. The second side will not evenly brown. Spray and reheat pan to the smoking point before cooking each crêpe. You may store well wrapped crêpes in the refrigerator with a piece of wax paper between each crêpe. These freeze well and are worth the time involved. This recipe is for meat or vegetable crêpes, not dessert.
Makes 25 to 30 6 or 7-inch crêpes or 20 8-inch crêpes

Cheese Grits

3½ cups water
1½ cups milk
1 teaspoon salt
1¼ cups quick grits, uncooked
1 stick butter
1 6-ounce roll garlic cheese
12 ounces medium Cheddar
  cheese, grated
1 Tablespoon Worcestershire
  sauce
¼ teaspoon garlic powder
½ teaspoon cayenne
Paprika

In a saucepan, bring water, milk, and salt to a boil. Add grits, reduce heat, and cook until done, stirring occasionally. Add butter, cheeses, Worcestershire, garlic powder, and cayenne. Stir until the butter and cheeses have melted. Put in greased 3-quart casserole and sprinkle with paprika. Bake in 350 degree oven for 15-20 minutes or until heated thoroughly.
12 side dish servings or 6 main dish servings

For the creamiest cheese grits ever, serve immediately from the stove.

Feta Cheese Pizza

1 recipe **Thin Pizza Dough**
1 recipe **Pesto Sauce**
1 cup Feta cheese, crumbled
4 tomatoes, sliced
½ cup shredded Mozzarella
  cheese
½ cup shredded Provolone cheese
½ cup grated Parmesan cheese

Prepare pizza crust according to directions. Generously spread pesto on crust. Follow with crumbled Feta cheese, slices of tomatoes, and remaining cheeses. Bake in 450 degree oven for 15 minutes.
Makes 2 12-inch pizzas

Ginger and Green Onion Lo Mein

1 pound fresh or dry Chinese
  Lo Mein Noodles
7 Tablespoons peanut oil
2 Tablespoons finely minced
  ginger root
1 cup coarsley chopped whole
  green onions
2 Tablespoons soy sauce
2 Tablespoons oyster-flavored
  sauce
4 teaspoons sesame oil
¼ cup chicken broth

Boil noodles in salted water. Drain, place in a large bowl, and toss with 3 Tablespoons peanut oil. In a wok, heat remaining 4 Tablespoons peanut oil on high. When hot, add ginger and onions, and cook about 1 minute until fragrant. In a bowl, combine soy sauce, oyster sauce, sesame oil, and chicken broth. Mix well. Add to the ginger-onion mixture. Pour over noodles and toss well. Serve hot.
12 servings

This may be prepared early in the day and served at room temperature.

Herbal Cheese Quiche

1 cup Pepperidge Farm Herb
  Seasoned Stuffing
1 cup freshly grated Parmesan
  cheese
6 Tablespoons butter, melted
3 8-ounce packages cream
  cheese, softened
2 cloves garlic, finely chopped
2 Tablespoons dried parsley
  flakes
1 teaspoon dried oregano leaves
1 teaspoon dried basil
½ teaspoon thyme
½ teaspoon cracked black pepper
1 teaspoon Worcestershire sauce
4 large eggs, at room
  temperature

Sauce:
2 cups **Garden Fresh Tomato
  Sauce**
1 10-ounce package frozen peas,
  thawed

Preheat oven to 350 degrees. In a small bowl, combine stuffing, Parmesan cheese, and 2 Tablespoons butter. Press mixture into bottom of greased 9⅝-inch spring-form pan. Bake for 10 minutes, remove, and leave oven on. In a large bowl, with an electric mixer at medium speed, beat cream cheese until fluffy. Beat in 4 Tablespoons butter, garlic, herbs, and pepper until well mixed. Beat in Worcestershire and then eggs, one at a time, mixing well after each addition. Pour filling over crust and bake for 1 hour. Turn off heat and leave in oven for 30 minutes with the door ajar. Serve wedges warm, topped with the sauce, and a tossed green salad. This cheese quiche, covered with plastic wrap, will keep several days in the refrigerator. Great warm or cold!

Sauce:
Combine sauce and peas and heat to serve. This is an easy, yet elegant, topping for Herbal Cheese Quiche.

This is an excellent accompaniment for a soup and salad luncheon.

Herbal Cheese Bits

Prepare Herbal Cheese Quiche in a greased 8 x 12 baking dish and bake as directed for the Quiche. Cool. Cut into small squares and serve.

Garden Party Pasta

1 stick unsalted butter
1 medium onion, minced
2 large cloves garlic, minced
1 pound thin asparagus, ends
  trimmed, cut diagonally into
  ½-inch slices, tips left intact
½ pound mushrooms, thinly
  sliced
1 cup cauliflower, broken into
  small flowerets
1 medium zucchini, cut into
  ¼-inch rounds
1 small carrot, halved
  lengthwise, cut diagonally into
  ⅛-inch slices
½ pint whipping cream
½ cup chicken stock
2 Tablespoons chopped fresh
  basil*
¼ cup chopped cooked smoked
  ham
5 green onions, chopped
Salt
Freshly ground black pepper
1 pound fettucine, cooked al
  dente, thoroughly drained
1 cup freshly grated Parmesan
  cheese

Reserve several pieces of asparagus tips, mushrooms, and zucchini for garnish. Heat wok or large, deep skillet over medium-high heat and melt butter. Add onion, garlic, and saute until onion is softened, about 2 minutes. Add asparagus, mushrooms, cauliflower, zucchini, and carrot. Stir-fry 2 minutes and remove vegetables. Increase heat to high. Add cream, stock, and basil. Allow mixture to boil until liquid is slightly reduced, about 2-3 minutes. Stir in ham and green onion. Cook 1 minute more. Season with salt and pepper. In a large bowl, toss pasta and cheese together until thoroughly combined. Add vegetables, liquid from wok, and toss until combined. Turn onto large serving platter. Garnish with reserved vegetables. Serve immediately. Pass additional Parmesan cheese. Vegetables may be chopped several hours in advance, wrapped, and refrigerated.
*Two teaspoons dried basil may be substituted.
4-6 main dish servings or 6-8 side dish servings.

For a light dish, omit ham and add 1 pound cooked, shelled shrimp.

Giant Ravioli

Spinach and Ricotta Filling:
½ stick butter
½ cup minced onion
1 10-ounce package frozen
    chopped spinach, thawed and
    minced
½ teaspoon salt
1 heaping cup Ricotta cheese
⅓ cup freshly grated Parmesan
    cheese
1 egg yolk
¼ teaspoon nutmeg
Salt
Freshly ground black pepper

Ravioli Dough:
3 cups flour
4 eggs

Cheese Sauce Rossi

Spinach and Ricotta Filling:
In a skillet, melt butter and sauté onion until lightly colored. Stir in spinach and salt, stirring until spinach is coated well. Add ricotta cheese, Parmesan cheese, egg yolk, and nutmeg. Season with salt and pepper and mix well. Cover with plastic wrap and chill for at least 4 hours or overnight.
Makes 2½ cups

Ravioli:
Place flour and egg in bowl of food processor and process until dough begins to stick together. Remove from processor, form into a ball, cover with a cloth and allow to rest 20-30 minutes. Pinch one piece of dough at a time and pass through the rollers of a pasta machine until very thin. To assemble the ravioli, place one strip of pasta on lightly floured board. Brush pasta with water and place filling, 2 Tablespoons at a time, at regular intervals on the pasta. Run another strip through the pasta machine and lay on top of the pasta with filling. Press the top piece down to seal around each mound of filling. With a ravioli cutter or pastry wheel, cut 3-inch squares around each mound of filling. Repeat until all pasta and filling is used. Allow ravioli to dry one hour. The ravioli may be frozen after they have been assembled. Place in a single layer on a cookie sheet to freeze individually. When frozen, place in a ziplock bag until ready to serve. They may be cooked frozen but cooking time will be longer.
To cook the ravioli, drop a few at a time in boiling salted water until they come to the surface, about 7 minutes. Remove from the water with a slotted spoon, drain well, and place in a large buttered bowl or chaffing dish.
To serve the ravioli, top with Cheese Sauce Rossi, sprinkle with pepper, and serve at once. Pass freshly grated Parmesan cheese, if desired.
6-8 servings

Continued

Cheese Sauce Rossi

1 stick butter
½ cup freshly grated Parmesan
cheese
¼ cup shredded Mozzarella
cheese
¼ cup shredded Provolone cheese
½ cup whipping cream

In the top of a double boiler, melt butter. Combine cheeses, add to butter and heat until melted. Slowly add cream and whisk until smooth.
Makes 1½ cups

This cheese sauce is not only delicious with **Giant Ravioli** *but any pasta. Add to cooked and drained noodles, toss, sprinkle with freshly ground black pepper and serve at once. Easy yet so good!*

Fettucine with Sun-Dried Tomatoes

2 Tablespoons butter
¼ cup freshly grated Parmesan
cheese
¼ cup freshly grated Romano
cheese
¼ cup shredded Mozzarella
cheese
½ cup whipping cream
2 Tablespoons chopped sun-dried
tomatoes
1 small garlic clove, pressed
½ pound fettucine, cooked al
denté and drained
¼ teaspoon freshly ground black
pepper

In the top of a double boiler, melt butter. Combine cheeses, add to butter and heat until melted. Slowly add cream to cheese mixture and whisk until smooth. Do not overheat or the cheeses will get stringy. Add tomatoes, garlic, and heat thoroughly. Toss with warm fettucine, season with freshly ground pepper, and serve at once.
2 main dish servings or 4 side dish servings ·

Pot Stickers

Dough:
3 cups white flour
1½ cups boiling water

Filling:
8 cabbage leaves, Bok Choi or
    Napa
Boiling water
1 pound boneless pork shoulder,
    finely chopped
3 green onions, finely chopped
1 sprig parsley, finely minced
½ teaspoon minced ginger root
1 clove garlic, minced
2 Tablespoons thin soy sauce
1 Tablespoon dry sherry
1 Tablespoon sesame seed oil
1 teaspoon sugar
½ teaspoon salt
2-3 teaspoons cornstarch

Cooking:
2 Tablespoons oil
1 cup boiling water

Sauce:
¼ cup dark soy sauce
1 Tablespoon sesame seed oil
½ teaspoon minced fresh ginger
1 green onion, finely minced,
    about 1 Tablespoon

Dough:
The pastry dough is a 2 to 1 mixture of flour and boiling water. The boiling water cooks the flour and makes a smooth pasty consistency. Combine the flour and boiling water until thoroughly blended, adding more water if necessary. Allow the dough to cool slightly, then knead it on a well-floured surface about 5 minutes until it is spongy. Completely cool and rest for 20-30 minutes. In the meantime, prepare the filling.

Filling:
Wash and break up the cabbage leaves. Place in a large bowl and pour boiling water over to wilt. Drain completely. In a food processor, finely mince the cabbage leaves, then drain the water that forms. In a bowl, combine pork, cabbage, green onions, and parsley. In a large mixing bowl, combine remaining filling ingredients and stir in the pork mixture. The filling should have the consistency of a thick, lumpy porridge. Add additional cornstarch if mixture is runny.

Dumplings:
Roll the rested dough to $\frac{1}{16}$ inch and cut into 3½-inch circles. Place a circle in the palm of 1 hand and form into a shallow cup. Moisten the outer edges with water or egg white. Put about 1 teaspoon filling in the center and fold the patty in half and pinch together to seal, forming a half moon. Pleat one side and pinch working from one end to the other. Place on a floured cookie sheet, pleated side up. At this point, the dumpling may be wrapped for freezing and will keep for several weeks.

Cooking:
Use a very large heavy frying pan with a lid. Heat to medium-high, and add 2 Tablespoons oil. When the oil is moderately hot, but not smoking, add the dumplings. Arrange snugly but not pressed together. Brown the bottoms slowly, and check as they cook. When the bottoms are medium brown, add 1 cup boiling water for 24 dumplings. As a rule of thumb, the water should be about halfway up the dumplings. Tightly cover the pan and cook at a very gentle boil until the water is absorbed, about 10 minutes. If working with frozen dumplings, it is not necessary to thaw first, though steaming time will be a little longer.

Sauce:
In a bowl, combine all ingredients and use to dip the dumplings.
12-14 servings.

Vegetables

PRAIRIE OF THE CANOES

Early French settlers named the area that would become known as Monroe *prairie des canots*, or "prairie of the canoes," because it was one of the early landing places where the Indians came to trade with the hunters and trappers. Throughout history our area has been known as a trading center for America's earliest inhabitants.

Northeastern Louisiana was home to the Indians at least as early as 2000-1500 B.C., long before the beginning of the Roman Empire. The settlement at Poverty Point in northeastern Louisiana is one of the oldest and most important archeological finds in the United States. At the time Poverty Point was settled, most Indians lived in small groups, rarely numbering more than 200 people. This village, however, contained 5,000 to 6,000 people. The Indians at Poverty Point were an advanced civilization. They lived on six miles of artificial ridges, ten feet high, seventy-feet wide and approximately one hundred feet apart. They also built three large mounds, nearly equal in weight to the Great Pyramid of Cheops.

Even these Stone Age Indians enjoyed the bounty of Louisiana. There is evidence that they ate fish, deer, birds, reptiles, small mammals, and native plants. Centuries later, their descendants taught the first French and Cajun settlers how to cook white potatoes, sweet potatoes, corn, beans, squash, peanuts, tapioca, and pecans. All of these foods were unknown in other parts of the world. To these new ingredients cooks added spices from Africa, foods brought to the new world by the Spanish, and classical French cooking techniques. This mixture blended to become Louisiana's distinctive cuisine.

In addition to food, Indians gave Louisiana places musical names — Ouachita, Tensas, Caddo — as well as many interesting legends. One of the most famous Indian stories concerns the origin of the Spanish moss which hangs from trees throughout much of the South. According to the legend, the daughter of a Chitimacha Indian chief died just before her marriage and her grief-stricken lover begged to be allowed to keep her hair. He took her braids and wandered away from the tribe along the bayous scattering the strands of her hair through the trees. Eventually the hair turned gray and was named "Spanish Moss."

Fresh Artichokes

Artichokes
Package Italian seasoning
Garlic pods, chopped
Lemon juice
Olive oil

Cut stems and tops from artichokes and trim the leaves. Season uncooked artichokes with Italian seasoning and place garlic in center of artichokes. Drizzle lemon juice and olive oil over top and into center. Steam 40 minutes to 1 hour, or until tender.

Allow one artichoke per person if served as a vegetable. Artichokes are also delicious as an appetizer with any number of dips such as horseradish, buttermilk, Bearnaise, Hollandaise, or simply lemon butter.

Ham and Asparagus Roll-Ups

24 fresh asparagus, trimmed
2 Tablespoons lemon juice
2 Tablespoons butter, melted
Lemon pepper
8 thin slices deli ham

Steam asparagus spears until tender. Season with lemon juice, butter, and lemon pepper. Roll 3 spears in a slice of deli ham. Place on platter and garnish with olives and peppers.
8 servings

Marinated Asparagus

2 pounds asparagus, trimmed
Best Vinaigrette Dressing

Steam asparagus for 8 minutes. Cool completely. Cover with **Best Vinaigrette Dressing.** Chill 2-4 hours.
8 servings

Roasted Asparagus

½ pound fresh asparagus,
    trimmed and peeled halfway
    up
2 teaspoons extra virgin olive oil
½ lemon, cut into wedges
Freshly ground black pepper

Preheat oven to 500 degrees. Place asparagus in a single layer on a baking sheet or shallow pan. Drizzle with olive oil. Roast asparagus in the middle of the oven, turning spears occasionally for even cooking and to avoid browning, about 8-10 minutes, depending on the thickness of the stalks. Serve hot with lemon wedges and a pepper mill at the table.
2 servings

"Horsey" Green Beans

2 pounds fresh green beans
Salt
Black pepper

Wash and snip off the ends of green beans. Steam green beans for 10-12 minutes or until desired degree of doneness. Chill. When ready to serve, arrange green beans on platter, season with salt and pepper, and top with horseradish sauce.
8 servings

Horseradish Sauce

½ cup horseradish
2 cups sour cream

Whisk horseradish and sour cream together. Refrigerate. This will keep for several days.
Makes 2½ cups

This may be served hot as a vegetable dish or cold as a salad.

Stir Fried Broccoli

1 bunch broccoli
2 Tablespoons oil
Salt
Black pepper
¼ cup water

Wash broccoli and cut off the flowerets. Peel the stems and cut into diagonal slices. In a heavy saucepan, heat the oil. When it is hot, add the broccoli, stirring constantly. Season with salt and pepper. Add water, cover immediately, and cook for 3 minutes, shaking the pan occasionally.
4 servings

Brussels Sprouts with Walnuts

3 cups firm fresh Brussels
  sprouts*
4 Tablespoons butter
1 Tablespoon flour
¾ cup chicken broth
1 teaspoon salt
Black pepper
1 cup coarsely chopped walnuts
½ cup bread crumbs

For fresh sprouts, peel off any wilted or yellowing leaves and shave off the base of the stem to rid it of any brown color. Cut a shallow cross in the bottom of the stems so that they will cook evenly. Boil whole sprouts for 5-7 minutes or steam whole for 15-20 minutes.

Melt 2 Tablespoons butter in a saucepan. Add the flour and stir to blend. Gradually add the chicken broth and bring to a boil. Stir constantly until thickened. Season with salt and black pepper. Taste for seasoning. Add the walnuts and sprouts and simmer partially covered for 10 minutes. In a small saucepan, melt the remaining 2 Tablespoons butter, stir in the bread crumbs, and cook for 4 minutes or until the crumbs are golden brown. Transfer the Brussels sprouts to a heated serving bowl and sprinkle top with browned crumbs.
*2 10-ounce packages frozen sprouts may be used, prepare according to package directions.
8 servings

Camouflaged Carrots

2 pounds carrots, sliced
1 Tablespoon sugar
2 teaspoons cornstarch
½ teaspoon salt
½ teaspoon ground ginger
½ teaspoon coriander
2 teaspoons candied ginger, minced
¾ cup freshly-squeezed orange juice
3 Tablespoons butter

Steam carrots until tender. Drain. In a saucepan, combine sugar, cornstarch, salt, ground ginger, coriander, candied ginger, and orange juice. Cook over medium-high heat, stirring constantly until thick. Add the butter, stir, and pour over the carrots.
10-12 servings

Cauliflower Au Gratin

1 medium cauliflower
1 cup sour cream
1½ cups grated sharp Cheddar cheese
Salt
Black pepper

Break cauliflower into flowerets. Cook covered in a small amount of boiling salted water until tender. Drain well. Place half of cauliflower in a 1-quart casserole dish. Combine sour cream and 1 cup cheese, season with salt and pepper, and mix well. Pour half of cheese mixture over cauliflower, add the remaining cauliflower, then top with remaining cheese mixture. Sprinkle with ½ cup cheese. Bake uncovered in a 350 degree oven until hot, about 15 minutes.
6 servings

Cauliflower and Broccoli Extraordinaire

1 head cauliflower, broken into flowerets
1 head broccoli, broken into flowerets
2 teaspoons grated onion
½ cup margarine
½ teaspoon salt
Black pepper to taste
4 Tablespoons flour
2 cups milk
1 8-ounce package cream cheese, cut into small pieces
2½ cups grated Cheddar cheese

Cook cauliflower and broccoli with grated onion in boiling water until tender. Drain well. Meanwhile in a saucepan, melt margarine. Add salt, pepper, and flour, stirring until smooth. Slowly add milk and cook until slightly thick. Add cream cheese and stir until completely melted and smooth. Put vegetables into a 9 x 13 baking dish. Pour the sauce over vegetables and mix lightly. Sprinkle with cheese. Cover with foil and bake at 350 degrees for 30-40 minutes. May be frozen.
10-12 servings

Great with grilled meat or fish.

French-Fried Cauliflower Au Gratin

1 head cauliflower, cut into
　flowerets
2 eggs
2 Tablespoons water
1 cup fine cracker crumbs
Vegetable oil
2 Tablespoons margarine
2 Tablespoons flour
1 cup milk
¼ teaspoon salt
Dash black pepper
1 cup grated Cheddar cheese

Cook cauliflower in salted water until just tender. Combine eggs and water and beat well. Dredge flowerets in egg mixture, then cracker crumbs, and deep fry in hot oil until brown. Keep warm while preparing sauce. Melt margarine, add flour, and stir until smooth. Cook a few minutes, then gradually add the milk. Cook over medium-low heat, stirring until thick and bubbly. Add salt, pepper, and cheese, stirring until the cheese melts. Serve over cauliflower.
4 servings

Cauliflower Puff

1 head cauliflower, cut into
　flowerets
½ cup mayonnaise
½ cup grated sharp Cheddar
　cheese
½ teaspoon dry mustard
¼ teaspoon salt
¼ teaspoon cayenne

Cook flowerets until crisp tender. Place cauliflower in a greased 8 x 8 dish. Combine remaining ingredients and spread over cauliflower. Bake, uncovered, at 400 degrees for 8-10 minutes until puffed and lightly browned.
4 servings

Corn on the Cob with Basil Butter

2 sticks butter
¼ cup chopped fresh basil
12 ears corn, cooked

Melt butter with basil. Pour over hot corn on the cob.
12 servings

Never-Fail Corn Pudding

½ stick butter, melted
6 eggs, beaten
1 cup milk
½ cup flour
2 Tablespoons sugar
¼ teaspoon salt
2 17-ounce cans cream style
    corn

Combine butter, eggs, milk, flour, sugar, and salt, and beat with a wire whisk. Add corn and whisk again. Pour into a greased 2-quart casserole. Bake in 325 degree oven for 70 minutes or until knife inserted is clean.
6-8 servings

Elegant Eggplant Bake

4 eggplants, peeled and cut into
    1-inch cubes
4 Tablespoons butter
2 onions, chopped
4 ribs celery, chopped
2 cups soda cracker crumbs
2 eggs
¼ cup milk
2 cups grated American cheese
1 cup freshly grated Parmesan
    cheese
2 Tablespoons butter

In a saucepan, parboil eggplants 10-15 minutes. Drain. In a large skillet, melt butter and sauté onion and celery until tender. Add eggplant and cracker crumbs and mix well. Beat the eggs with milk then add to eggplant mixture. Pour ½ eggplant mixture into a greased 9 x 13 baking dish. Spread the American cheese. Pour the remaining mixture, follow with the Parmesan cheese, and dot the top with butter. Brown in 350 degree oven for 20-25 minutes.
12 servings

So good with game.

Mushroom Ratatouille

2 medium zucchini, unpeeled
3 medium tomatoes, unpeeled
1 medium green bell pepper,
    seeded
1 pound fresh mushrooms
1 medium onion
¼ cup PLUS 2 Tablespoons
    vegetable oil
2 cloves garlic, pressed
1½ teaspoons salt
¼ teaspoon black pepper
½ teaspoon thyme

Cut zucchini into ½-inch slices, tomatoes into large chunks, mushrooms in half, and pepper into 1-inch pieces. Thinly slice the onion. In a skillet, add ¼ cup oil and sauté the green pepper, onion, and garlic until tender. Add 2 Tablespoons oil, zucchini, tomatoes, mushrooms, salt, pepper, and thyme. Cover and simmer for 5 minutes or until desired doneness. Serve hot.
12 servings

Vegetables

Southern Summer Peas

1 *quart fresh shelled purple-hull,
crowder, or lady peas*
1 *whole onion, peeled*
2 *teaspoons salt*
1 *teaspoon black pepper*
1-2 *teaspoons sugar*
4 *slices bacon*
5-6 *cups water*

Clean peas and rinse thoroughly. In a large saucepan, place all
ingredients and bring to a boil. Reduce heat and simmer uncovered
for 2 hours. At the end of cooking time you may separate onions
into pieces and let sit covered until serving time.
6-8 servings

*When summer peas are plentiful — buy a bushel, blanch, and freeze. A
special treat in winter.*

Country-Style Okra and Tomatoes

3 *pounds fresh young okra*
10 *slices bacon*
2 *medium onions, chopped*
2 *teaspoons salt*
8 *medium firm ripe tomatoes,
peeled and chopped*
½ *teaspoon cayenne*

Wash okra, let dry completely, and cut into 1-inch pieces. In a skillet,
fry the bacon until crisp and brown. Remove bacon, drain, and set
aside. Add okra, onion, and salt to the bacon drippings in the skillet.
Cook for 10 minutes over high heat. Lower heat, add tomatoes and
cayenne and cook for 2 minutes, stirring constantly. Reduce heat and
simmer for about 45 minutes, stirring frequently. Taste for seasoning.
Serve topped with crumbled bacon.
12 servings

Truly Southern.

Okra-Corn-Tomato Medley

1 *medium onion, chopped*
3 *Tablespoons butter or
margarine*
½ *pound fresh okra, sliced,
about 2 cups*
3 *medium ears fresh corn, cut
from cob, about 2 cups*
4 *medium tomatoes, peeled and
chopped, about 3 cups*
1 *teaspoon sugar*
1 *teaspoon salt*
¼ *teaspoon black pepper*

In a Dutch oven, sauté onions in butter until tender, add okra, and
cook 5 minutes, stirring occasionally. Add remaining ingredients and
stir well. Cover and simmer 15 minutes or until corn is tender.
6-8 servings

Roasted Peppers

3 *green or red bell peppers*
3 *garlic cloves, halved*
⅓ *cup vegetable or olive oil*
Salt
Freshly ground black pepper
Juice of ½ lemon

Char peppers over gas flame or under broiler until skins blister and blacken. Place in tightly sealed plastic container and let steam for 10 minutes. Peel skins and remove seeds. Cut peppers lengthwise into strips. Layer with garlic in bowl. Cover with oil and season to taste with salt, pepper, and lemon juice. Cover and refrigerate. Can be prepared up to one week ahead of time. Bring peppers to room temperature before serving.
6-8 servings

Dressed New Potatoes

1-2 *potatoes per person*

Toppings:
Butter
Grated Cheddar cheese
Grated Parmesan cheese
Chopped green onions
Sour cream
Bacon bits
Herbs

Buy smallest, most uniform potatoes that can be found. Arrange potatoes in single layer on baking sheets. Bake in 350 degree oven 40-45 minutes, or until tender. Potatoes may be kept hot in an insulated cooler for up to 6 hours, though the crispness is reduced. Potatoes may be recrisped in the oven just before serving if desired. Serve with a combination of various toppings.

These potatoes will be the talk of your party. Kids love these "little baked potatoes" — just their size.

Man-Pleasing New Potatoes

14-18 *new potatoes, about 2*
  pounds, unpeeled
3 *cups water*
1 *teaspoon salt*
1 *stick butter*
4-6 *green onions, chopped*
¼ *cup chopped parsley*
2 *large cloves garlic, finely*
  chopped
½ *teaspoon salt*
½ *teaspoon black pepper*

In a baking dish, cover potatoes with water, add salt, and seal tightly with a lid. Bake at 350 degrees for 1 hour and 15 minutes or until tender. In a saucepan, melt butter and add green onions, parsley, garlic, salt, and pepper. Drain water off potatoes. Pour butter sauce over potatoes. Return to oven and bake for 10 minutes.
8 servings

Basilico Potatoes

⅓ cup extra virgin olive oil
3-4 medium baking potatoes,
  unpeeled and sliced ¼-inch
1 teaspoon salt
½ teaspoon freshly ground black
  pepper
½ cup chopped fresh basil

Preheat broiler. Line baking sheet with foil and coat with
2 Tablespoons olive oil. Arrange potato slices on baking sheet,
overlapping as little as possible. Drizzle remaining olive oil over the
potatoes and season with salt and pepper. Turn potatoes to coat
generously. Broil 5-6 inches from heat about 10 minutes on each
side or until golden brown. Watch to avoid burning. Remove
potatoes from pan and toss quickly in bowl with basil. Serve
immediately.
4 servings

Superb with grilled steak or chicken.

Potatoes Savoyard

6 large potatoes, peeled
1 medium white onion, cut in
  thin strips
2 cloves garlic, crushed
½ teaspoon oregano
1 Tablespoon lemon pepper
1 stick butter
6 ounces Gruyére or Swiss
  cheese, thinly sliced
½ pint whipping cream

Slice potatoes into thin rounds and parboil in 2 cups water for 5
minutes. Drain and set aside. Sauté onion, garlic, oregano, and lemon
pepper in butter until onions are clear. In a 9 x 13 baking dish layer
potatoes, then the onion mixture, cheese, and whipping cream. Be
sure to end last two layers with potatoes and cheese. The onion
mixture does not look pretty on top. Bake at 350 degrees for 30
minutes.
8 servings

This is a wonderful addition to pork or beef tenderloin.

Southern Sweet Potato Ring

8 medium sweet potatoes
1 stick plus 1 Tablespoon
  butter, softened
½ cup light brown sugar
1 5-ounce can evaporated milk
1 teaspoon nutmeg
1 teaspoon cinnamon
1 teaspoon vanilla
1 egg, slightly beaten
¾ cup raisins, optional
½ cup dark brown sugar
½ cup pecan halves

Bake sweet potatoes in 350 degree oven for 1 hour 30 minutes.
Remove peeling. In a large bowl, mash potatoes with a fork. Add
1 stick butter, light brown sugar, milk, nutmeg, cinnamon, vanilla, and
egg. Mix well. Fold in raisins. Generously spray a bundt pan or 9-cup
mold with cooking spray and lightly grease with 1 Tablespoon soft
butter. Sprinkle dark brown sugar in bottom of pan, follow with
pecan halves, then gently spoon in the sweet potato mixture. Bake at
350 degrees for 60 minutes. After baking, let cool 15 minutes and
unmold onto a warmed platter.
12 servings

An elegant presentation for a holiday buffet.

Creole Rice Pilaf

2¼ cups chicken broth
¼ cup white wine
1 stick butter
1 cup brown rice
¼ cup finely chopped onion
Salt
1¼ cups sliced fresh mushrooms
½ teaspoon finely chopped garlic
2 tomatoes peeled, seeded, and
    diced
½ teaspoon oregano
Black pepper
1 ripe avocado
Lemon juice
½ teaspoon dried parsley

In a saucepan, add broth, wine, and 6 Tablespoons butter. Bring to a boil. Add rice, onion, and season with salt. Cover tightly and cook over low heat for about 50 minutes until water is absorbed. In another saucepan, melt remaining butter and sauté mushrooms for 3 minutes. Add garlic, tomatoes, and oregano. Season to taste with salt and pepper. Simmer 5 minutes. Peel and dice avocado and toss with lemon juice. Combine all with rice, tossing gently. Sprinkle with dried parsley and toss once again. If dry, add additional butter.
6 servings

Outstanding.

Spicy Louisiana Spinach

3 10-ounce packages frozen
    chopped spinach
6 Tablespoons butter
3 Tablespoons flour
½ cup chopped onion
¾ cup evaporated milk
¾ cup vegetable liquor, from
    spinach
¼ teaspoon cayenne
½ teaspoon black pepper
½ teaspoon celery salt
1 teaspoon garlic salt
1 8-ounce package Monterey
    Jack cheese, grated
1 teaspoon Worcestershire sauce
½ cup bread crumbs, optional
¼ cup sliced almonds, optional

Cook spinach according to package directions. Drain and reserve liquor. In a large saucepan, melt butter over low heat. Add flour stirring until blended and smooth, but not brown. Add onion and cook until soft, but not brown. Add liquids slowly, stirring constantly to avoid lumps, until smooth and thick. Add seasonings, cheese, and Worcestershire, stirring until cheese is melted. Add spinach to cheese mixture. Pour into a greased 8 x 12 casserole. Top with bread crumbs and sliced almonds, if desired. Bake at 350 degrees for 25 minutes or until hot.
10-12 servings

This spicy spinach is perfect with grilled meats.

Vegetables

Spinach-Artichoke Casserole

1 stick butter
½ cup finely chopped onion
2 10-ounce packages frozen
   chopped spinach, thawed and
   drained well
2 14-ounce cans artichoke
   hearts, drained and chopped
1½ pints sour cream
10 shakes hot pepper sauce
1 Tablespoon lemon juice
1 teaspoon Worcestershire sauce
¼ teaspoon garlic powder
Salt
Black pepper
½ cup Italian bread crumbs
½ cup freshly grated Parmesan
   cheese

In a large skillet, melt butter, add onion, and sauté until wilted. Add spinach and artichoke hearts and mix well. Simmer 3-4 minutes. Remove from heat. Add sour cream, hot pepper sauce, lemon juice, Worcestershire, and garlic powder. Season with salt and pepper and mix well. Pour into a greased 2-quart casserole and sprinkle with bread crumbs and Parmesan cheese. Bake uncovered in 350 degree oven for 20-30 minutes or until hot.
10 servings

Greens Roman Style

1 bunch greens*
4-6 pods garlic, pressed
¼-½ cup extra virgin or French
   olive oil
½ teaspoon salt

Pick leaves from greens and wash thoroughly. Steam for 10 minutes or until tender. Heat oil over moderately high heat. Add garlic and stir fry quickly until lightly browned. Add greens and stir fry for 5 minutes. Season with salt. Serve immediately.
*Chickory, broccoli flowerets, mustard, or beet greens may be used.
6-8 servings

Squash Pirogues

6 medium yellow squash
8 slices bacon, diced
1 small onion, chopped
¾ cup Italian bread crumbs
1 cup grated sharp Cheddar
   cheese
Salt
Black pepper
Paprika

In a saucepan, boil whole squash in boiling salted water, 8-10 minutes or until tender. Cool, split squash lengthwise, scoop out and reserve pulp. Fry bacon until crisp and set aside. In 2 Tablespoons bacon drippings, sauté onion until tender. Add bacon, bread crumbs, squash pulp and season well with salt and pepper. Stuff shells with the dressing, top with cheese and sprinkle with paprika.
8-10 servings

A real hit with non-squash lovers.

Cajun Summer Squash

3 medium zucchini
3 medium yellow squash
6 Tablespoons butter
2 teaspoons Cajun vegetable
   seasoning
½ teaspoon salt
½ teaspoon black pepper

Cut zucchini and squash into julienne strips. In a large skillet, melt the butter over high heat, add Cajun seasoning, and stir until dissolved. Add zucchini and squash. Cook about 2 minutes, until somewhat tender but still crispy, stirring frequently. Be sure that all of the vegetables are coated with butter and seasoning. Add salt and pepper. Serve immediately.
8-10 servings

Baked Tomatoes with Pesto

6 large tomatoes
Pesto Sauce
Olive oil
Salt
Black pepper
Grated Parmesan cheese

Cut tomatoes into ¾-inch slices. Spread pesto sauce on top of each slice. Drizzle with olive oil and season with salt and pepper. Top with cheese. Bake at 350 degrees for 15 minutes.
8-10 servings

Broiled Tomatoes Basil

Tomatoes
Olive oil
Salt
Black pepper
Sugar
Crumbled basil
Marjoram
Creole seasoning
Buttered bread crumbs
Grated Parmesan cheese

Slice tomatoes in half. Drizzle with a small amount of olive oil. Sprinkle with salt, pepper, a tiny bit of sugar, crumbled basil, marjoram, Creole seasoning, and buttered bread crumbs. Top with cheese. Bake at 350 degrees until tender.

Roasted Zucchini

6 large zucchini*
¼ cup olive oil
Salt
Black pepper

Halve zucchini and slice lengthwise into 1-inch strips. Place in shallow baking dish. Drizzle olive oil over zucchini and season with salt and pepper. Bake in 375 degree oven for 30 minutes. Garnish with sprig of rosemary or basil. This also is excellent cooked on the grill with a cooking time of about 20 minutes.
*May substitute yellow squash.
12 servings

Baked Zucchini

5 medium zucchini, grated
1 stick butter, melted
1 cup Bisquick
⅔ cup chopped onion
½ cup freshly grated Parmesan
  cheese
2 Tablespoons chopped parsley
1 large clove garlic, minced
½ teaspoon oregano
½ teaspoon salt
½ teaspoon black pepper
4 eggs, beaten

In a large bowl, combine all ingredients and mix well. Pour into a greased 8 x 8 casserole. Bake in a 350 degree oven for 45-50 minutes or until heated thoroughly.
6 servings

Zucchini Boats with Spinach

1 10-ounce package frozen
  chopped spinach
4 medium zucchini
3 Tablespoons finely chopped
  onion
3 Tablespoons butter
3 Tablespoons flour
1 cup Half and Half
½ cup milk
½ cup grated Swiss or Gruyére
  cheese
5 drops hot pepper sauce
1 Tablespoon Worcestershire
  sauce
½ teaspoon garlic powder
1 teaspoon salt
¼ teaspoon white pepper
1 Tablespoon grated Parmesan
  cheese

Cook spinach according to package directions, drain and press dry. Set aside. Cook whole zucchini in boiling salted water for about 5 minutes. Drain, cool, and trim off stems. Cut zucchini in half lengthwise, remove and reserve pulp, leaving ¼-inch thick shells. Drain shells and set aside. Chop pulp, drain well, and set aside. In a saucepan, sauté onion in butter. Reduce heat to low and add flour, whisking until smooth. Cook 1 minute, stirring constantly. Gradually add Half and Half and milk. Cook over medium heat, stirring constantly until thick and bubbly. Add spinach, zucchini pulp, cheese, hot pepper sauce, Worcestershire, and seasonings. Place zucchini shells in an 8 x 12 baking dish. Spoon spinach mixture into shells and sprinkle with Parmesan cheese. Bake uncovered at 350 degrees for 15 minutes or until thoroughly heated.
8 servings

Veggies on Safari

This is an African recipe which uses vegetables from the garden in the abundant variety. It is a "one-dish" vegetable offering and is highly seasoned. For a milder taste, one hot chili pepper might be more acceptable than two.

4 large carrots, scraped
8 small new potatoes, peeled
4 baby squash, sliced
½ pound fresh string beans*
¼ cup vegetable oil
2 Tablespoons butter or
   margarine
2 medium onions, chopped
1-2 whole hot chilies, seeded
   and chopped
1 Tablespoon finely chopped
   garlic
2 teaspoons finely chopped
   ginger root
1 teaspoon salt
¼ teaspoon white pepper
¼ cup finely chopped peanuts,
   optional
½ red bell pepper, cut into thin
   strips

Cut carrots lengthwise and crosswise into 2-inch lengths. Place potatoes in lightly salted boiling water. Add carrots, squash, and string beans. Boil for 5 minutes. Drain, then run cold water over the vegetables to prevent further cooking. In a heavy saucepan, heat the oil and butter, add onions and chilies, and cook 5 minutes, stirring frequently. Add garlic, ginger, salt, pepper, and peanuts, stirring to coat. Next, add carrots, potatoes, squash, string beans, and bell pepper and coat thoroughly with the oil mixture. Reduce heat to medium-low and cook covered for 10 minutes. Serve hot.

*One 10-ounce package frozen string beans may be used.

10 servings

Vegetable Tien

The beauty of this casserole is that it can have more or fewer of the vegetables listed. Measurements of the vegetables do not have to be exact. Use what you have on hand or what is in season.

5 medium zucchini, unpeeled
3 medium baking potatoes,
   unpeeled
4 medium tomatoes*, unpeeled
2-3 white or purple onions
¼-⅓ cup olive oil
Seasoned salt
Black pepper
1¼ teaspoons fines herbes

Thinly slice zucchini, potatoes, tomatoes, and onions. Arrange in a lightly oiled 9 x 13 casserole dish, alternating slices of vegetables for color. Drizzle with olive oil and bake in a 400 degree oven for 30-40 minutes or until potatoes are done. Sprinkle with salt, pepper, and herbs. Serve hot.

*If fresh tomatoes are not available, use whole Italian plum tomatoes.

10-12 servings

If fresh basil is available, this dish is excellent using 8-10 chopped basil leaves in place of the fines herbes.

Vegetables and Herb Julienne

Vinaigrette:
1 cup olive oil
½ cup vegetable oil
½ cup red wine vinegar
⅓ cup chopped fresh parsley
2 Tablespoons fresh lemon juice
1 garlic clove, minced
2 teaspoons dried basil,
  crumbled, or fresh
½ teaspoon salt
¼ teaspoon freshly ground black
  pepper

Vegetables:
1½ pounds carrots, cut into
  julienne strips and steamed
1½ pounds French green beans,
  cut in same length as carrots
  and steamed
½ pound fresh mushrooms,
  sliced
1 red bell pepper, cut into thin
  rings

Combine oils, vinegar, parsley, lemon juice, garlic, basil, salt, and pepper. Place carrots, beans, mushrooms, and bell pepper in a large bowl. Pour vinaigrette over vegetables and stir gently. Cover and marinate 3 hours at room temperature or refrigerate overnight. To serve, line platter with Bibb lettuce leaves and arrange vegetables over lettuce leaves.

10-12 servings

For the **Rehearsal Dinner,** double this recipe.

Entrées

SPORTSMAN'S PARADISE

Louisiana is a perfect place for anyone who loves the outdoors. It is no accident that she is called "the Sportsman's Paradise." The semi-tropical climate and pleasant weather encourage year-round fishing and hunting.

Wherever you prefer to fish — in a pond, lake, river, bayou, or the Gulf — you can find a place you like not too far away. The freshwater specialist can find bass, crappie, bream, and catfish. For the saltwater enthusiast, Louisiana has miles of coastline along the Gulf of Mexico and the Intercoastal Canal. There he may take speckled trout, red snapper, and flounder. From cane poles along the bayou bank to high-tech ocean vessels, the Louisiana fisherman finds his fun.

One unique form of sport for Louisiana is crawfishing. In spite of the commercialization of the crawfish industry that has made these small lobster-like creatures readily available in the markets, many families prefer catching their crawfish the old-fashioned way. They bait traps with bits of bacon or other delicacies and set them out in the marshes and bayous during the spring months. More enterprising sportsmen take nets and just scoop up the "mudbugs." Once enough crawfish are caught, it's time for a "Crawfish Boil," a party long present on the Louisiana social scene. Here the fare is crawfish, "new" potatoes, and corn on the cob all boiled in a spicy seasoning and eaten with or without sauce. All of this spice is washed down with ice cold beer, of course!

Not all of our reputation as a sportsman's paradise is based on our water sports, however. Louisiana also boasts a wildlife population of considerable diversity and abundance. Louisiana hunters list the four seasons of the year as "squirrel, quail, duck, and deer." Especially enjoyable are the cool, crisp mornings of fall and winter when hunters crouch in blinds and wait for the migrating duck and geese. Turkey, dove, woodcock, and snipe are also popular for sport.

Lucky fishermen and hunters enjoy the sport while their families and friends anticipate the feasting. Whatever your favorite sport, you're sure to enjoy coming to Louisiana to relax and have fun, or — as the Cajuns say — to "Pass a good time!"

Irish Brisket

3 pounds corned beef brisket
4 cups chicken broth
1 small head cabbage, cut into
    6 wedges
10 medium red potatoes, in
    jackets

Sauce:
¼ cup butter
¼ cup flour
2 Tablespoons Creole mustard
¼ cup chopped parsley

Simmer beef in chicken broth 3-4 hours or until tender. Remove from liquid and chill. Add cabbage and potatoes to broth and cook 30-40 minutes or until tender. Transfer vegetables and meat to serving platter and keep warm. Skim excess fat from broth and reserve 1½ cups for sauce. Blend butter, flour, and mustard and stir in reserved broth. Cook over medium heat, stirring constantly, until sauce comes to a boil and is slightly thickened. Serve with meat and vegetables. Garnish with parsley.

The secret to this recipe is cooking the corned beef in the chicken stock. For a St. Patrick's Day Feast, serve with Irish Whiskey and Creme de Menthe parfaits.

Country Cajun Roast

4-5 pounds roast, any cut
Creole seasoning
Garlic cloves
Jalapeño pepper, sliced
Worcestershire sauce
Flour
Water

Preheat oven to 400 degrees. Make slits in roast, making sure all areas are covered. In each slit stuff with Creole seasoning, a garlic clove, and a pepper slice. Bathe in Worcestershire and dust with flour. Place in Dutch oven and brown on top of stove. Add water halfway up sides of roast and cover. Bake in oven at 325 degrees for three hours. Check for tenderness after that time and continue cooking if meat is not falling off bone. Serve with rice.
8-10 servings

A turkey is also delicious prepared this way. Stuff as for roast but omit Worcestershire sauce and flour. Do not add water to Dutch oven. Bake as for any poundage of turkey.

Grilled Eye Roast

3-4 pounds eye of round roast
Salt
Black pepper
1½ sticks margarine
½ cup reconstituted lemon juice
3 bunches shallots, chopped
Coarse ground black pepper to
    taste

Season roast with salt and pepper. In a saucepan, melt margarine over low heat. Add lemon juice, shallots, and coarsely ground pepper. Cover and cook, stirring frequently, until shallots are soft. Place roast on a covered barbecue grill to the side of a hot fire, turning frequently and basting with sauce each turn. Cook for 1-1½ hours.
6-8 Servings

Breard's Outdoor Rib Eyes

8-14 pounds well-marbled,
  prime grade, whole rib eye
  roast
Vegetable oil
Salt
Black pepper

Trim roast of excess fat. Liberally rub with oil, and heavily salt and pepper. In a pit or barrel-style barbecue, put 8-10 pounds charcoal in a pyramid pile at one end of pit. Light and let burn with pit open for 10-14 minutes until charcoal is white ash on the outside and fire is very hot. Add 1-2 handfuls of presoaked hickory chips and close pit, leaving both top vents open to preheat pit to 425 degrees. Place prepared roast directly over fire to sear for 5-10 minutes. Roll roast to sear other side for 5-10 minutes. After searing both sides, move roast to center of pit, closing the top vent over the fire. Cook for 1½ hours or so, depending on size of roast, rotating the roast every 15-20 minutes so that it cooks evenly end-to-end and side-to-side. Replenish hickory chips with 1-2 handfuls every 30-45 minutes as needed. Note that one end can be cooked rarer than the other to accommodate a variety of tastes. Remove and serve hot when desired doneness is achieved. When cooking more than one roast at a time, extend the cooking period by about ½ hour, and remove roast at different times to achieve varying degrees of doneness and to serve hot. If an oven or pit to keep the meat warm is not available at the location of the party, one may place the roast in a large disposable roasting pan. Loosely cover with aluminum foil, and place inside a 48-quart ice chest that has been preheated by filling it with very hot tap water. Thinly slice hot meat with a very sharp knife from ½ of the roast at a time.

Grilled Sirloin with Cucumber Yogurt Sauce

2 pounds top sirloin*

Marinade:
½ cup olive oil
Juice of 3 lemons, about ½ cup
¼ cup red wine vinegar
2 cloves garlic, halved
2 bay leaves
1 teaspoon dried oregano,
* crumbled*
½ teaspoon dried basil, crumbled
½ teaspoon salt
¼ teaspoon freshly ground black
* pepper*

Trim sirloin of fat and gristle and cut into 1½-inch cubes. In a large bowl, combine marinade ingredients. Add meat and stir gently to coat. Cover mixture and refrigerate, stirring occasionally, for at least 6 hours or, preferably overnight. Prepare barbecue. Thread meat onto 6 to 8-inch skewers. Brush with marinade. Grill, turning and brushing frequently with marinade, about 8-10 minutes or to desired doneness. Transfer to platter. Garnish with onions, tomatoes, and lemon wedges. Pass sauce separately.
*Tender cuts of lamb or pork can be substituted for top sirloin.
6-8 servings

Cucumber Yogurt Sauce

½ cucumber, peeled, seeded, and
* diced*
½ teaspoon salt
⅓ cup plain yogurt
¼ cup sour cream
½ clove garlic, minced
¼ teaspoon fresh lemon juice
¼ teaspoon dill weed
Salt to taste
Freshly ground black pepper to
* taste*

Place cucumber in colander and sprinkle with salt. Let drain 20 minutes. Rinse and pat dry with paper towels. Transfer to a bowl. Combine remaining ingredients and gently stir into cucumbers. Cover and refrigerate at least 1 hour before serving.
Makes 1 cup

Stuffed Tenderloin

1 7-pound whole filet mignon
Worcestershire sauce
Fresh lemon juice
½ stick butter, melted
Cracked black pepper
Salt

Stuffing:
1½ sticks unsalted butter
1 pound fresh mushrooms, sliced
3 green onion tops, finely
    chopped
2 4-ounce cartons crumbled
    Bleu cheese

Early in the day, liberally coat tenderloin with Worcestershire, lemon juice, butter, pepper, and a little salt. Allow to marinate 4-5 hours at room temperature. In a saucepan, melt butter and sauté mushrooms and onions until tender. Drain. Slit tenderloin deeply and stuff Bleu cheese into the meat slit. Top with sautéed vegetables and close *tightly* with toothpicks. Grill on a *very* hot fire in this manner: Sear meat with left side of slit down, then right side of slit down. It cannot be turned slit-side down or stuffing will drip out! Remove meat to other end of pit from fire, close lid, and cook approximately 20 minutes until rare or longer for more well-done meat. It is recommended that this be grilled to rare or medium-rare only. This may also be broiled.
8-10 servings

L. C. Scally's Award Winning Crawfish Stuffed Tenderloin

For a twist on ''Steak and Tails'', prepare this blue ribbon creation from L. C. Scally's Eatery. Scally's has a casual pub atmosphere that lends itself to offering Louisiana regional specialties in not so traditional presentations.

1 7-8 pound beef tenderloin
1 stick butter
1 pound crawfish tails with fat
½ cup chopped green onions
½ cup chopped celery
½ cup sliced mushrooms
3 Tablespoons Cajun seasoning
1 recipe **Crawfish Etouffe Pie**
    filling

Trim excess fat from tenderloin. Cut tenderloin lengthwise to within ½-inch of other edge, leaving one long side connected. Make a slit lengthwise in each half, making sure not to cut through the tenderloin. In a skillet, melt butter and sauté crawfish, onions, celery, mushrooms, and Cajun seasoning. Fill cavities of tenderloin with crawfish mixture, roll as tightly as possible, and tie with a string. Grill on the barbecue pit for 1 hour turning every 15 minutes. Top with crawfish etouffe.
12-14 servings

The best on the bayou!

Tenderloin Perfect'

4 pounds beef tenderloin
Salt
Cracked black pepper
3 cloves garlic
½ stick butter

Bring tenderloin to room temperature. Salt and pepper the meat. Crush garlic into butter, making a paste. Spread garlic butter mixture over top of tenderloin. Bake uncovered at 500 degrees for 22 minutes. Remove from oven and wrap in foil. Let sit for 20 minutes.
8 servings

Simple but superb.

Oriental Tenderloin

2 pounds boneless beef
  tenderloin
4 Tablespoons butter
2 Tablespoons olive oil
1 teaspoon salt
½ teaspoon coarse ground black
  pepper
Dash of ground sage
Dash of ground cumin
1 pound mushrooms, trimmed
  and quartered
2 cloves garlic, finely chopped
2 medium onions, peeled and
  cut into 8 wedges
2 medium green bell peppers,
  halved, seeded, and cut into
  1-inch pieces
½ cup soy sauce
2 Tablespoons cider or white
  wine vinegar
2 Tablespoons tomato paste
2 medium tomatoes, peeled and
  cut into 8 wedges each

Dice beef into ¼-inch wide strips. In a large frying pan, sauté quickly a few pieces at a time in 2 Tablespoons butter and 1 Tablespoon olive oil. Place in a 4-quart casserole, sprinkle with salt, pepper, sage, and cumin. Toss lightly to mix. In the same frying pan, sauté mushrooms in remaining butter and olive oil for 2 minutes and add to meat. Stir garlic, onions and peppers into drippings in pan. Sauté for 2 minutes, then add to meat. Combine soy sauce, vinegar, and tomato paste in frying pan. Heat to boiling, stirring constantly. Pour over meat and toss lightly to mix. Place tomato wedges around edge of casserole as decoration. Cover with heavy duty foil and bake in a 350 degree oven for 30 minutes. Serve over rice with orange spiced peaches.
6-8 servings

Meats

Grilled Flank Steaks

Marinade:
½ cup **Best Vinaigrette Dressing**
½ cup soy sauce
½ cup dry red wine

Steaks:
4 1½-pound flank steaks, best quality not tenderized
Greek seasoning
Garlic powder
Coarse black pepper

Combine marinade ingredients. Season flank steaks well with Greek seasoning, garlic powder, and pepper. Pour marinade over steaks and marinate overnight or at least 4 hours. Prepare barbecue. Meanwhile, soak hickory chips in water for 30 minutes. When fire is ready, add hickory chips to coals. Grill steaks over hot fire six inches from the coals for 7-10 minutes on each side. Baste frequently with marinade. Serve with Sautéed Red Onions on the side.
12 Servings

Sautéed Red Onions

4-6 red onions, thinly sliced
½ stick butter
2 Tablespoons sugar

In a skillet, melt butter and sauté onions until tender. Add sugar and continue to cook until onions are slightly tender.

Leftover Steak? Try **Marinated Beef Salad** in a pita round.

Grillades and Grits

2½ pounds beef or veal round
Salt
Black pepper
½ cup flour
3 Tablespoons vegetable oil
2 Tablespoons butter
2 large onions, coarsely chopped
1 large green bell pepper, coarsely chopped
½ cup coarsely chopped celery
3 cloves garlic, minced
2 cups chicken stock
2 tomatoes, chopped
1 bay leaf
2 teaspoons salt
1 teaspoon black pepper
6 servings grits, uncooked

Pound the beef or veal rounds, cut into 2 x 3 inch pieces and season with salt and pepper. Dredge meat in flour, and shake off the excess. In a heavy skillet, heat oil and brown meat. Remove meat from skillet and set aside. Pour off remaining fat in skillet, add butter and melt it over moderate heat. When foam begins to subside, add onions, green bell pepper, celery, and garlic. Cook for about 5 minutes, stirring frequently, or until the vegetables are tender. Stir in stock, tomatoes, bay leaf, salt, and pepper and bring to a boil. Reduce heat to low, partially cover the skillet, and simmer for 20 minutes. Return meat and accumulated liquid to the skillet, stirring well. Simmer partially covered for about 1 hour or until meat is tender and sauce is thickened. Adjust seasonings. Half an hour before grillades are done, cook grits according to package directions. Mound grits on warm plates and ladle grillades over grits.
6 servings

A Louisiana brunch favorite.

Veal Benedict

1½ pounds veal cutlets, 12
   slices, ¼-inch thick
1 teaspoon salt
1 teaspoon white pepper
3 Tablespoons flour
3 Tablespoons butter
1 Tablespoon olive oil

Crawfish Topping:
½ stick butter
6 Tablespoons chopped green
   onions
1 pound crawfish tails
½ teaspoon Creole seasoning or
   to taste
¼ cup white wine

6 toasted English Muffins, split
   in half
2 recipes **Hollandaise Sauce**

Have butcher prepare cutlets as for scallopini. Combine salt, pepper, and flour. Dredge cutlets on both sides in flour mixture. Shake off excess flour. In a large skillet, over moderately high heat, heat butter with oil. When very hot, sauté cutlets for 2 minutes on each side. As veal is browned, transfer to warmed serving platter, and keep warm in 140 degree oven. May be made ahead to this point and reheated in microwave oven.

Crawfish Topping:
In a skillet, melt butter and sauté green onions until limp. Add crawfish tails, Creole seasoning, white wine, and sauté 5 minutes. Drain. Keep warm. May be made ahead to this point and reheated. To assemble Veal Benedict, place toasted English muffins on serving platter. Top with a veal cutlet and 2 Tablespoons crawfish mixture. Cover with Hollandaise Sauce and serve.
12 servings

Trout fillets may be substituted for veal, but cooking time will be a bit longer. Crabmeat or shrimp may be substituted for the crawfish.

Veal Milanese

2-3 veal chops or veal scallopini
1 egg beaten
Fine dry bread crumbs*
⅓ stick butter
Salt
Lemon wedges

Trim chops, making nicks around edge so they will not curl when cooking. Dip into beaten egg and coat well with bread crumbs. In a large skillet, heat butter and add all the chops at the same time. Cook briskly, without moving them, until a golden crust forms on underside. Turn carefully and let a crust form on the other side. Lower heat and continue to cook gently for another 5 minutes to make sure they are well done. Just before serving, sprinkle lightly with salt. Arrange chops on a serving dish and garnish with lemon wedges.
*May substitute Italian bread crumbs.
2 servings

Meats

Italian Meatballs

1 medium onion, chopped
3 cloves garlic, minced
1 Tablespoon oil
2 8-ounce cans tomato sauce
1 6-ounce can tomato paste
4 cups water
⅛ teaspoon oregano
2 teaspoons sugar
½ teaspoon basil
½ teaspoon salt
½ teaspoon black pepper

Meatballs:
1 pound ground chuck,
   crumbled
2 Tablespoons dried parsley
4 Tablespoons freshly grated
   Parmesan cheese
2 eggs, slightly beaten
½ cup Italian bread crumbs
½ teaspoon salt
½ teaspoon black pepper

Sauté onions and garlic in oil. Add tomato sauce, tomato paste, water, and spices. Bring to a boil. Prepare meatballs by combining meat, parsley, Parmesan cheese, eggs, bread crumbs, salt, and pepper. Shape mixture into balls. While the sauce is boiling, drop in meatballs, cover, reduce heat, and cook on low for 1½ hours, stirring occasionally. This can be cooked for up to three hours. Serve over cooked spaghetti with crusty bread and a green salad.
6-8 servings

To make **Reindeer Noses** for the Children's Christmas Party make 1-inch meatballs. This will make 3½ dozen.

Hearty Manicotti

2 pounds ground chuck
1 medium onion, chopped
½ green bell pepper, chopped
2 cloves garlic, minced
2 16-ounce cans tomato sauce
1 6-ounce can tomato paste
1 cup water
2 Tablespoons sweet basil
1½ teaspoons sugar
Salt
Black pepper
1 8-ounce package manicotti shells
1 16-ounce carton Ricotta
   cheese
2 cups shredded Mozzarella
   cheese
½ cup grated Parmesan cheese

In a skillet, brown beef with onion, bell pepper, and garlic. Drain. Add tomato sauce, tomato paste, water, basil, and sugar. Season with salt and pepper and mix well. Simmer for 45 minutes, stirring occasionally. Meanwhile, cook manicotti shells according to package directions. Drain and set aside. Place ½ cup sauce in a 9 x 13 baking dish. Combine the Ricotta and Mozzarella cheeses. Stuff the cooked shells and place on the sauce lined casserole. Pour remaining sauce over the shells and sprinkle with Parmesan cheese. Bake in a 350 degree oven for about 30 minutes.
8 servings

Serve with Italian salad and French bread.

Lasagna

1 recipe **Basic Pasta**

Meat Sauce:
3 pounds ground chuck
1 teaspoon salt
1 Tablespoon celery salt
½ teaspoon black pepper
2 cloves garlic, crushed
2 Tablespoons olive oil
2 large onions, chopped
1 green bell pepper, chopped
8 ounces mushrooms, sliced
1 15-ounce can tomato sauce
1 6-ounce can tomato paste
4 cups water
½ cup grated Parmesan cheese
¼ cup grated Romano cheese
¼ teaspoon nutmeg
Dash of oregano
⅛ teaspoon basil

Spinach Filling:
1 10-ounce package frozen
   chopped spinach, thawed
1 16-ounce carton Ricotta
   cheese
1 cup grated Parmesan cheese
1 egg

Grated Parmesan cheese

Noodles:
Prepare the pasta and cut into 2 x 10-inch strips. Place in boiling water that has a little olive oil added to it. Boil noodles approximately 4 minutes, remove and rinse in colander under cold water. To dry, hang noodles on a pasta rack or place noodles flat on wax paper. Several layers of cooked noodles may be layered this way. At this point, the noodles may be frozen. Take a cardboard paper towel tube and roll layers of noodles around the tube, placing wax paper between each layer. Wrap the entire roll in plastic wrap, tape and freeze. Thaw noodles at room temperature or in the microwave.

Meat Sauce:
Mix and mash together meat, salt, celery salt, pepper, and garlic and set aside. In a large Dutch oven, heat olive oil and sauté onions until tender. Add meat mixture and brown well. Stir in bell pepper, mushrooms, tomato sauce, tomato paste, and water. Coat the top of the mixture with Parmesan and Romano cheeses. Sprinkle in nutmeg, oregano, and basil and stir well. Bring to a boil, reduce heat, and simmer on lowest possible setting for 3½-4 hours.

Spinach Filling:
Squeeze all the water out of the spinach. Add cheeses, egg, and mix well.

To assemble Lasagna:
If frozen, thaw noodles. Grease two 9 x 13 baking pans. Place three noodles on bottom of pan, spoon a layer of meat sauce, dot with spinach filling and sprinkle with Parmesan cheese. Repeat layers to ¼ inch from top of pan. Bake in 400 degree oven for 20-30 minutes or until heated thoroughly.
16 servings

This recipe for lasagna should be made over several days. By doing this in stages, it does not seem like so much work. The pasta, meat sauce and spinach filling will freeze well individually or as casseroles. This meat sauce is also excellent over **Giant Ravioli** *or plain spaghetti.*

Basic Pasta

2½ cups flour
2 eggs
2-4 Tablespoons water

Place flour, eggs, and water in bowl of food processor. Blend until dough begins to stick together. Remove from processor, form into a ball, cover with a cloth and allow to rest 10 minutes. Divide dough into thirds, rolling one third at a time. Run dough through pasta machine and cut into desired shapes.

Louisiana-Style Country Ham

Whole ham, approximately
15-25 pounds

Remove outside rind by slitting it down the middle and peeling it off in one big sheet. Remove all of the fat from outside of ham. Cut as much off as possible. Scrape remaining fat off with the edge of a large knife. Place rind back around ham and skewer it in place with metal turkey lacers or a few toothpicks. Put whole ham onto the grill of a covered smoker. The bottom pan should be filled with a combination of charcoal and pre-soaked hickory or mesquite wood chunks. The waterpan located between fire and ham must not be allowed to dry out. Add charcoal and soaked wood every 4 hours. Cook 18-24 hours.

This method of cooking a ham results in a flavor similar to a "Smithfield" ham. It is very dense and richly flavored and is excellent served on biscuits or small party rolls.

Skewered Spiced Pork

Marinade:
½ cup vegetable oil
¼ cup red wine vinegar
1 onion, sliced
4 garlic cloves, halved
3 bay leaves
2 teaspoons salt
½ teaspoon dried oregano,
*   crumbled*
¼ teaspoon freshly ground black
*   pepper*

2 pounds pork loin, trimmed
*   and cut into 1½-inch cubes*
Bay leaves, broken in half

Combine all ingredients for marinade in large bowl. Add pork stirring to coat well. Cover bowl and refrigerate for at least 6 hours, or preferably, overnight. Prepare grill. Thread pork onto 6 or 8-inch skewers, placing ½ bay leaf between every other cube. Brush with marinade and grill, basting several times, turning as necessary until pork is cooked thoroughly, about 10-20 minutes. Make sure pork is done, but not cooked to point of drying out. Transfer to platter. Garnish with chopped onions, peppers, and cucumber slices. Serve immediately.
8 servings

Short Bill's Grilled Pork Loin

1 5½-6½ pound boneless whole
 pork loin
2 large onions, quartered
2-3 cloves garlic, slivered
1 8-ounce bottle Wishbone
 Italian Dressing
2 cups white wine
¾ cup Worcestershire sauce
Morton Nature's Seasoning
Seasoned pepper
8-10 pounds charcoal
5-6 hickory chunks

Early in the day place pork loin in a heavy duty aluminum foil pan. Place onions and garlic in split part of loin. Pour Italian dressing, wine, and Worcestershire over loin. Sprinkle seasonings completely over loin. Cover and let sit at least 3-4 hours before grilling. Place charcoal in one end of grill, let it burn down until coals are gray. Soak wood chunks in water for at least 30 minutes. When fire is ready, set pan on opposite end of pit from fire. Add hickory chunks and close lid. Cook about 4½-5 hours. *Do not pick up lid for 4 hours!* Loin should fall apart at the touch of a fork.

Put this on the grill and go to the ballgame. You'll be the winner at the post game celebration!

Grilled Pork Tenderloin
"When a man cooks, who measures!"

Marinade:
1 8-ounce jar Caesar Salad
 Dressing
Cavender's Greek seasoning
Garlic salt
Freshly ground black pepper
Hot pepper sauce

1½ pounds pork tenderloin

Pour Caesar salad dressing, 10 "shakes" of Greek seasoning, 8 "shakes" of garlic salt, and 15 "seconds" of freshly ground black pepper into a bowl and stir. Add hot pepper sauce to taste. Pour the marinade over pork tenderloin and place in refrigerator 4-6 hours. Place on grill, cover, and cook until slightly blackened on all sides, about 30 minutes. Each time you rotate tenderloin, dip it in the marinade. This should be served well-done. Remove from grill and let tenderloin cool for 10-15 minutes. Slice in ¼ to ½-inch slices.

4 servings

As cocktail fare, allow 2 ounces meat per person.

Honey-Roasted Pork Tenderloin

1½ pounds pork tenderloin
Olive oil
Salt
Black pepper
Creole seasoning
Lemon pepper
Worcestershire sauce
Soy sauce
Pickapeppa sauce
Honey
½ cup white wine

Rub tenderloins with olive oil and season with salt, pepper, Creole seasoning, and lemon pepper. Place seasoned tenderloins in baking pan with sides touching. Drizzle Worcestershire, soy sauce, Pickapeppa sauce, and honey over each tenderloin. Add white wine for moisture in pan. Bake uncovered at 350 degrees for 45 minutes to one hour.

4 servings

Mu Shu Pork

2 Tablespoons sherry
2 Tablespoons soy sauce
2 teaspoons cornstarch
2 teaspoons sugar
1 pound pork tenderloin or
  center pork chops, cut into
  julienne strips
10 Tablespoons peanut oil
2 eggs, slightly beaten
8 ounces fresh bean sprouts
14 black mushrooms, soaked in
   warm water for 30 minutes,
   drained and cut into julienne
   strips
6 green onions with tops, sliced
2 teaspoons salt
1 cup dried lily buds, soaked in
  warm water for 30 minutes
  and drained
8 ounces fresh spinach, washed
  and cut into julienne strips
2 teaspoons sesame oil
2 dozen Mandarin pancakes*

Scallion Brushes:
2 dozen scallions or green
  onions

Hoisin Sauce:
1½ cups hoisin sauce
¼ cup water
4 teaspoons sesame oil
4 teaspoons sugar

Combine first four ingredients, add pork and marinate for 30 minutes. In a wok, heat 2 Tablespoons peanut oil until hot. Add egg and scramble, shredding with a fork. Add 4 Tablespoons peanut oil to wok, add pork and stir fry 5-6 minutes. Remove and set aside. To wok, add remaining 4 Tablespoons peanut oil and heat until hot. Add bean sprouts, and stir fry for 3-4 minutes. Add mushrooms, green onions, and salt and stir fry an additional 1 minute. Add spinach and lily buds. Stir in reserved pork and sesame oil. Prior to serving, heat pancakes either by steaming for 10 minutes in a steamer coated with non-stick cooking spray or warming them, wrapped in foil, in a preheated 350 degree oven for 10 minutes. To serve, use scallion brushes to paint hoisin sauce on Mandarin pancakes, add pork filling, place scallion brush on top of pork filling, and roll up. Happy eating!
*Purchase Mandarin pancakes at an Oriental market.

Scallion Brushes:
Cut off the root and trim the stalk to make about 2 inches of scallion. With a sharp knife cut thin slivers, almost but not quite, through both stalk and root end so the slivers are held together in the middle. Place scallions in ice and water. Refrigerate until cut parts curl into brushlike fans.

Hoisin Sauce:
In a saucepan, combine all ingredients, bring to a boil, and simmer on low 3 minutes.
12 servings

Roast Leg of Lamb

1 5-6 pound leg of lamb
2 cloves garlic
Salt
Black pepper

Gravy:
Pan juices
1 cup water
1 Tablespoon flour
1 teaspoon chopped fresh mint,
   optional
½ teaspoon chopped fresh basil,
   optional
Salt
Black pepper

Stuff lamb with slivered garlic pieces. Salt and pepper all sides of lamb. Place lamb, fat side up, on rack in open roasting pan. Roast in preheated 450 degree oven for 10 minutes. Reduce heat to 325 degrees and roast for 20-30 minutes per pound. Test for doneness with a meat thermometer. Rare will be 140 degrees; well-done will be 170 degrees. Skim fat from pan juices. Add water to pan juices in roasting pan and cook over medium heat, stirring to loosen bits of lamb left in pan. Whisk in flour and cook briskly until gravy is thickened. Add chopped mint and basil. Season well with salt and pepper.
8 servings

Perfect lamb every time.

Butterflied Leg of Lamb

"This is an easy and elegant recipe that even confirmed lamb-haters love. It should be cooked either rare or medium-rare and sliced thinly."

Marinade:
½ cup olive oil
1 teaspoon ground black pepper
2 cloves garlic, crushed
1 Tablespoon minced parsley
2 medium onions, finely
   chopped
2 teaspoons salt
2 lemons, juice and rind
½ teaspoon thyme
½ teaspoon oregano
1 bay leaf, broken
2 cups red wine

5-6 pound leg of lamb, boned
   and flattened

Combine marinade and pour over lamb. Marinate for at least 6 hours or overnight, turning frequently. Remove lamb from marinade. Prepare hot coals for grilling. The lamb is grilled 10 minutes on the cut side and 15 minutes on the fell side. These instructions are for rare. The result will be lamb which is charred on the outside and very rare on the inside. Increase cooking time as desired. For more evenly cooked lamb, grill lamb 4 inches above coals about 20 minutes on a side, basting frequently with marinade. Check for doneness after 30 minutes grilling.
8-10 servings

Lamb Marinade with a little ginger is wonderful on beef shish-ka-bobs.

Cheesy Bacon Loaf

2 18-inch loaves French bread
1-1½ sticks butter
½ cup chopped onions
4 Tablespoons prepared mustard
2 Tablespoons poppy seed
12 ounces Monterey Jack cheese, sliced
1 pound bacon

Slice top crust from bread and discard. Slice each loaf in 1½-inch sections almost through to the bottom. Sauté butter, onions, mustard, and poppy seed. Place in freezer for 15 minutes until ''pasty.'' Spoon butter mixture between each slice and on top. Place sliced cheese between each bread section. Half each bacon slice and place on top of each bread slice. Bake uncovered in 375 degree oven for 20-30 minutes.
Makes 24 slices

Very hearty!

Baker's Deli Loaf

3¼ cups flour
1 Tablespoon sugar
1 teaspoon salt
1 package yeast
1 cup very hot water, 125 degrees
1 Tablespoon butter
¼ cup Dijon mustard
6 ounces ham*, thinly sliced
¼ pound Swiss cheese*, thinly sliced
1 egg white, beaten
Caraway seed, optional

In a large bowl, mix 2¼ cups flour, sugar, salt, and yeast. Stir in hot water and butter. Mix in only enough of the remaining flour to make a soft dough. On floured surface, knead for 4 minutes. On a greased baking sheet, roll dough to 14 x 10-inches. Spread mustard down the center third of dough length. Top this center third with layers of ham and cheese. Cut 1-inch wide strips from the filling to the dough edge. Alternating sides, fold strips at an angle across the filling. Cover the dough with a towel. Place the baking sheet over a large pan, half-filled with boiling water, for 15 minutes. The dough will rise to twice its size. Brush with egg white and sprinkle with caraway seed. Bake at 400 degrees for 25 minutes. Preparation time is 60 minutes from start to finish. The loaf will keep and reheat well.
*Any meat and cheese combination may be used.
6 servings

This makes a great ''tailgate party'' contribution or picnic entrée.

Stromboli

3 loaves frozen bread dough
¾ pound ham, thinly sliced
1 pound Swiss cheese, grated
¾ pound Genoa salami, thinly
  sliced
1 pound Mozzarella cheese,
  grated
¾ pound pizza style pepperoni,
  thinly sliced
Garlic salt
Oregano

Allow bread dough to thaw in refrigerator overnight. Lightly coat bread with non-stick cooking spray and cover with wax paper. Allow bread to rise for about 4 hours. Knead out air bubbles and roll dough into a rectangular shape 17 x 11-inches. In this order layer ham, Swiss cheese, salami, Mozzarella cheese, and pepperoni. Sprinkle with garlic salt and oregano. Fold over and seal. Do not put more than 2 loaves on a baking sheet. Bake in 325 degree oven for 30 minutes or until loaves are golden brown.
24 servings

For a bolder flavor, add chopped green olives.

Tortilla Wrapped Mexican Sandwiches

Fresh Avocado Dip*:
1 small tomato, finely chopped
4 medium avocados, mashed
2 Tablespoons finely minced
  onion
2 teaspoons olive oil
4 drops hot pepper sauce
Salt

Sandwiches:
3-ounce package cream cheese,
  softened
6 8-inch flour tortillas, softened
8 ounces cooked roast beef or
  turkey, thinly sliced
Shredded leaf lettuce
1 cup shredded Monterey Jack
  cheese
Alfalfa sprouts, optional
Salsa or taco sauce

Combine all the dip ingredients and mix well. In a small bowl, combine avocado dip and cream cheese. Blend well. Spread each tortilla evenly with avocado dip to within ½ inch of the edge. Arrange slices of meat, lettuce, cheese, and sprouts, over dip. Spoon on a thin layer of salsa. If sandwiches are made ahead of time omit salsa and spoon onto sandwiches just before serving. Roll each tortilla, secure with two toothpicks, cover securely with plastic wrap and refrigerate until serving time.
*In a hurry, a 6-ounce container of frozen avocado dip may be used.
4-6 servings

*For a fun "South of the Border" menu start with **Apache Cheese Bread**, combine the sandwiches with **Zesty Corn Salad** and finish with **Country Vanilla Ice Cream** and **Out-Of-This World Chocolate Sauce** or **English Toffee Nut Sauce**.*

Grilled Quail with Mustard Butter

8 quail
Creole seasoning
1 stick butter
2 Tablespoons prepared mustard
2 teaspoons fresh lemon juice

Cut each quail down the back. Flatten each bird to allow for maximum surface area to heat. Season well with Creole seasoning. In a saucepan, melt butter, add mustard and lemon juice. Dip each bird into sauce. Cook on grill, 20-30 minutes over hot coals, basting with sauce and turning frequently. To cook indoors, preheat the broiler to maximum heat. Broil about 4 inches from heat until browned, basting frequently. Turn over and brown other side. The less-meaty side will take less time. To serve, arrange on a platter and pour on any remaining sauce.
8 servings

This is undoubtedly the very best way to eat quail.

Venison Chili

Beans:
1 pound package red beans
Bacon drippings
1 clove garlic, minced
1 onion, chopped
1 Tablespoon salt
1 Tablespoon black pepper
½ teaspoon cayenne
1 teaspoon sugar
8 cups water

Chili:
¼ cup oil
1 onion, chopped
2 cloves garlic, chopped
2 pounds ground venison
3 heaping Tablespoons flour
2 Tablespoons chili powder
2 Tablespoons ground cumin
2 teaspoons salt
6 cups hot water
1 8-ounce can tomato sauce

Beans:
Cover beans with water and soak 24 hours. Drain. In a large stock pot, combine beans, bacon drippings, garlic, onion, salt, pepper, cayenne, sugar, and water. Simmer uncovered until beans are tender, about 2 hours, stirring occasionally.

Chili:
In a Dutch oven, sauté onion and garlic in oil until tender. Add meat and brown. Pour off fat, then add flour, chili powder, cumin, and salt to meat, stirring well. Add water and tomato sauce and simmer uncovered 15 minutes. Add meat mixture to beans. Bring to a boil, simmer on low heat uncovered for at least 2 more hours, stirring as needed to prevent sticking. Refrigerate. Reheat to serve. This freezes well and may be doubled. To ensure the best flavor, prepare chili at least 2-3 days prior to serving.
8 servings

Perfect for taking on winter outings.

Grilled Venison Backstrap

Marinade:
2 cups red wine
1½ cups oil
½ cup soy sauce
¼ cup Worcestershire sauce
2 medium onions, chopped
2 cloves garlic, crushed
2 Tablespoons dry mustard
1½ teaspoons parsley flakes
¼ teaspoon salt
1 Tablespoon cracked black
   pepper
Pinch of cayenne

1 4-5 pound venison tenderloin
Lemon pepper
8 pounds charcoal
4 chunks hickory or pecan,
   soaked

Combine all marinade ingredients and mix well. Pour marinade over meat and refrigerate overnight. Piercing the meat also helps the marinade work better. Place charcoal on one end of grill and let burn down until coals are gray. Season meat with lemon pepper. Char venison on each side. Then place meat on opposite side of grill from fire. Place hickory chunks on coals and cook meat 1 hour.
8 servings

To grill the venison, quail, and zucchini for the **Hunt Dinner**, first cook the venison, remove from grill and wrap in foil. This will stay warm for 1 hour if tightly wrapped. Then grill the quail and zucchini according to directions.

Venison Parmesan

3 pounds boneless venison
   backstrap, any cut may be
   substituted
Salt
Black pepper
2 eggs
4 teaspoons water
⅓ cup grated Parmesan cheese
½ cup Italian bread crumbs
½ cup olive oil
2 onions, finely chopped
2 6-ounce cans tomato paste
4 cups hot water
2 teaspoons salt
1 teaspoon marjoram
1 pound Mozzarella cheese,
   thinly sliced

Be sure to remove and clean outer membrane of venison well. Cut tenderloin into ½-inch slices and season with salt and pepper. Beat eggs with water. Combine cheese and breadcrumbs. Dip meat in egg, then roll in breadcrumb mixture. Heat oil in skillet and fry steaks until golden brown on each side. Place steaks in two 8 x 8 baking dishes. In the same skillet, cook onions until tender in remaining oil. Combine tomato paste and water. Add tomato paste, salt, and marjoram to onions and mix well. Boil a few minutes, scraping all of the brown bits from bottom. Pour most of sauce over steaks. Top with slices of cheese, then pour over the remaining sauce. Bake in a 350 degree oven for 30 minutes or until hot and bubbly. This freezes well, thaw ahead of time in the refrigerator and bake.
8 servings

A gourmet treat.

Game

Davis Island Venison Stew

Davis Island was formed when the Mississippi River changed course. It is an area famous for hunting and fishing.

1½ pounds boneless venison
    roast or backstrap, cubed
½ pound sliced link sausage
2 Tablespoons oil
1 onion, chopped
¾ cup chopped celery
2 14½-ounce cans stewed
    tomatoes, chopped
2 14½-ounce cans tomatoes,
    chopped
1 12-ounce can beer
1 Tablespoon Worcestershire
    sauce
1 Tablespoon salt
1 teaspoon sugar
½ teaspoon rosemary
½ teaspoon basil
1 teaspoon black pepper
2 potatoes, peeled and sliced
2 carrots, sliced

In a large deep pot, brown venison and sausage in oil. Add onion and celery and cook until tender. Add tomatoes, beer, Worcestershire, salt, sugar, rosemary, basil, and pepper and mix well. Cover and simmer 30 minutes, stirring occasionally. Add potatoes and simmer uncovered, stirring occasionally for 30 more minutes. Add carrots and simmer 1 more hour, stirring occasionally. Adjust seasonings.
6-8 servings

Favorite fare at the ''deer camp''. A hearty stew that is a one dish meal.

Venison Teriyaki

1½ pounds venison steak or
    tenderloin

Marinade:
½ cup vegetable oil
¼ cup soy sauce
¼ cup honey
2 Tablespoons vinegar
2 Tablespoons chopped green
    onions
1 large clove garlic
1½ teaspoons ginger
¼ cup white wine

Punch holes in steak to allow for absorption of marinade. Combine marinade ingredients. Pour over steak and marinate 4 hours or overnight, turning occasionally. Cook over hot coals on grill, turning once, about 5 minutes on each side for medium rare. Baste occasionally with marinade while cooking.
4 servings

Leftovers make a great sandwich on a French bread roll.

Chicken Cacciatore

½ cup diced bacon
1 medium onion, finely chopped
1 medium green bell pepper,
  finely chopped
1 14½-ounce can tomatoes,
  chopped
1 6-ounce can tomato paste
2½ teaspoons salt
1½ teaspoons freshly ground
  black pepper
½ teaspoon oregano
¼ teaspoon minced garlic
½ cup dry red wine
2 fryers, cut up
½ cup flour
6 Tablespoons olive oil

In a skillet, fry bacon until tender and crisp. Remove bacon and sauté onion and bell pepper until golden. Add tomatoes, tomato paste, bacon, salt, pepper, oregano, and garlic. Simmer 20 minutes, then add wine and stir well. Shake chicken with flour in paper bag. In another skillet, heat oil and brown chicken on all sides. Add chicken to sauce. Simmer 1 hour or until chicken is tender. Serve over rice or pasta.
6-8 servings

A *family favorite.*

Chicken Saltimboca

2 pounds boneless chicken
  breasts
2 Tablespoons butter
2 Tablespoons olive oil
1 pound fresh mushrooms, sliced
6 ounces Mozzarella cheese,
  thinly sliced
1 Tablespoon flour
¾ cup chicken stock
Salt
Black pepper
½ cup Madeira wine
Chopped parsley

Trim chicken breasts of fat and pound until thin. In a heavy skillet, melt butter with olive oil until foam subsides. Brown chicken quickly on each side. Place in a flat ovenproof dish and set aside in a warm place. In the same skillet, sauté mushrooms. Cover chicken with cheese and top with mushrooms. If fat is depleted in the skillet, add more using the same butter and oil proportions. Add flour to fat and stir constantly until the roux is brown. Add stock to make a moderately thick sauce. Season with salt and pepper. Add Madeira at the last moment after the sauce has thickened. Do not boil after this point. Pour sauce over chicken and decorate with chopped parsley. The chicken and sauce should melt the cheese, but if this has cooled run it under the broiler until the cheese melts.
6 servings

Chicken Tetrazzini

5 pounds chicken breasts
5 quarts water
2 strips bacon
1 Tablespoon Creole seasoning
1 Tablespoon salt
Garlic powder
Black pepper
1 pound fresh mushrooms
2 Tablespoons butter
Garlic
1 pound thin spaghetti
1½ sticks butter
¾ cup flour
½ pint whipping cream
1 cup freshly grated Parmesan
    cheese
Salt to taste
Black pepper to taste

First Day:
In a stock pot, combine chicken, water, bacon, Creole seasoning, salt, garlic powder, and pepper. Bring to a boil, reduce heat, cover, and simmer for 1½ hours. Cool chicken in broth. When cool, remove skin and bone, then cut chicken into bite-size pieces. Chill broth. Remove all fat from top and reserve broth.

Second Day:
Sauté whole mushrooms in butter and lots of garlic. Drain and set aside. Bring reserved broth to a boil, add spaghetti, and cook al denté. Drain spaghetti, reserving broth, and set aside. There should be 8-10 cups broth remaining, if not, add as many cans of broth as necessary to reach this amount. Bring broth to a boil, reduce heat, and simmer until reduced to 5 cups. In another saucepan, melt butter and stir in flour until smooth. Add broth, stirring constantly, until thickened. Add cream and cook until it is a rich cream sauce. In a shallow 3-quart casserole, layer ½ of spaghetti, chicken, mushrooms, cheese, salt, and pepper, then ½ of sauce. Repeat layers and top with Parmesan cheese. Garnish with chopped parsley. Bake in 350 degree oven 30-45 minutes or until very hot. Freezes beautifully.
12-14 servings

Chicken Fajita Filler

Marinade:
½ cup **Best Vinaigrette
    Dressing**
½ cup soy sauce
½ cup white wine

4½ pounds boneless chicken
    breasts
Cavender's Greek Seasoning
Garlic powder
Coarse black pepper
Pita bread
Avocados
Lemon juice
Lemon pepper
Alfalfa sprouts

Combine marinade ingredients. Season chicken with Greek seasoning, garlic powder, and black pepper. Pour marinade over chicken. Marinate for 4-6 hours. Prepare barbecue pit. Grill chicken over hot fire approximately 6 inches from coals. Grill 7-10 minutes on each side. Cut chicken into strips. Slice avocados and toss with lemon juice and lemon pepper seasoning. Stuff chicken into pita bread and garnish with avocados and sprouts.
16 servings

A super yet simple grilled chicken recipe. Great not only for pita sandwiches, but excellent for fajitas or an easy, light chicken on the grill.

Chicken Enchiladas

Filling:
10 chicken breast halves
6 cups chicken broth
2 carrots, coarsely chopped
½ large onion
4 cloves garlic
4 sprigs parsley
2 bay leaves

Sauce:
1 stick butter
6 Tablespoons flour
1 Tablespoon vegetable oil
2 medium onions, chopped
2 bunches spinach, stemmed and
   coarsely chopped
4 green onions, cut into pieces
2 4-ounce cans diced jalapeño
   chilies, drained
Salt
Freshly ground black pepper

1½ pounds Monterey Jack
   cheese, grated
Vegetable oil if frying tortillas
24 6-inch tortillas
Sour cream

Filling:
In a large saucepan, combine chicken, chicken broth, carrots, onion, garlic, parsley, and bay leaves. Bring to a boil. Cover, reduce heat and simmer 30 minutes. Turn off heat and let stand until chicken is cooked, about 30 minutes. Remove chicken from broth and cool slightly. Strain cooking liquid, return to saucepan and boil until reduced to 3 cups. Skin and debone chicken. Shred meat and place in medium bowl. Chill.

Sauce:
In a heavy medium saucepan over low heat, melt butter. Add flour and cook until light brown, stirring frequently, about 5 minutes. Whisk in 2¾ cups reserved cooking liquid. Increase heat to medium and cook until sauce thickens, stirring occasionally. Cool. In a heavy large skillet, heat oil, add onions, and cook until soft, stirring occasionally, about 5 minutes. Add spinach and stir until wilted, about 2 minutes. Transfer to processor. Add sauce, sour cream, green onions, and 1 can chilies and purée until smooth. Season with salt and pepper. Add remaining can of chilies, if desired.

To Assemble Enchiladas:
Grease two 9 x 13 baking dishes. Spread ½ cup sauce over bottom of each dish. Add one cup sauce to chicken. Mix in 5 cups grated cheese and ¼ cup reserved cooking liquid. Soften tortillas in hot oil or heat a few seconds in buttered dish in microwave oven. Divide chicken filling among tortillas and roll up. Arrange seam side down in prepared dishes. Spoon remaining sauce over tortillas. Cover with foil. Can be prepared 1 day ahead. Refrigerate enchiladas and remaining cheese separately. Bring enchiladas to room temperature before baking. Preheat oven to 400 degrees. Bake covered until just heated through, about 20 minutes. Uncover, sprinkle with remaining cheese and bake until cheese melts, about 5 minutes. Serve with sour cream.
12 servings

Perfect for luncheon fare with a fruit salad.

Mesquite Grilled Chicken with New Potato Skewers

Marinade:
1 Tablespoon Greek seasoning
1 teaspoon garlic powder
1 teaspoon coarse ground black
  pepper
½ cup soy sauce
Juice of 1 lemon
¼-½ cup olive oil

12 boneless chicken breast
  halves
6-9 mesquite chips
36 small new potatoes
Vegetable oil
3 purple onions, quartered

Combine marinade ingredients, mix well. Pour over chicken, and let stand for 1 hour. Soak mesquite chips in water. Prepare grill for moderately high fire. Rub each potato with 1 Tablespoon vegetable oil. Thread 3-4 potatoes on each skewer, alternating with onion quarters. When fire is ready, place mesquite chips in coals. Put potatoes on grill and cook 15 minutes, basting with marinade as they cook. Place chicken breasts on grill for 20-30 minutes, depending on the size of breasts. Baste chicken once or twice while cooking.
8 servings

Chicken may be cubed and added to skewers with potatoes and onion for shish-ka-bobs. Adjust marinade ingredients accordingly by tasting for salt.

Chicken, Mushroom and Artichoke Bake

4-6 boneless chicken breast
  halves
Salt
Black pepper
Paprika
½ cup butter
½-1 pound mushrooms, sliced
2 Tablespoons flour
1 10-ounce can condensed
  chicken broth
½ cup sherry
1 14-ounce can artichoke hearts,
  drained

Season chicken with salt, pepper, and paprika. In a large skillet, melt butter and sauté chicken until lightly brown. Remove to a baking dish. In the same skillet, sauté mushrooms, add flour and mix well. Stir in broth and sherry. Season with salt and pepper. Simmer for 5-10 minutes and pour over chicken breasts. Bake in 375 degree oven for 1 hour. Top with artichoke hearts and cook for 20-30 minutes.
4 servings

Rosemary-Lemon Chicken

1 cup olive oil
Juice of 3 lemons, about ½ cup
3 cloves garlic, minced
3 bay leaves
1 Tablespoon dried rosemary, crumbled
1 teaspoon salt
½ teaspoon white pepper
2 3½-pound fryers, quartered

In a bowl, combine olive oil, lemon juice, garlic, bay leaves, rosemary, salt, and pepper and mix well. Arrange chicken pieces in a large shallow dish. Pour marinade evenly over chicken, turning to coat. Cover and refrigerate overnight, turning occasionally. Prepare barbecue. Grill chicken, basting frequently, until juices run yellow when pricked, about 10-15 minutes on each side. Transfer to platter. Garnish with lemon wedges and rosemary sprigs. Serve immediately.
8 servings

Shanghai Red-Cooked Chicken

3-4 pound whole frying chicken, washed and dried
½ cup dark soy sauce
1½ cups oil
2 Tablespoons peanut oil
4 green onions, chopped into 2-inch sections
½ teaspoon fresh ginger root, minced
4 cups water
½ cup sherry
½ cup thin soy sauce
1 clove star anise
1 teaspoon salt
Cornstarch paste, 1 Tablespoon cornstarch mixed with 2 Tablespoons water
1 Tablespoon sesame seed oil

Place chicken in a snug bowl and brush dark soy sauce into skin. Let stand in bowl for 30 minutes. Repeat brushing several times. Heat 1½ cups of oil in wok over medium heat then quickly lower chicken in oil. With a large spoon, baste chicken with hot oil and turn it so that skin browns evenly, about 10-15 minutes. The chicken should be a dark brown color. Carefully remove chicken from wok, trying not to break skin. In a Dutch oven, heat 2 Tablespoons peanut oil. When hot, add green onions and lightly brown. Then add ginger root, water, sherry, thin soy sauce, star anise, and salt, and bring to a boil. While liquid is heating, tie legs of chicken together with twine. Lower chicken into boiling liquid, bring to a boil again, and then reduce heat to a slow simmer. The chicken should actually be floating free in liquid. Cover and simmer for 1 hour or until chicken is very tender. Leave chicken in pot covered until 5 minutes before ready to serve. Carefully remove it to a serving platter and reserve one cup of liquid for sauce. Bring reserved liquid to a boil, thickening slightly with the cornstarch paste. Add sesame seed oil and pour over chicken.
8 servings

Poulet á la Bearnaise

8 chicken breast halves, skinned
   and boned
2 large eggs, beaten
⅓ cup milk
Salt to taste
Black pepper to taste
1½ cups cracker crumbs
1½ sticks butter
2 Tablespoons Half and Half

Bearnaise Sauce:
1 stick butter
2 Tablespoons lemon juice
4 egg yolks, beaten and at room
   temperature
¼ cup light cream
1 teaspoon dry mustard
¼ teaspoon salt
Dash hot pepper sauce
¼ cup tarragon vinegar
3 Tablespoons chopped onion
2 Tablespoons tarragon leaves,
   crushed
2 Tablespoons minced parsley

Wash chicken and pat dry. Combine eggs, milk, salt, and pepper. Dip chicken in egg mixture and turn to coat, then dip in cracker crumbs to completely cover. Chill. In a large skillet, melt butter over medium heat. When foam subsides, cook chicken breasts on each side until brown. Keep warm. When ready to serve, reheat sauce with an additional 2 Tablespoons Half and Half. Microwave on high for 1 minute, stirring every 15 seconds until hot. Whisk until smooth. Place chicken on serving platter and spoon 1-2 Tablespoons of sauce on each piece.

Bearnaise Sauce:
Place butter in a 5 cup measure. Microwave on high for 1 minute. Stir in lemon juice, egg yolks, cream, mustard, salt, and hot pepper sauce. Microwave on high 1½ minutes, stirring every 15 seconds. Beat with a whisk until smooth. Set aside. Place vinegar, onion, tarragon leaves, and parsley in a saucepan. Simmer and reduce liquid completely. Cool and blend in sauce. Cover and refrigerate.
4-6 servings

For variation, lightly sauté ½ pound lump crabmeat in ½ stick of butter and spoon on top of chicken with sauce. The crabmeat mixture and sauce are also wonderful over sautéed or broiled trout fillets.

Smoked Turkey

Turkey
Cooking oil
Salt
Black pepper

Brush turkey with cooking oil. Use salt, pepper, and other seasonings to your taste.

TURKEY	CHARCOAL	HOT WATER	HICKORY CHUNKS	COOKING TIME	TEST FOR DONENESS
8-10 pounds	10 pounds	5 quarts	3	4-6	185 degrees
11-13 pounds	Full pan	6 quarts	3	6-7½	or leg moves
14-16 pounds	Full pan	6 quarts	4	6-8	easily in joint

Soak dry hickory chunks for an hour. Prepare smoker with amount of charcoal from chart. Light fire. Allow coals to burn about 15-20 minutes or until coals are without flames and beginning to gray. Place wet hickory chunks on top of burning coals. Fill pan with amount of hot water recommended by chart. When cooking time is longer than six hours, more hot water may need to be added to the pan. Place turkey on grid. Put lid on smoker. (Do not remove lid more times than necessary.) The turkey is smoking properly when the heat indicator needle is in the "ideal" range. If the needle drops to "cool," add more charcoal to the fire. If the needle is in the "hot" range, add more water to the pan. Add charcoal, water and hickory by opening door in front of smoker. Do not leave door open any longer than necessary. Smoke turkey according to time on chart. Basting or turning is not necessary once the meat is placed on grid — the meat bastes itself during cooking. Turkey is done when leg moves easily in joint.

Turkey Jambalaya

2 *pounds hot Jimmy Dean*
  sausage
2 *large onions, chopped*
2 *6-ounce packages long grain*
  and wild rice mix
1 *pound fresh mushrooms, sliced*
2 *Tablespoons margarine or*
  butter
4 *cups turkey meat, 1½ pounds*
2 *2¼-ounce cans sliced black*
  olives
2 *8½-ounce cans artichoke*
  hearts, sliced
⅓ *cup chopped green onions*

In a Dutch oven, brown sausage. Add onions and cook until clear. Drain off any excess fat. Add wild rice to sausage and cook according to package directions. Meanwhile in a saucepan, saute´ mushrooms in margarine and drain. Add mushrooms, turkey, black olives, and artichoke hearts to cooked rice. Garnish with chopped green onions. Bake in a 350 degree oven for 30 minutes or until heated throughout.
8-10 servings

Leftover turkey never tasted so good. A spicy Louisiana treat.

Marie Louise's Turkey and Gravy

This is a classic recipe from **the Cotton Country collection** — a best-selling cookbook from The Junior League of Monroe, Inc.

1 turkey
Dry mustard
Worcestershire sauce
Olive oil
Salt
Black pepper
Vinegar
1 onion, cut in half
Celery
Parsley
Bacon
Butter
2 cups chicken stock

Gravy:
Turkey giblets
4 to 5 cups water
2 ribs celery, chopped
1 onion
Salt
Black pepper
1 Tablespoon oil or butter
1 Tablespoon flour
1 onion, chopped
1 rib celery, chopped
Chopped parsley
Bay leaf
Salt and pepper to taste
2 cups giblet stock

If you buy a frozen turkey, be sure that the turkey is well-thawed. A few hours before you propose to cook it, the day before if possible, rub the turkey well inside and out with a paste which you make up of dry mustard, Worcestershire sauce, olive oil, salt, pepper, and a little vinegar in the proportions to make it into a soft paste. Rub the bird well inside and out with this, then place inside it a whole onion cut in half, a couple of pieces of celery, and a little parsley. Across the breast of the turkey lay 2 pieces of bacon and in the crevice between the drumstick and the body of the turkey stick hunks of butter, about a stick of butter all together. Soak a dishtowel or cheesecloth in olive oil and lay it over the turkey and put it in an uncovered roaster. To this you can add about one to two cups of stock in the roaster, or if you have any gravy left, that is fine, too. In cooking the turkey, you cook it according to the following scale using a 300 degree oven:

7 to 10 pounds, 30 minutes per pound
10 to 15 pounds, 20 minutes per pound
15 to 18 pounds, 18 minutes per pound
18 to 20 pounds, 15 minutes per pound
20 to 23 pounds, 13 minutes per pound

You may baste the turkey only once or twice during the course of cooking. This browns the turkey beautifully and makes it completely tender when you eat it.

Gravy: While the turkey is cooking, take the neck and giblets and cook them all in about 4 to 5 cups of water with celery, onion, salt, and pepper and let them boil until they are thoroughly done. In the meantime, you take a Tablespoon of grease or butter and one Tablespoon of flour and make a roux by browning the flour. Add one chopped onion, 1 piece of chopped celery, some chopped parsley, a bay leaf, salt and pepper to taste. Saute' this until soft and add the stock to this roux. Let it simmer down to make the gravy as you desire. Add the giblets, which have been chopped, to the gravy.

A perfect turkey for the "first Thanksgiving" celebration at your house—the juiciest and most flavorful turkey ever.

Down Home Cornbread Dressing

1 recipe **Grandma's Cornbread**

2 cups Pepperidge Farm Herb Seasoning Stuffing Mix

2 sticks margarine

1½ cups chopped onion

1½ cups chopped green onion

1½ cups chopped celery

1½ cups chopped green bell pepper

2 Tablespoons poultry seasoning

1 Tablespoon sage

Salt

Black pepper

2 14½-ounce cans chicken broth*

Prepare cornbread recipe ahead of time. Let cool. Crumble cornbread, add stuffing mix and combine well. In a skillet, melt margarine and sauté vegetables until tender, add to cornbread and mix well. Add seasonings to taste. Pour broth over all and mix well. Pour into a 9 x 13 casserole and bake at 350 degrees for 30 minutes.

*Additional chicken broth may be added if mixture is too dry.

12 servings

A southern staple.

Cornbread Rice Dressing

1 black iron skillet of cornbread

2 cups cooked rice

1 bunch green onions, chopped

1 large onion, chopped

3 ribs celery, chopped

¾ cup margarine

4-5 slices wheat bread, crumbled

¼-⅓ cup finely chopped parsley

2 eggs, beaten

2 chicken bouillon cubes

1 cup boiling water

1 14½-ounce can chicken broth

1 teaspoon salt

1 teaspoon poultry seasoning

½ teaspoon pepper

⅛ teaspoon cayenne

Prepare cornbread and rice ahead of time. In a Dutch oven, sauté onions and celery in ½ cup margarine until vegetables are tender. In a large bowl, crumble together cornbread, rice, bread, and parsley. Add vegetables and eggs and mix well. Dissolve bouillon cubes in water. Add bouillon and chicken broth to dressing, mixing well. Melt 2 Tablespoons margarine in Dutch oven, add dressing and seasonings. Cook for 10 minutes or until it is light brown, stirring occasionally. Place in greased 2-quart casserole, dot with remaining butter, and bake in 350 degree oven for 30 minutes or until heated thoroughly.

12 servings

Just like at grandmother's house. Very moist.

Italian Stuffed Crabs

1 stick unsalted butter
1 cup minced onion
½ cup minced green bell pepper
½ cup minced celery
3 cloves garlic, minced
½ cup minced green onion tops
2 Tablespoons chopped fresh
    parsley
Juice of 1 lemon
1 teaspoon salt
¼ teaspoon cayenne
4 dashes hot pepper sauce
1 teaspoon Worcestershire sauce
¼ cup water
1 pound crab claw meat
⅓ cup Italian bread crumbs
⅓ cup grated Parmesan cheese

In a skillet, melt butter and saute onions, pepper, celery, and garlic until soft. Add green onion tops, parsley, and lemon juice and saute 5 minutes. Add salt, pepper, hot pepper sauce, Worcestershire, water, and crabmeat, stirring well. Fill twelve 4-ounce ramekins or crab shells. Combine bread crumbs and cheese and top crabmeat mixture. Bake in a 350 degree oven until bubbly.

12 servings

Crabmeat and Artichoke Supreme

1 cup mayonnaise
1 cup freshly grated Parmesan
    cheese
1 cup chopped green onions
1 cup sliced fresh mushrooms
3 14-ounce cans artichoke
    hearts, drained and sliced
1 pound fresh crabmeat
Juice of 1 lemon
½ teaspoon cayenne

Combine all ingredients, pour into a 3-quart casserole, and bake at 350 degrees for 30 minutes. This is so easy and divine! It is great for a ladies' brunch or cocktail party dip.

8 Servings

For brunch, serve in pastry shells with frozen fruit salad, and baby asparagus spears and **Asphodel Bread.**

Creole Italian Crab

1 cup sliced fresh mushrooms
½ cup finely chopped celery
½ cup finely chopped onion
¼ cup chopped fresh parsley
2-3 Tablespoons olive oil
1 pound lump crabmeat
½ stick unsalted butter
1 2-ounce jar chopped
  pimiento*
½ cup red wine
Juice of 1 lemon
Hot pepper sauce to taste
¼ teaspoon white pepper
Creole seasoning to taste
1 teaspoon oregano
1 teaspoon basil

Cream Sauce:
2 cups milk
½ cup flour
Salt
Black pepper
1 stick unsalted butter
½ wedge freshly grated
  Parmesan cheese

In a skillet, saute mushrooms, celery, onions, and parsley in olive oil. Add remaining ingredients, blend and set aside. To prepare cream sauce, blend milk and flour in a double boiler until smooth. Season with salt and pepper. Cook until thick. Remove from heat and add butter, mixing well. Pour cream sauce over crab mixture, stirring gently so as not to break lumps. Divide into 8 individual ramekins or scallop shells. Cover with Parmesan cheese. Bake 325 degrees for 20-25 minutes.
*2 Tablespoons chopped red bell pepper may be used.
8 servings

Crawfish ''Tout Etouffe''

3 pounds peeled crawfish tails
Creole seasoning
1 cup vegetable oil
¾ cup flour
2 large onions, chopped
1 green bell pepper, chopped
1 stalk celery, chopped
4 green onion tops, chopped
12 sprigs parsley, chopped
1 clove garlic, chopped
2 dashes hot pepper sauce
1 8-ounce package cream cheese
2 Tablespoons cornstarch
2 cups water

Sprinkle crawfish with Creole seasoning. In an aluminum pot, make a roux with oil and flour by cooking over medium-low heat, stirring constantly, until the color of peanut butter. Add onions, bell pepper, celery, green onions, parsley, garlic, and hot pepper sauce and saute until vegetables are tender. Add crawfish and cook 5 minutes. Add cream cheese and stir until melted. Mix cornstarch with water and add to crawfish. Cook on low heat for 15-20 minutes.
12 main course servings

This is wonderful in so many ways — as a dip in a chaffing dish, over pasta or rice, or simply on patty shells — like the name says ''Crawfish Everything.''

Crawfish Fettucine

3 sticks butter
3 onions, chopped
2 green bell peppers, chopped
3 stalks celery, chopped
3 pounds crawfish tails
3 cloves garlic, minced
1 Tablespoon chopped parsley
½ cup flour
1 pint Half and Half
1 pound Kraft Jalapeño cheese, cubed
12 ounces fettucine

In a saucepan, melt butter and sauté onion, bell pepper, and celery until tender. Add crawfish and simmer 10 minutes, stirring occasionally. Add garlic, parsley, flour and Half and Half and mix well. Simmer on low heat for 30 minutes, stirring occasionally. Add cheese and stir until melted. Meanwhile, cook noodles, drain, and cool. Combine noodles and sauce. Pour into a greased 6-quart casserole or two greased 3-quart casseroles. Bake uncovered in a 300 degree oven for 20 minutes or until heated thoroughly. Freezes well.
12 servings

A *delicious first course.*

Crawfish Etouffe Pie

2 bunches green onions
1 stick margarine
½ cup flour
2 cloves garlic, minced
1 onion, chopped
1 green bell pepper, chopped
1 cup celery, chopped
3 Tablespoons tomato sauce
2 teaspoons salt
1 teaspoon paprika
¼ teaspoon white pepper
¼ teaspoon onion powder
¼ teaspoon garlic powder
¼ teaspoon dry mustard
1 teaspoon cayenne
¼ teaspoon black pepper
3 cups water
1 bunch parsley, chopped
3 pounds crawfish tails with fat
1 recipe **Flaky Pastry**

Chop green onions separating tops and bottoms. In a saucepan, melt margarine. Add flour and brown lightly, stirring constantly. Add garlic, green onion bottoms, onion, green pepper, celery, and tomato sauce. Cover and simmer about 1 hour, stirring frequently, to keep from sticking. Add seasonings and water. Simmer for additional 2-3 hours. If mixture thickens too much, add more water. Mixture should be creamy and as thick as a paste when tails and fat are added. Add tails and fat. Cook 15 minutes or until tails are tender. Add onion tops and parsley. Pour filling into two pie shells. Cover with another layer of dough. Cut slits in top. Bake at 350 degrees for 35 minutes or until golden brown. When removed from oven, allow pies to cool for at least 20 minutes. Cooling time is important for the filling to set before serving. It is best to make the etouffe the day ahead and fill the pies the day you plan to serve them. The filling freezes well.
8 servings

The etouffe may also be served over fluffy white steamy rice.

Flaky Pastry

4 cups sifted flour
½ teaspoon salt
½ pound unsalted butter, chilled
    and cut in ¼-inch pieces
½ pound shortening, chilled
10-12 Tablespoons ice water

Mix flour and salt. Cut in shortening and butter using metal blade of food processor. Add 10 Tablespoons of water and process until dough makes balls the size of peas. Work with the dough as little as possible at this stage. Use the other 2 Tablespoons of water if necessary. Press out on a lightly floured board into a 21 x 12-inch rectangle. Do this procedure a total of four times. At this point you may wrap in plastic wrap and store in the refrigerator for up to three days. When you are ready to roll the dough out, divide it into four pieces, a top and bottom for two pies. Flour surface lightly and roll pie crust out to ⅛-inch. For thinner crust, roll dough out between two pieces of wax paper. Place in buttered pie plates. Fill with desired filling. Place top crust over filling, seal, and cut slits to release steam. Bake in a preheated 350 degree oven for 35 minutes or until golden brown.

New Orleans Oysters

This recipe is served by the Lotus Club of Monroe, which was founded in 1920 and remains today one of the finest men's clubs in the South.

Batter:
1 *pound package Louisiana fish fry*
1 *Tablespoon garlic salt*
½ *teaspoon cayenne*
¼ *cup flour*

4-6 *dozen oysters, freshly shucked or from gallon containers*
Peanut oil or pure vegetable oil, enough to fill frying container used

Mix together first three batter ingredients. Add flour. Remove each oyster from shell or directly from liquor and roll in batter. Drop immediately in hot oil. Fry approximately 1½ minutes or until crispy. If this takes longer than 2 minutes, the oil is not hot enough. These are great plain, but are also delectable with any remoulade sauce or lemon mayonnaise.

The secret to this recipe is to have good hot grease for frying—the temperature should be at least 350 degrees. This method used is to "flashfry", resulting in a crisp but not overcooked oyster.

Don Juan Oysters

1 *stick butter*
½ *cup olive oil*
½ *cup chopped green onion*
½ *cup chopped white onion*
2 *Tablespoons minced garlic*
2 *Tablespoons chopped fresh parsley*
1 *cup Italian bread crumbs*
1 *cup freshly grated Parmesan cheese*
Salt to taste
Black pepper to taste
¼ *teaspoon cayenne*
1 *teaspoon basil*
1 *teaspoon oregano*
4 *dozen oysters, well-drained, reserving liquid*
2 *slices bacon, fried and crumbled*

In a large skillet, melt butter. Add olive oil and onions and sauté onions until clear. Add garlic and parsley. In a bowl, combine bread crumbs, ½ cup cheese, salt, pepper, cayenne, basil, and oregano. Add to skillet mixture and mix well. Add oysters and stir until oysters curl. If mixture is too dry, add a bit of reserved oyster liquid. Add crumbled bacon and stir. Place in a 2-quart casserole and top with remaining ½ cup cheese. Cook in 425 degree oven for 15 minutes, until crusty.
6-8 servings

Serve as a casserole with green salad and good French bread or as appetizer with melba rounds. Garnish with fresh artichoke leaves and bottoms. This is a wonderful combination.

Oyster Rockefeller Casserole

4 dozen small oysters
3 10-ounce packages frozen
   chopped spinach
3 sticks butter
1 teaspoon thyme
1⅔ cups chopped green onions
1 cup chopped celery
1 large clove garlic, crushed
1 Tablespoon Worcestershire
   sauce
1 teaspoon anchovy paste
1½ cups seasoned bread crumbs
¾ cup chopped parsley
½ cup freshly grated Parmesan
   cheese
2 Tablespoons Pernod*
½ teaspoon salt
¼ teaspoon black pepper
¼ teaspoon cayenne

Drain oysters, reserving liquid and chop. Set aside. In a saucepan, prepare spinach according to package directions, drain and set aside. In a large skillet over moderate heat, melt butter and add thyme, green onion, celery, and garlic. Sauté for 5 minutes. Add Worcestershire, anchovy paste, and bread crumbs. Stir well for 5 minutes until bread crumbs are toasted. Gently stir in oysters, ½ cup of reserved oyster liquid, parsley, cheese, and Pernod. Cook for 3 minutes or until oysters curl. Add spinach and season with salt, pepper, and cayenne. Place in a 3-quart casserole and bake at 375 degrees for 20-25 minutes.
*Anise liquor
10 servings

This can also be served in a chafing dish with French bread rounds for a cocktail party or in individual ramekins as an appetizer.

Seafood Spectacular

1 8-ounce package cream cheese
1 stick plus 2 Tablespoons
   butter
1 pound raw shrimp, peeled
1 large onion, chopped
1 green bell pepper, chopped
2 ribs celery, chopped
1 10¾-ounce can cream of
   mushroom soup
1½ teaspoons garlic salt
Creole seasoning to taste
1 teaspoon hot pepper sauce
½ teaspoon cayenne
1 pint crabmeat
2 cups cooked rice
1 cup grated Cheddar cheese
4-6 saltine crackers, crushed

In a small saucepan, melt cream cheese and 1 stick butter. Set aside. In a large skillet, melt 2 Tablespoons butter and sauté shrimp, onion, bell pepper, and celery. Add cream cheese mixture to shrimp and vegetables. Then add soup and seasonings, mixing well. Stir in crabmeat and rice. Pour into a greased 9 x 13 baking dish. Top with cheese and cracker crumbs. Bake at 350 degrees for 20-30 minutes until heated thoroughly.
8 servings

Seafood and Fish

Seafood Manicotti

Pasta:
2 large eggs
1½ cups flour
Olive oil

Filling:
2 8-ounce packages cream
  cheese
1 stick unsalted butter
7 dashes hot pepper sauce
1½-2 teaspoons Worcestershire
  sauce
2 pounds lump crabmeat

1 pound medium raw shrimp,
  peeled
⅓ cup slivered red bell pepper
8 slices bacon, fried and
  coarsely chopped
Creole seasoning
Salt
White pepper
¾ cup freshly grated Parmesan
  cheese
12 ounces Mozzarella cheese,
  grated

Mix eggs and flour in food processor pulsing on and off for 10-15 seconds. Remove and form into a ball. Pinch off one piece of dough at a time and pass through the rollers of pasta machine until strips are very thin. Cut noodles into 3 x 4-inch rectangles. In a skillet of boiling water, add a little olive oil then add noodles and cook for about 2 minutes. You can cook 5-6 noodles in a skillet at one time. Spread cooked strips on wax paper to cool.

Filling:
Place cream cheese and butter in a 4-quart glass container, cover, and cook in microwave for 10 minutes on 50% power or until melted and smooth. To cream cheese mixture, add hot pepper sauce and Worcestershire. Set aside ½ cup of this sauce. Fold crabmeat into remaining cream cheese mixture. Roll about 2 Tablespoons of crabmeat mixture in pasta and place manicotti in greased casserole.

Toss shrimp, bell pepper, bacon, Creole seasoning, salt, and pepper together. Spread over manicotti and pour remaining ½ cup sauce over noodles. Sprinkle with cheeses. Cover with foil and bake in 350 degree oven for 20-30 minutes or until the shrimp are pink and the casserole is hot and bubbly throughout.
12 servings

You may use 20 commercially prepared shells and will make 10 servings. An unusual way to serve the bayou's best.

Twin City Sautéed Shrimp

2 pounds large headless shrimp
2 Tablespoons butter
Juice of 1 lemon
8 ounces whole mushrooms
Lemon pepper
Creole seasoning
Paprika

Peel, devein, and butterfly shrimp. In a skillet, melt butter, then add lemon juice and shrimp. When heated, add mushrooms and season well with lemon pepper and Creole seasoning. When shrimp are pink and bubbly, increase heat and stir gently, but continuously, for 2-3 minutes. Place on plate and sprinkle with paprika.
4 servings

Serve with French bread to soak up the extra sauce. Delicious!

Captain Avery's Easy-Peel Boiled Shrimp

Captain Avery Seafood Restaurant has brought the tasty delights from the Louisiana Gulf Coast to our part of the state. A family operation that provides the finest oysters, shrimp, fish, and crabs—guaranteed fresh and always cooked to perfection.

1 gallon water
1 3-ounce bag Zatarains Crab
   Boil
1 head garlic
1 lemon
12 mini ears of corn
2 pounds "B" size potatoes
4 pounds large headless shrimp
3-4 trays ice
Seasoned salt
Hot pepper sauce

In a 12 or 16 quart stockpot, place water, crab boil, garlic, and lemon. Bring to a boil. Add potatoes and boil for 3-4 minutes. Add corn and boil for 5 minutes. Add shrimp and boil for 2½-3 minutes. Remove pot from heat and add ice. Let stand 3-4 minutes, then drain. Sprinkle liberally with seasoned salt and hot pepper sauce. Serve with cocktail sauce.

6 servings

Shrimp and Artichoke Orleans

1 14-ounce can artichoke
   hearts*
1½ pounds large boiled shrimp,
   peeled and deveined
1 stick butter
8 ounces large fresh mushrooms,
   sliced
4½ Tablespoons flour
½ pint whipping cream
½ cup milk
1 teaspoon salt
½ teaspoon white pepper
¼ cup dry sherry
1 Tablespoon Worcestershire
   sauce
¼ cup freshly grated Parmesan
   cheese
¼ teaspoon paprika

Drain and quarter artichoke hearts and place in bottom of well-greased 1½-quart casserole. Cover with shrimp. In a skillet, melt 3½ Tablespoons butter and saute mushrooms for 6-8 minutes. Drain and place over shrimp. In a medium saucepan, melt remaining butter and add flour. Cook over low heat for 3-5 minutes, stirring constantly. Gradually add cream and milk and cook until thick. Sauce should be thick enough to coat a spoon heavily. Add salt, pepper, sherry, Worcestershire and stir until smooth. Pour over casserole. Top with cheese and sprinkle with paprika. Bake uncovered in 350 degree oven for 25 minutes, until light brown and bubbly.

*You may use 6-8 fresh artichoke hearts.

6 servings

Shrimp DeSiard

1 pound large raw shrimp,
   peeled
¼ cup white wine
5 green onions, chopped
2 cloves garlic, finely chopped
½ stick butter
2 teaspoons peanut oil
2 cups sliced fresh mushrooms
½ pound snow peas, cleaned
½ cup pine nuts
1 teaspoon salt

Fettucine:
8 ounces fettucine noodles
1 Tablespoon olive oil
½ cup whipping cream
½ cup grated Romano cheese
1 cup grated Parmesan cheese
2 Tablespoons shrimp liquid
4 Tablespoons chopped parsley
Freshly ground black pepper

Marinate shrimp in white wine for 1 hour. In skillet or electric wok over medium heat, stir fry onions and garlic in butter and peanut oil for 1 minute. Add mushrooms, snow peas, and pine nuts. When vegetables are still slightly crisp, add shrimp and sauté until shrimp are pink. Season with salt, cover, and keep warm. Meanwhile, cook noodles in salted boiling water with 1 Tablespoon olive oil until tender, about 10 minutes. Drain well. Place noodles in a large bowl and toss with cream, cheeses, and shrimp liquid. Drain shrimp mixture and add to pasta mixture. Mix well. Add parsley, toss and serve immediately. Pass freshly ground black pepper.
6-8 servings

Shrimp Cardinale

3 sticks butter
4 bunches green onions, mostly
   white part, finely chopped
8 ribs celery, finely chopped
4 pounds medium shrimp,
   peeled, deveined, and boiled*
½ cup flour
1 quart whipping cream
1 cup ketchup
8 ounces mushrooms, sliced
1 teaspoon salt
1½ teaspoons white pepper
5 ounces brandy or to taste

In a Dutch oven, melt 2 sticks butter. Add green onions and celery and sauté until very limp and clear. Add shrimp and set aside. In another saucepan, melt remaining 1 stick butter and stir in flour. Whisk in whipping cream. Cook, stirring over low heat until sauce is thickened. Add ketchup, mushrooms, salt, and pepper. Combine with shrimp mixture. This may be frozen at this point. When ready to serve, add brandy and heat thoroughly. Do not allow to overcook or shrimp will be tough.
*The shrimp are easier to peel raw.
12 servings

Serve over noodles along with toasted French bread

Cajun Fried Fish

Catfish or trout fillets, allow two
    fillets per person
Creole seasoning
Cayenne
Hot pepper sauce
Prepared mustard
Zatarain's Fish Fry, a spiced
    corn meal

Season fillets with Creole seasoning and a little cayenne. About 15 minutes before frying, pour a liberal amount of hot pepper sauce and a little prepared mustard on fillets, making sure the fillets are coated. Shake the fillets in fish fry that has been seasoned with Creole seasoning and a little cayenne. Drop a few fillets at a time into hot grease. Too many fillets at once will cool the grease and the fish will not be crispy. The fish are done when they float. All ingredients in this recipe are ''to taste.''

So easy after a day of fishing.

Cajun Catfish Bits

Cut fillets into bite-size pieces and prepare as above.

Catfish Parmesan

1 cup grated Parmesan cheese
½ cup flour
½ teaspoon seasoned salt
¼ teaspoon black pepper
1 teaspoon paprika
1 egg, beaten
½ cup milk
6 catfish fillets
½ stick butter or margarine,
    melted
Paprika
Black pepper

Combine cheese, flour, salt, pepper, and paprika, mixing well. Combine egg and milk and stir well. Dip fillets in egg mixture, then dredge in flour mixture. Arrange fillets in a lightly greased 9 x 13 baking dish, and drizzle with butter. Top with a light coating of paprika and pepper. Bake in 350 degree oven for 40 minutes or until fish flakes.
6 servings

Quick and easy. Kids love this fish.

Domangue's Grilled Fish

½ stick butter, melted
Juice of 1 lemon
6 8-ounce fish fillets*
Cajun seasoning
Lemon pepper
3-4 wood chunks, soaked
    (mesquite, hickory, or pecan)

Prepare grill. Meanwhile in a saucepan, melt butter. Remove from heat, add lemon juice, and baste fish. Sprinkle with Cajun seasoning and lemon pepper. When heat is medium to low, add 3 or 4 wood chunks to hot coals, and place fish on grill, skin side up. Cover fish to trap heat and smoke. Cook 6-8 minutes, baste, flip gently, baste again, and cover. Cook another 6 minutes or until flaky. Garnish with paprika, parsley, and thin lemon slices.
*Red fish, snapper, catfish, striper, or bass.
6 servings

A wonderful alternative to fried fish.

Chef Hans' Poached Salmon

Chef Hans, far from his boyhood home in the Swiss Alps, brings European flair to Cajun cooking. His restaurant and catering enterprises are renowned for elegant presentations of fine food in Monroe, Louisiana.

1 7-12 *pound salmon*
2 *yellow onions, diced*
2 *carrots, diced*
3 *celery stalks, diced*
1 *Tablespoon whole black peppercorns, crushed*
4 *whole bay leaves*
½ *cup salt*
½ *teaspoon cayenne pepper*

Scale and wash salmon thoroughly leaving heads, fins, and tail intact. In order to keep a nice presentable form, roll aluminum foil the length of the belly, insert in cavity so salmon will be in upright position (as in natural swimming position). Place on a small wooden board the size of the salmon (like from vegetable crate) and secure with twine to the board in upright position. It is advisable to wrap salmon in small tablecloth before placing on board.

Have all above ingredients in large enough container to have adequate water to cover salmon. Put all vegetables and ingredients in water and simmer 15 minutes before placing salmon into it. Put salmon into bouillon, making sure it is not a strong boil, only simmer, and simmer approximately 20-25 minutes, depending on size. Turn heat off and let cool completely, leaving overnight in refrigerator to maintain firmness. DO NOT take fish out before it is completely cooled.

Carefully remove wrappings and leave foil inside fish. Then remove skin with sharp knife from main body, leaving fins and head intact. Bottom and top fins may be removed, if desired. All tissues should be carefully removed so the salmon will have beautiful, splendid color.

After skinning, carefully place on a large mirror or silver tray for decorating. Can be decorated using a variety of different colors and decorations such as stuffed olives, cucumber slices, black olives, red pimento, parsley, and cooked egg whites.

In cold state, cover fish entirely with aspic or clear gelatin to glaze it. Fish must be cold and aspic ready to be gelled so all decorations will stay in place. Decorations should also be covered in aspic or gelatin. Serve with Parsley Vodka Sauce on the side.

Continued

Parsley Vodka Sauce

½ quart mayonnaise
2 bunches parsley, no stems
2 Tablespoons Worcestershire
   sauce
1 Tablespoon hot Mango
   Chutney
Juice of ½ lemon
1 Tablespoon Chef Hans
   Jalapeño Hot Sauce
Salt to taste
Black pepper to taste

Blend all ingredients in mixer and serve chilled.

Grilled Salmon Steaks

6 ½-pound salmon steaks
3 Tablespoons lemon juice
¼ cup white wine
½ stick butter, melted
Salt
Black pepper
1 recipe **Hollandaise Sauce**
Capers
Dill sprigs

Prepare barbecue grill. Meanwhile, marinate steaks in 1 Tablespoon lemon juice and wine. Combine remaining lemon juice, butter, salt, and pepper. For easy handling, place steaks in a double grill rack. Grill fish about 5-6 inches above hot coals for 5-6 minutes per side, basting with lemon butter. Remove steaks from rack and place on a warmed platter. Pour Hollandaise Sauce over fish and sprinkle with capers. Garnish with dill sprigs.
6 servings

So easy and delicious.

Trout Burre Blanc

6 trout fillets
Salt
Black pepper
1 cup self-rising flour
1 teaspoon paprika
1½ cups buttermilk
1 stick butter
½ cup slivered almonds, toasted
Freshly chopped parsley

Burre Blanc Sauce:
2 shallots, minced
½ cup white wine
½ cup cold butter, cut into
  pieces

Season trout with salt and pepper. Combine flour and paprika. Dip trout in buttermilk, then in flour mixture and coat well. In a large skillet, heat 4 Tablespoons butter and sauté trout until lightly brown, add more butter if necessary. Do not over cook! Drain on paper towel and place on hot serving platter. Top with toasted almonds and chopped parsley. Serve with Burre Blanc Sauce.
6 servings

Burre Blanc Sauce:
In a saucepan over medium heat, combine shallots with wine and cook until liquid is reduced to about 2 Tablespoons. Into the reduced liquid, whisk in one piece of butter at a time, whisking until melted.
Makes ½ cup

To serve as cocktail fare, arrange fillets on a circular platter, placing Burre Blanc Sauce in bowl in center of platter. Provide a fish knife for slicing fish and French bread rounds to place fish pieces on. Adjust amount of fish and sauce to number of guests.

Desserts

POLITICS: LOUISIANA'S GREATEST SPECTATOR SPORT

The old adage, "Never discuss politics or religion at dinner" doesn't hold true in Louisiana, for here politics is a way of life. Almost everything about Louisiana politics is unique.

What other state had its incoming governor plan a trip to Paris, including a dinner-dance at Versailles, as a means of retiring his campaign indebtedness? What other state has a former governor hosting an annual "Dinner on the Grounds" at his family's tabernacle? What other state has produced two brothers who both became governor and have both been the subject of several motion pictures?

Tales of flamboyant governors and their colorful campaigns fill shelves of books. . .and many hours after dinner as Louisianians retell the old stories. The most well-known of these political figures is probably the "Kingfish" himself, Huey Long. With his incredible ability to hold an audience and his skillful use of power, Long pushed his "Share the Wealth" program beyond Louisiana to national attention. Promising a "chicken in every pot" and proclaiming "every man a king," Long captured the imagination of even the poorest citizens of the state and gave them hope.

Less well known but no less colorful was Huey Long's brother, Earl K. Long. Perhaps "Uncle Earl" didn't have the charisma of his brother, but he did have a way of getting people's attention. For one thing, he was often sloppy in his attire. When chided about his appearance, Long would reply that putting a $200 suit on him would be like putting "socks on a rooster."

Politics in Louisiana has only recently become a media event. For many years, the politicians went out among the people, "stumping" for votes. They would travel across the state, stopping at the small towns and rural areas, climb up on a truck or a tree stump (hence the name) and give fiery promise-filled speeches. Today there may be fewer stumps and perhaps the candidates are more accountable to the voters, but passions still run deep. As an astute news commentator remarked, "In Louisiana, politics is a spectator sport" where the people get involved, if for no other reason than to enjoy the process.

Apple Dapple Cake

3 eggs
1½ cups vegetable oil
2 cups sugar
2 teaspoons vanilla
3 cups flour
1 teaspoon salt
1 teaspoon soda
3 cups chopped baking apples
1½ cups chopped pecans

Topping:
1 cup brown sugar
¼ cup milk
1 stick butter or margarine

Preheat oven to 350 degrees. Mix eggs, oil, sugar, and vanilla, and blend well. Sift together flour, salt, and soda. Add flour to egg mixture, then add apples and pecans. Pour into a greased tube pan or bundt pan. Bake for 1 hour and 20 minutes.

Topping:
In a saucepan, combine brown sugar, milk and butter, and cook 2½ minutes. While cake is still hot, pour topping over the cake in the pan. Allow cake to cool completely before removing from the pan.

Carrot Cake Supreme

2 cups flour
2 teaspoons cinnamon
1 teaspoon salt
2 teaspoons soda
2 cups sugar
1½ cups vegetable oil
4 eggs
3 cups carrots, grated

Icing:
2 sticks butter
1 16-ounce box powdered sugar
1 8-ounce package Neufchâtel
  or cream cheese, softened
2 teaspoons vanilla
1 cup chopped pecans, optional

Preheat oven to 325 degrees. Combine dry ingredients, then add oil and mix well. Add eggs, one at a time, mixing well after each. Fold in carrots. Pour into two greased and floured 9-inch round pans. Bake for 1 hour or until done.

Icing:
Cream butter and sugar. Add remaining ingredients. Ice the cooled cake. For a fun Easter cake, cut one layer as shown in diagram and ice. Use carrot rings for eyes and raisins for nose and mouth.

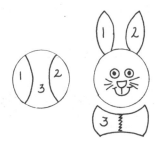

Chocolate Strawberry Cheesecake

Crust:
48 graham cracker squares,
    ground into crumbs
½ cup sugar
1 cup butter, melted
4 teaspoons Grand Marnier
    Liqueur
2 teaspoons cinnamon

Strawberry Layer:
1 quart fresh strawberries, stems
    removed
½ cup powdered sugar
4 Tablespoons Grand Marnier
    Liqueur
2 teaspoons cornstarch
2 teaspoons water

Cheesecake:
3 8-ounce packages cream
    cheese, softened
3 eggs
¼ cup sugar
1½ cups sour cream
4½ teaspoons flour
1½ teaspoons vanilla
3 Tablespoons Grand Marnier
    Liqueur

Chocolate Glaze:
2 1-ounce squares unsweetened
    chocolate
1 teaspoon butter
1 cup sifted powdered sugar
3 Tablespoons water

Crust:
Combine all ingredients, mix well, and press onto bottom and sides of a greased 10-inch spring-form pan. Chill.

Strawberry Layer:
Purée first 3 ingredients in a blender or processor, then place in top of a double boiler over hot water. Add cornstarch and water and cook until thickened, stirring constantly. Cool to room temperature and set aside.

Cheesecake:
Preheat oven to 350 degrees. Cut cream cheese into small pieces and place in the processor with remaining cheesecake ingredients. Blend just until smooth. Pour almost half the cheesecake mixture into crust. Carefully spoon strawberry layer over cheesecake, covering entirely. Carefully spoon remaining cheesecake over strawberry layer, covering completely, but not overlapping crust. Bake on cookie sheet for 1 hour and 10-15 minutes, or until cake no longer shakes in center. Turn oven off. Leave door ajar, and allow the cake to remain inside for 1 hour. Leave cake in pan, cover with plastic wrap, and refrigerate overnight. The following day, remove cake from pan and set aside.

Chocolate Glaze:
In a double boiler over hot water, melt chocolate and butter. Add sugar and water and mix well. Beat with wire whisk until smooth. While chocolate is still warm, spoon evenly over top of cheesecake and chill until glaze hardens.

Whipped Cream:
Place ingredients in a chilled bowl, and with chilled beaters, whip until soft. Spoon into pastry bag with small rosette tip and decorate cheesecake. If desired, cream may be served on the side. Serve cake circled with whole fresh strawberries.

Continued

Whipped Cream:
½ cup whipping cream, chilled
2 Tablespoons powdered sugar
1 Tablespoon Grand Marnier
   Liqueur
1 teaspoon vanilla

Whole fresh strawberries, stems
   removed

Cream Cheese Cake

1 cup coarsely ground walnuts
¾ cup finely crushed graham
   crackers
4 Tablespoons unsalted butter,
   melted
4 8-ounce packages cream
   cheese, softened
4 eggs
1¼ cups sugar
1 Tablespoon fresh lemon juice
1 teaspoon grated lemon rind
2 teaspoons vanilla
2 cups sour cream
¼ cup sugar
1 teaspoon vanilla

Position rack in center of oven and preheat to 350 degrees. Lightly butter a 9 or 10-inch spring-form pan. Combine walnuts, graham cracker crumbs, and butter. Press into bottom of pan. In large bowl of electric mixer, beat cream cheese until smooth. Add eggs, sugar, lemon juice, lemon rind, and vanilla, and beat thoroughly. Spoon over crust. Set pan on baking sheet to catch any batter that may drip. Bake 10-inch cake 40-45 minutes or 9-inch cake 50-55 minutes. Remove from oven and let stand at room temperature 15 minutes. Retain oven temperature at 350 degrees. For the topping, combine sour cream, sugar, and vanilla, and blend well. Cover and refrigerate. When cake has finished baking, spoon topping over cake, starting at center and extending to within ½-inch of edge. Return to oven and bake 5 minutes longer. Let cool. Refrigerate cheesecake for at least 24 hours or, preferably, 2-3 days.

Top with fresh strawberries.

Cheesecake with Raspberry Drizzle

Prepare the filling for **L. C. Scally's Cheesecake**, pour into a greased 9 or 10-inch spring-form pan, and bake at 350 degrees for 45 minutes. **Turn off heat** and allow cheesecake to cool in oven for 1 hour. Cover and refrigerate at least 3 hours. Slice and top with Raspberry Drizzle.

Raspberry Drizzle:

1 cup raspberry preserves
½ cup sour cream
1½ cups miniature
   marshmallows

In a double boiler, combine all ingredients and stir until marshmallows melt. Serve hot or cold.

Makes 2 cups

Desserts

L. C. Scally's Cheesecake

Crust:
15 Oreo cookies, crushed
½ stick butter, melted

Filling:
4 8-ounce packages cream
   cheese, softened
6 eggs, at room temperature
1 cup sugar
3 Tablespoons flour
1 teaspoon vanilla

Topping:
1 cup sour cream
¼ cup sugar
1 teaspoon vanilla

Crust:
Combine cookies and butter and press into the bottom of a 9 to 10-inch spring-form pan.

Filling:
Preheat oven to 350 degrees. Beat cream cheese and eggs until smooth. Blend in sugar, flour, and vanilla. Pour into crust and bake for 45 minutes. The center may ''jiggle'' a little, but it will be ready for the topping.

Topping:
Combine sour cream, sugar, and vanilla. Pour over cheesecake, place back in **turned off** oven, and cool for 1 hour. Cover and refrigerate at least 3 hours.

Coca-Cola Cake

2 cups flour
2 cups sugar
2 sticks butter
1 cup Coca-Cola
3 Tablespoons cocoa
½ cup buttermilk
2 eggs, beaten
1 teaspoon baking soda
1 teaspoon vanilla
2 cups miniature marshmallows

Icing:
1 stick butter
6 Tablespoons Coca-Cola
1 16-ounce box powdered sugar
1 teaspoon vanilla
3 Tablespoons cocoa
1 cup toasted pecans or
   almonds, or both

Preheat oven to 350 degrees. In a large bowl, combine flour and sugar, mixing well. In a saucepan, heat butter, Coca-Cola, cocoa, and bring to a boiling point. Pour over flour and sugar. Add buttermilk, eggs, baking soda, and vanilla. Mix well. Then add marshmallows and pour into a 9 x 13 greased cake pan. Bake for 30-35 minutes. The marshmallows will rise to the top during the baking.

Icing:
Cream butter. Add remaining ingredients and beat well. Pour over cake while still in the pan. This cake will keep for days if left in the pan in which it was cooked.

Cutting calories? Make this cake with Diet Coke.

Creme de Menthe Chocolate Cake

Cake:
1 cup unsifted, unsweetened cocoa
2 cups boiling water
2¾ cups sifted flour
2 teaspoons baking soda
½ teaspoon salt
½ teaspoon baking powder
2 sticks butter, softened
2½ cups sugar
4 eggs
1½ teaspoons vanilla

Filling:
6 Tablespoons butter, softened
3½ cups unsifted powdered sugar
6 Tablespoons green Creme de Menthe

Frosting:
1 6-ounce package semi-sweet chocolate chips
½ cup Half and Half
2 sticks butter
2½ cups unsifted powdered sugar
1 6-ounce box chocolate-coated square mints

Cake:
In medium bowl, combine cocoa with boiling water, mixing with wire whisk until smooth. Cool completely. Sift flour with baking soda, salt, and baking powder. Preheat oven to 350 degrees. Grease and lightly flour three 9-inch cake pans. In large bowl of electric mixer at high speed, beat butter, sugar, eggs, and vanilla, scraping bowl occasionally until light, for 5 minutes. At low speed beat in flour mixture in fourths, alternating with cocoa mixture in thirds, beginning and ending with flour mixture. Do not overbeat. Pour batter into pans, dividing evenly. Smooth tops. Bake for 25-30 minutes, or until surface springs back when gently pressed with fingertip. Cool in pans for 10 minutes. Carefully loosen side with spatula, remove from pans, and cool on racks.

Filling:
In medium bowl, combine butter, powdered sugar, and Creme de Menthe. Using mixer or wooden spoon, beat until smooth and fluffy. On cake stand put layers together, using half of Creme de Menthe filling between each two layers.

Frosting:
In medium saucepan, combine chocolate chips, Half and Half, and butter. Stir over medium heat until smooth. Remove from heat. With a wire whisk, blend in sugar. Pour into a bowl, set over ice, and beat until it holds its shape. With a metal spatula, frost the side of the cake, making vertical rows. Use the rest of the frosting on top, swirling decoratively. Cut the mints in half and decorate the top of the cake. Chill well before slicing.
16 servings

The taste and the comments from others make this cake worth the trouble!

Chocolate Mousse Cake

7 *ounces semi-sweet chocolate*
1 *stick unsalted butter*
7 *eggs, separated and at room*
temperature
1 *cup sugar*
1 *teaspoon vanilla**
⅛ *teaspoon cream of tartar*
2-3 *Tablespoons Amaretto,*
optional

Whipped Cream Frosting:
½ *pint whipping cream*
⅓ *cup powdered sugar*
1 *teaspoon vanilla**

Preheat oven to 325 degrees. In a small saucepan, melt the chocolate and butter over low heat. In a large bowl, beat egg yolks and ¾ cup sugar until very light and fluffy, approximately 5 minutes. Gradually beat in warm chocolate mixture and vanilla. In another large bowl, beat egg whites with cream of tartar until soft peaks form. Add remaining ¼ cup sugar, 1 Tablespoon at a time, beating until stiff. Fold egg whites carefully into chocolate mixture. Pour ¾ of the batter into ungreased 9-inch spring-form pan. To remaining batter, add Amaretto, cover, and refrigerate. Bake cake 35 minutes. Remove from oven and cool. Cake will drop as it cools. Remove outside ring of spring-form pan. Stir refrigerated batter to soften slightly. Spread on top of cake and refrigerate until firm, approximately 2-5 hours. Spread frosting over top and sides. Refrigerate several hours or overnight. Garnish each slice with chocolate curls. May be frozen.
*May use 1 teaspoon Amaretto.

Whipped Cream Frosting:
In a small bowl, beat whipping cream until soft peaks form. Add sugar and vanilla. Beat until stiff, cover, and refrigerate until ready to ice cake.
*May use 1 teaspoon Amaretto.

An elegant finale to any celebration.

Ornamental Chocolate Leaves

12-14 *non-poisonous leaves such*
as camellia, rose, ivy, grape
½ *cup semi-sweet chocolate*
pieces
2 *teaspoons solid shortening*

Clean the leaves well. In a double boiler over hot water, melt chocolate and shortening. With a table knife or spatula, spread the melted chocolate over the underside of the leaves. Place the leaves, chocolate side up, on a wax paper lined baking sheet. Freeze until chocolate is firm. Leaves may be stored in freezer. When ready to use, peel the leaf away from the chocolate very slowly and carefully. Grasp the leaf's stem and pull gently. The chocolate and the leaf will separate. Use to garnish desserts.

Blueberries or cranberries may be rolled in corn syrup and tossed with sugar as garnish to leaves.

Chocolate Sheet Cake

2 cups flour
2 cups sugar
½ teaspoon salt
1 stick margarine
1 cup water
½ cup oil
3 Tablespoons cocoa
1 teaspoon soda
½ cup buttermilk
2 eggs
2 teaspoons Mexican vanilla

Icing:
1 stick margarine
6 Tablespoons milk
3 Tablespoons cocoa
1 16-ounce box powdered sugar
2 teaspoons Mexican vanilla
1 cup chopped nuts

Preheat oven to 350 degrees. Lightly grease 11 x 16 x 1 jelly roll pan. Mix together flour, sugar, and salt. In a saucepan, melt margarine. Add water, oil, and cocoa. Pour over flour mixture and stir well. Add soda to buttermilk and stir into chocolate mixture. Beat eggs with vanilla and add to chocolate mixture. Pour into cookie sheet. Bake for 20 minutes.

Icing:
Melt together margarine, milk, and cocoa, and remove from heat. Add powdered sugar, vanilla, and chopped nuts. Pour over hot cake.

High Cotton Chocolate Cake

2 cups sugar
2 sticks margarine
2 eggs
¾ cup cocoa
½ teaspoon salt
1 teaspoon vanilla
1 cup buttermilk
1 teaspoon baking soda
2½ cups sifted flour
1 cup boiling water

Icing:
1 stick butter
3 Tablespoons cocoa
6 Tablespoons milk
1 16-ounce box powdered sugar
1 teaspoon vanilla
½ cup chopped pecans

Preheat oven to 350 degrees. In a large bowl, cream sugar, margarine, and eggs. Add cocoa, salt, and vanilla. Combine buttermilk and baking soda and add to mixture alternately with flour. Slowly pour in the boiling water. Bake in two 9-inch round cake pans that have been greased and lined with wax paper for 30-35 minutes. This recipe doubles easily.

Icing:
In a saucepan, bring the butter, milk, and cocoa to a boil. Remove from heat. Add sugar, vanilla, and pecans and mix well. Pour over cake while icing is still warm.

For the **Groom's Cake,** *double the recipe twice. This will make a two layer 16 x 20-inch cake.*

Desserts

White Chocolate Cake

¼ pound white chocolate or
  almond bark
½ cup hot water
2 sticks butter
2 cups sugar
4 eggs, separated
1 teaspoon vanilla
1 teaspoon baking soda
1 cup buttermilk
2½ cups cake flour
1 cup chopped pecans
1 cup flaked coconut

Icing:
2 5-ounce cans evaporated milk
2 cups sugar
1 stick butter
6 egg yolks, slightly beaten
2 teaspoons vanilla
2 cups chopped pecans
2 cups flaked coconut

Preheat oven to 350 degrees. Melt chocolate in hot water. Cool. Cream butter and sugar. Beat in egg yolks and vanilla. Dissolve soda in buttermilk and add alternately into creamed mixture with flour and chocolate. Beat egg whites until stiff and fold into batter. Stir in pecans and coconut. Pour into three or four 9-inch pans that have been sprayed with non-stick cooking spray. Bake for 25-30 minutes. Cool and ice.

Icing:
In a saucepan, combine milk, sugar, and butter, and heat until just before reaching the boiling point. Slowly blend egg yolks into cooked mixture. Add vanilla and cook over low heat for 15 minutes. Remove from heat, add pecans and coconut, and beat at high speed until thick.
12-15 servings

Orange Walnut Cake

2 cups sugar
2 sticks unsalted butter, softened
2 large eggs
2 cups flour
½ teaspoon salt
1 teaspoon baking powder
½ teaspoon cinnamon
1 cup sour cream
1 teaspoon vanilla
2 Tablespoons orange-flavored
  liqueur
1¼ cups finely chopped walnuts
1 Tablespoon freshly grated
  orange rind
2 teaspoons powdered sugar

Preheat oven to 350 degrees. Cream together the sugar and butter until light and fluffy. Beat in the eggs one at a time until well combined. Into a small bowl, sift together the flour, salt, baking powder, and cinnamon. In another small bowl, stir together the sour cream, vanilla, and liqueur. Add the flour and sour cream mixtures alternately to the butter mixture, beating until the batter is well combined. Beat in the walnuts and rind, and spoon into a greased and floured 10-inch bundt pan. Bake for 1 hour or until an inserted toothpick comes out clean. Let the cake cool in the pan on a rack for 20 minutes, turn out onto the rack, and let cool completely. Transfer to a plate and sift the powdered sugar over it lightly.

This is an unusual, absolutely delicious, pound cake.

Hummingbird Cake

3 cups flour
2 cups sugar
1 teaspoon salt
1 teaspoon baking soda
1 teaspoon ground cinnamon
3 eggs, beaten
1 cup vegetable oil
1½ teaspoons vanilla
1 8-ounce can crushed
   pineapple, drained
1½ cups chopped pecans
2 cups chopped bananas

Frosting:
1 8-ounce package cream cheese,
   softened
½ cup butter, softened
1 16-ounce box powdered sugar,
   sifted
1 teaspoon vanilla

Preheat oven to 350 degrees. In a large mixing bowl, combine the flour, sugar, salt, baking soda, and cinnamon. Add eggs and oil, stirring until dry ingredients are moistened. **Do not beat.** Stir in vanilla, pineapple, 1 cup pecans, and bananas. Batter will be thick. Spoon batter into three greased and floured 9-inch round pans. Bake for 25-30 minutes or until inserted toothpick comes out clean. Cool. Cream together icing ingredients. Put a generous amount of icing between layers, then cover tops and sides. Top with remaining chopped pecans.

Red Velvet Cake

1½ cups vegetable oil
1½ cups sugar
2 eggs
1 teaspoon soda
1 teaspoon vinegar
1 cup buttermilk
2½ cups flour
1 Tablespoon cocoa
1 teaspoon salt
2 Tablespoons red food coloring
1 teaspoon vanilla

Icing:
1 8-ounce package cream cheese,
   softened
1 stick margarine
1 16-ounce box powdered sugar
1 teaspoon vanilla
1 cup chopped nuts

Preheat oven to 300 degrees. Mix together oil, sugar, and eggs. In a separate bowl, add soda and vinegar to buttermilk and set aside. Sift together flour, cocoa, and salt. Alternately add dry ingredients and buttermilk mixture into the first mixture. Add food coloring and vanilla. Pour into two floured and greased 9-inch cake pans and bake for 45 minutes. For the icing, beat cream cheese and margarine until smooth. Add powdered sugar and vanilla. Add pecans and frost.

Desserts

Date Nut Cake

4 sticks butter, melted
2½ cups sugar
4 eggs, separated
3 Tablespoons lemon extract
4 cups flour
1 pound chopped dates
3 cups chopped pecans

Preheat oven to 225 degrees. Combine butter, sugar, well-beaten egg yolks, and lemon extract and mix well. Add 3 cups flour, mixing well. In a bowl, combine 1 cup flour, dates, and pecans, then add to the butter mixture. Blend this thick mixture well. Beat the egg whites until stiff. Fold the batter into the egg whites. Pour into a greased bundt pan and bake for 3-3½ hours or until done.

This is a very old Southern recipe. When made in small loaf pans, it makes a terrific ''Friendship Cake'' for gift giving.

Louisiana Blue-Ribbon Peach Cake

1 Duncan Hines Butter Cake mix
5 cups peaches, peeled and sliced
½ cup water
1½ cups sugar
4 Tablespoons cornstarch
1 cup sour cream

Bake cake according to package directions in two 8-inch round pans. Cool. Divide to make 4 layers. In a saucepan, combine peaches, water, sugar, and cornstarch, and cook until thick. Set aside and allow to cool. On the first cake layer, spread ¼ of the peach mixture, then spread ¼ cup sour cream. Repeat for remaining layers. Refrigerate. Garnish slices with mint sprigs. This cake is best made a day ahead to let the flavors mingle.

Peanut Sponge Cake

Cake:
4 eggs, separated
1 cup sugar
1 cup flour
1½ teaspoons baking powder
¼ teaspoon salt
½ cup boiling water
½ teaspoon vanilla

Butter Cream Frosting:
3¾ cups powdered sugar
4 Tablespoons butter
3 Tablespoons milk
2 teaspoons vanilla
¼ teaspoon salt
⅔ cup salted peanuts, coarsely ground

Preheat oven to 350 degrees. Beat egg whites until stiff peaks form and set aside. Beat yolks with rotary beater until thick and lemon colored. Add sugar gradually, beating continuously. Sift flour, baking powder, and salt together. Alternately add dry ingredients with boiling water to egg mixture. Add vanilla and beat well. Fold in stiffly beaten egg whites. Bake 20-25 minutes in a greased shallow 11 x 15 jelly roll pan. While cake bakes, prepare frosting.

Butter Cream Frosting:
Combine sugar, butter, and milk. Cream until smooth and soft. Add vanilla and salt, mixing well. Ice cooled cake with frosting and sprinkle with peanuts. Slice into squares.
Makes 2-3 dozen squares

This is wonderful topped with coffee ice cream!

Prize-Winning Pound Cake

1 8-ounce package cream cheese,
  softened
2 sticks margarine, softened
1 stick butter, softened
3 cups sugar
6 eggs
3 cups cake flour
2 teaspoons vanilla*

Preheat oven to 350 degrees. Grease and flour a 12-cup bundt pan. Beat cream cheese, margarine, butter, and sugar in a large bowl until smooth. Add eggs, one at a time, alternately with flour, blending well after each addition. Blend in vanilla. Pour batter into prepared pan. Bake 30 minutes. Reduce heat to 325 degrees and continue cooking until cake tests done, about 40-50 minutes. Cool in pan on rack. Invert onto platter.
*May use 1 teaspoon almond flavoring and 1 teaspoon vanilla.

*Delicious with fruit and whipped cream or **Out-Of-This-World Chocolate Sauce**.*

Mardi Gras King Cake

1 stick butter plus 1
  Tablespoon butter
⅔ cup evaporated milk
½ cup sugar
2 teaspoons salt
2 envelopes dry yeast
⅓ cup warm water
4 eggs
6 cups flour

Filling:
½ cup brown sugar
¾ cup sugar
1 Tablespoon cinnamon
1 stick butter, melted and
  divided evenly

Topping:
1 egg, beaten
1 cup sugar, colored (⅓ cup
  each of yellow, purple, and
  green)

2 plastic babies (¾-inch) or 2
  beans

In a small saucepan over low heat, melt 1 stick butter with milk, ⅓ cup sugar, and salt, stirring occasionally. Then allow mixture to cool to lukewarm. In a large mixing bowl, combine 2 Tablespoons sugar, yeast, and the warm water. Let stand until it is foaming, about 5-10 minutes. Beat the eggs into the foaming yeast, then add the cooled milk mixture. Stir in the flour, ½ cup at a time, reserving 1 cup flour for the kneading surface. Knead dough until it is smooth, about 5-10 minutes. Place in a large mixing bowl which has been greased with 1 Tablespoon butter. Turn dough once to grease the top, cover, and let rise in a warm place until doubled, about 1½-2 hours. While dough is rising, mix the filling.

Mix sugars and cinnamon and set aside. When the dough is doubled, punch down and divide in half. On a floured surface roll one of the halves into a rectangle about 30 x 15. Brush with half of the melted butter and cut into 3 lengthwise strips, leaving one free for sealing. Fold each strip lengthwise toward the center, sealing the seam. Braid the three 30-inch strips and make a circle by joining the ends. Repeat with the other half of the dough. Place each cake on a 10 x 15 baking sheet, cover with a damp cloth, and let rise again until double, about 1 hour. When doubled, brush each cake with beaten egg and sprinkle the top with colored sugars, alternating colors. Bake in a preheated 350 degree oven for 20 minutes. Remove cakes and insert plastic babies from underneath the cake.
Makes 2 cake rings

Tradition states that the person who eats the slice with the "baby" brings the king cake next year.

Peanut Brittle

½ cup water
1 cup light corn syrup
1½ cups sugar
½ teaspoon salt
1 teaspoon baking soda
2 cups raw peanuts

In a heavy saucepan, combine water, corn syrup, and sugar, and cook until it spins a thread, 234 degrees. Add peanuts and salt, stirring until the peanuts are parched, 305 degrees. Remove from heat, add soda, and stir vigorously until well mixed. Pour on a greased cookie sheet. Cool. Crack into pieces. This recipe may be doubled.

Peanut Butter Pumpkin Balls

2 sticks butter
1 16-ounce box powdered sugar
1 16-ounce jar crunchy peanut butter
½ cup pecans, ground
½ block paraffin
12-ounces white chocolate or almond bark, grated

In a large bowl, combine butter, powdered sugar, peanut butter, and pecans, and roll into 1-inch balls. Chill until firm, about 1 hour. Melt paraffin in double boiler. Add grated white chocolate to paraffin, a little at a time, stirring constantly until smooth. Leave chocolate mixture over heat, insert toothpick into each ball, and dip into chocolate. Drain on wax paper. Decorate using decorator tip with orange icing to make grooves and green icing for a stem. Easily doubles.
Makes 6 dozen

These balls may be prepared using dark chocolate when a pumpkin decoration is not needed.

Scaramel Crunch

5 quarts popped, unsalted popcorn
2 cups brown sugar
1 cup butter or margarine
½ cup light corn syrup
1 teaspoon salt
½ teaspoon baking soda
1 cup pecan halves*

Warm popcorn in 250 degree oven while making sauce. In a saucepan, mix sugar, butter, syrup, and salt. Bring to a boil, reduce heat, and gently boil for 5 minutes. Remove from heat and add soda. Mixture will foam. Pour sauce over popcorn, sprinkle nuts on top, and mix well. Put in 250 degree oven for 45 minutes, stirring every 15 minutes. Pour on wax paper and let cool. Store in an air-tight container.
*Unsalted roasted peanuts may be substituted for pecan halves.
Makes 5 quarts

Winter White Pecans

½ stick butter, melted
2½ cups pecans
Salt
½ pound white chocolate or
   almond bark

Preheat oven to 325 degrees. Pour butter over pecans then bake 15 minutes. After removing from oven, sprinkle with salt. In the top of a double boiler, melt chocolate. Using a toothpick, dip pecans in white chocolate. Place on wax paper and cool.

Surprise your child's teacher with a tin of these at Christmas.

Toffee Almond Squares

1½ cups almonds, slivered
1 pound butter
2 cups sugar
¼ cup light Karo syrup
6 to 10 1.55-ounce Hershey
   Bars
1 cup finely chopped pecans

Lightly toast almonds in a 300 degree oven for 5 minutes. In a heavy pan, cook butter, sugar, almonds, and Karo until mixture reaches 300 degrees on a candy thermometer, or approximately 40 minutes on low setting of electric stove. Pour into a greased 15½ x 10½ baking pan. Place Hershey Bars on top while hot and sprinkle with pecans. Let cool and score. Break into pieces. Store in an airtight container.

A rich, crunchy candy. Perfect for Christmas gifts.

Turtle Candy

1 12-ounce package semi-sweet
   chocolate morsels
2 Tablespoons shortening
30 Kraft caramels
3 Tablespoons butter
2 Tablespoons water
1 cup chopped pecans

In a double boiler, melt chocolate with shortening over hot, *not boiling*, water, stirring occasionally until smooth. Line an 8 x 8 pan with foil. Pour ½ of chocolate into foil-lined pan and refrigerate until firm, for about 15 minutes. In a double boiler, melt caramels, butter, and water, stirring occasionally until smooth. Mix in nuts and pour over firm chocolate. Refrigerate about 15 minutes or until "tacky." Pour remaining chocolate over caramel nut layer and refrigerate at least 1 hour. To serve, cut into small squares.

Bite-size bits of sheer chocolate pleasure.

Desserts

Bayou Brownies

¾ cup flour
¼ teaspoon baking soda
¼ teaspoon salt
⅓ cup butter
¾ cup sugar
2 Tablespoons water
1 12-ounce bag semi-sweet
   chocolate chips
2 teaspoons vanilla
2 eggs
½ cup chopped pecans

Preheat oven to 325 degrees. Combine flour, soda, and salt in a small bowl. In a saucepan melt butter. Add sugar and water. Bring just to a boil and remove from heat. Add 1 cup of chocolate chips and vanilla, stirring until melted and smooth. Transfer to a large bowl. Add eggs, one at a time, beating well after each addition. Gradually blend in flour mixture. Stir in remaining chips and pecans and spread into a greased 10 x 7 baking pan. Bake for 30-35 minutes. Let cool and cut into squares.
Makes 1 dozen large or 2 dozen small brownies

Chewy and chocolately.

Brownie Surprise

2 sticks butter
4 ounces unsweetened chocolate
4 eggs
2 cups sugar
1 cup flour
1 teaspoon vanilla
1 teaspoon salt
½ cup chopped pecans
1 14-ounce package caramels
⅓ cup evaporated milk

Preheat oven to 350 degrees. Melt butter and chocolate. Allow to cool. Beat eggs and sugar, then add to chocolate. Stir in flour, vanilla, salt, and pecans. Put half of mixture into greased 9 x 13 pan. Bake 15 minutes. While this is baking, heat caramels and milk, stirring constantly until caramels are melted. Spread caramels on brownies and top with remaining half of batter. Bake 30 minutes. Cool and cut.

Swamp Bottom Brownie

1 cup flour
2 teaspoons baking powder
1½ Tablespoons cocoa
½ teaspoon salt
¾ cup sugar
½ cup milk
1 teaspoon vanilla
2 Tablespoons butter, melted
½ cup brown sugar
½ cup white sugar
2 Tablespoons cocoa
1 cup hot water

Preheat oven to 350 degrees. In a large bowl, sift together flour, baking powder, cocoa, salt, and sugar. Combine milk, vanilla, butter, and add to sifted ingredients. Pour into a greased 8 x 8 pan. In a saucepan, combine the remaining ingredients and boil for five minutes. This makes a thin syrup. Pour over batter. Bake for 40 minutes. While baking, the syrup sinks to the bottom and makes a fudge sauce. Serve warm, upside down. Garnish with whipped cream, if desired.
8-10 servings

Almond Butter Cookies

1 cup butter
½ cup sugar
1 teaspoon almond extract
¼ teaspoon salt
2 cups flour
Granulated sugar

Preheat oven to 350 degrees. In a large bowl, cream butter and sugar. Add almond extract, mixing well, then add salt and flour. Chill dough. Roll in 1-inch balls, then roll each ball in granulated sugar. Stamp with a cookie stamp or press flat with the tines of a fork. Bake for 12-15 minutes.
Makes 4 dozen

If you have a set of cookie stamps, this recipe is perfect to show off a design.

Christmas Sugar Cookies

1 pound butter
2 cups sugar
3 eggs
4 cups flour
2 teaspoons baking powder
¼ teaspoon salt
1 Tablespoon vanilla

Preheat oven to 375 degrees. Cream butter and sugar. Add eggs, mixing well. Sift flour, baking powder, and salt. Combine with creamed mixture, then add vanilla. Chill dough at least four hours. Work with cool dough. Sprinkle a board with flour and powdered sugar to prevent dough from sticking. Roll out dough approximately ¼-inch. Cut cookies. Bake on ungreased cookie sheet until lightly browned, 8-10 minutes. Sprinkle with sugar.
Makes 3 dozen cookies

Sugar Cookies

1 cup butter
2 cups sugar
2 eggs
2 teaspoons vanilla
4 cups sifted flour
2 teaspoons baking powder
½ teaspoon salt

Preheat oven to 375 degrees. Combine butter and sugar. Add eggs, mixing well. Stir in vanilla. Sift flour with salt and baking powder. Add flour to egg mixture, kneading toward the last, if necessary. Refrigerate 1 hour. Lightly dust board with a combination of flour and powdered sugar to prevent the dough from sticking. Roll dough to little more than ¼-inch thick. Cut with desired-shaped cutters. Bake until lightly browned, 10-12 minutes.
Makes about 3 dozen

*To make **Ghost Cookies**, use a ghost-shaped cookie cutter. Bake, coat with white icing, and paint faces on the cookies with chocolate icing using a toothpick.*

Desserts

Butter Bits

1 cup butter
⅔ cup sugar
2 egg yolks
1 teaspoon almond extract
2⅔ cups sifted flour

Preheat oven to 350 degrees. In a large bowl, cream butter, slowly stir in sugar, and beat well. Add egg yolks, one at a time, beating well after each addition. Stir in almond extract and flour, working with a wooden spoon to make a smooth, stiff dough. Shape into ½-inch balls. Place on ungreased cookie sheet and flatten to desired thickness. Bake 10 minutes or until pale brown. Remove from cookie sheet and cool on wire rack.
Makes 6½ dozen

Straight from grandmother's kitchen. An easy cookie for any occasion.

Cottonland Cheesecakes

Crust:
1½ cups graham cracker crumbs,
    finely ground
1 stick butter, softened

Filling:
3 8-ounce packages cream
    cheese, softened
1 cup sugar
5 eggs, room temperature
1 teaspoon lemon extract
2 Tablespoons fresh lemon juice

Topping:
1 pint sour cream
3 Tablespoons sugar
1 teaspoon vanilla

Crust:
Preheat oven to 375 degrees. Combine graham cracker crumbs and butter and press into the bottom of a greased 9 x 13 pan.

Filling:
Beat the cream cheese and gradually add the sugar. Beat in eggs, one at a time, beating well after each addition. Add lemon extract and lemon juice and beat until smooth. Pour into prepared crust. Bake for 20-25 minutes. Remove from oven and cool 10 minutes before adding topping.

Topping:
Combine sour cream, sugar, and vanilla, and mix well. Spread topping over filling and return to a 375 degree oven for 7-8 minutes. Remove and cool completely. Store in refrigerator. Cut into bite-size pieces. May be topped with fresh strawberries or other seasonal fruits.

Chocolate Earthquake Cookies

2 cups flour
½ cup cocoa
1 teaspoon baking soda
½ cup butter or margarine
½ cup solid shortening
1 cup packed brown sugar
1 cup white sugar
2 eggs
1½ teaspoons vanilla
1 12-ounce bag chocolate chips
1 12-ounce bag peanut butter
   chips
Powdered sugar

Preheat oven to 375 degrees. Combine flour, cocoa, and baking soda. In a large mixing bowl, beat the butter and shortening for 30 seconds. Add the sugars and beat until fluffy. Add eggs and vanilla and beat well. Add the flour mixture, beating until well combined. Stir in the chips. Roll teaspoon-size balls of dough in powdered sugar. Place on an ungreased cookie sheet. Bake for 8 minutes. Cool on a wire rack.
Makes 6 dozen cookies

This cookie is so good with a glass of cold milk. Warm in microwave for a soft and chewy sensation.

Cookie Monster Delight

½ cup softened butter
½ cup brown sugar
1 egg
2 teaspoons vanilla
¾ cup flour
Pinch of salt
½ teaspoon baking powder
½ teaspoon baking soda
1 cup crushed granola cereal
1 cup semi-sweet chocolate chips
½ cup chopped pecans
½ cup raisins
½ cup M & M's

Preheat oven to 350 degrees. Grease a 12-inch aluminum pizza pan. Beat together butter, sugar, egg, and vanilla until fluffy. Add flour, salt, baking powder, and baking soda to sugar mixture. Add granola cereal and mix well. Spread dough evenly on the pan. Sprinkle on chocolate chips, pecans, and raisins. Bake 13-15 minutes or until golden brown. While still very soft, garnish with M & M's. Cool and cut in wedges.
12-14 servings

Children will love to help make this cookie pizza.

Crispy Date Bars

Crust:
2 cups sifted flour
1 cup margarine
4 Tablespoons sugar

Filling:
1 cup chopped dates
½ cup sugar
½ cup margarine
1 egg, well-beaten
2 cups Rice Krispies
1 cup chopped nuts
1 teaspoon vanilla

Frosting:
2 cups sifted powdered sugar
1-2 teaspoons milk
½ teaspoon vanilla
1 3-ounce package cream cheese,
  softened

Preheat oven to 350 degrees. To prepare crust, mix flour, margarine, and sugar and press into a slightly greased 9 x 13 pan. Bake for 25 minutes.

Filling:
In a medium saucepan, combine dates, sugar, and margarine. Cook over medium heat until mixture boils, stirring constantly. Simmer 3 minutes. Blend ¼ cup of hot mixture into beaten egg, then return egg mixture to pan. Mix and cook until bubbles appear. Remove from heat. Add cereal, nuts, and vanilla, then spread over warm crust.

Frosting:
Combine powdered sugar, milk, vanilla, and cream cheese. Add enough milk to make frosting of spreading consistency. Spread over cooled bars. Refrigerate until firm, then slice in 1 x 2-inch bars. The frosting recipe can be doubled for thicker frosting.
Makes 24 bars

Ginger Jumbles

1½ sticks butter, melted
1 cup granulated sugar
¼ cup molasses*
1 egg, slightly beaten
1¾ cups flour
½ teaspoon ground cloves
½ teaspoon ground ginger
1 teaspoon ground cinnamon
½ teaspoon salt
½ teaspoon baking soda

Preheat oven to 350 degrees. Combine butter, sugar, and molasses, and mix thoroughly. Add egg to butter mixture and blend well. Sift flour, spices, salt, and baking soda together. Add to sugar mixture and mix well. Drop by heaping teaspoons on a foil-covered cookie sheet. Bake for 6-8 minutes.
*Cane syrup may be substituted for molasses.
Makes 4 dozen 2-inch cookies

Hearty Oatmeal Cookies

1½ sticks butter
1⅓ cups brown sugar
2 eggs
1 teaspoon vanilla
1 cup flour
2 teaspoons baking soda
½ teaspoon salt
1 teaspoon cinnamon
¼ teaspoon nutmeg
2 cups oatmeal
1 cup raisins
1 cup chopped nuts

Preheat oven to 350 degrees. In a large bowl, cream butter and brown sugar. Add eggs and vanilla and beat until smooth. Sift flour, baking soda, salt, cinnamon, and nutmeg together, and slowly add to sugar mixture. Fold in oatmeal, raisins, and nuts. Drop by spoonfuls onto a greased cookie sheet. Bake for 10-15 minutes or until lightly browned.
Makes 6 dozen

Louisiana Sin-de-Bars

1 stick butter
½ cup sugar
5 Tablespoons cocoa
1 teaspoon vanilla
1 egg, beaten
1½ cups graham cracker crumbs
1 cup chopped pecans*

Custard filling:
2 cups powdered sugar
1 stick butter, softened
3 Tablespoons instant vanilla
  pudding mix
2 Tablespoons milk

Icing:
6 ounces semi-sweet chocolate
1 Tablespoon butter

In a saucepan, combine the butter, sugar, cocoa, and vanilla, and cook, stirring until the sugar is dissolved. Then add the egg and mix well. Remove from heat and add graham cracker crumbs and nuts. Pack the crust into a greased 8 x 12 baking pan and chill.
*Walnuts may be substituted for the pecans.

Custard filling:
Combine the sugar, butter, pudding mix, and milk. Beat well, then spread over crust and chill.

Icing:
In a small saucepan, combine the chocolate and butter, stirring over very low heat until chocolate melts. Spread over custard filling. Cool for 30 minutes. Cut into 2-inch squares, then cover and store in refrigerator until ready to serve. It is important to allow the bars to come to room temperature before cutting. Refrigerate uneaten bars to maintain proper consistency.
Makes 48 2-inch squares

Rich and chewy and positively divine for a real sweet tooth!!!

Desserts

Lace Cookies

2 cups old-fashioned rolled oats
1 Tablespoon flour
2 cups sugar
½ teaspoon salt
2 sticks butter, melted
2 eggs, beaten
1 teaspoon vanilla

· Preheat oven to 325 degrees. Combine the oats, flour, sugar, and salt. Pour very hot butter over the mixture and stir until the sugar has melted. Add the eggs and vanilla, stirring well. Cover cookie sheets with aluminum foil and coat with non-stick cooking spray. Place teaspoonfuls of dough 1 inch apart on cookie sheet. Bake for 10-12 minutes. When baking is completed, slide aluminum foil with cookies onto a cooling rack. Let cool completely before removing the cookies from the foil.
Makes 6 dozen cookies

Priscilla Cookies

2 sticks margarine, softened
5½ Tablespoons powdered sugar
¾ cup cornstarch
1 cup flour

Topping:
¾ cup powdered sugar
2 Tablespoons orange juice

Preheat oven to 350 degrees. Cream the margarine and powdered sugar. Add the cornstarch and flour and beat well. Chill dough 3 hours. Roll into nickel-size balls. If too sticky, add extra flour. Indent the top of the cookies with a baby spoon or your thumb. Bake for 15-20 minutes or until just brown. Combine the powdered sugar and orange juice and drizzle over the cookies.
Makes 6½ dozen

Wonderful!

Pattycake Cookies

1 pound butter, softened
2 cups dark brown sugar
2 cups white sugar
2 teaspoons vanilla
4 eggs, slightly beaten
4 cups flour
2 teaspoons soda
2 teaspoons baking powder
2 cups minute oatmeal
2 cups crushed corn flake cereal
1 12-ounce package chocolate chips
1-2 cups chopped pecans

In a large bowl, cream butter and sugars. Add vanilla to eggs and blend with sugar mixture. Combine flour, soda, and baking powder, and add to sugar mixture. Mix oatmeal, cereal, chocolate chips, and pecans. In a very large bowl, gently combine the two mixtures. Place heaping Tablespoons on a lightly greased cookie sheet. Mash dough flat. These are large cookies, and you can only get 6 on a cookie sheet. Bake at 300-325 degrees for 10-12 minutes.
Makes 48 large cookies

Super cookies!

Lemon Tarts

Filling:
2 cups sugar
2 teaspoons grated lemon rind
1 cup lemon juice
1 cup butter
4 eggs, beaten

Tarts:
2 cups flour
½ cup sugar
2 pinches salt
2 sticks butter, softened
2 egg yolks
1 teaspoon almond extract

Combine sugar, lemon rind, lemon juice, and butter in top of a double boiler and bring water to a boil. Reduce heat to low and cook until butter melts, stirring constantly. Gradually stir about ¼ of hot mixture into eggs, then return to hot mixture, stirring constantly. Cook in top of double boiler, stirring constantly for 20 minutes or until thickened. Chill 2 hours. To serve, spoon filling into tart shells and garnish with decorator frosting or whipped cream if desired.

Tarts:
In the bowl of a food processor, sift together flour, sugar, and salt and process until it forms a ball. Remove to a lightly floured board and work until dough is smooth. Chill. Pinch off 1-inch balls of dough and press into tart molds. Bake in a 400 degree oven for 12-15 minutes or until lightly brown.
Makes about 8 dozen

Fresh Fruit Tart

Crust:
1 cup flour
¼ cup light brown sugar
1 cup ground pecans
1 stick butter, melted

Filling:
1 8-ounce package cream cheese
½ pint sour cream
⅓ cup sugar
4 ounces Cool Whip
2 teaspoons vanilla

Fruit:
Peaches
Strawberries
Kiwi
Cantaloupe
2 Tablespoons orange juice

Preheat oven to 350 degrees. Mix flour, brown sugar, pecans, and butter. Press into a 9 to 11-inch tart/quiche pan, making the crust very thin. Bake for 10 minutes or until lightly brown.

Filling:
Whip together cream cheese, sour cream, and sugar. Fold in Cool Whip and vanilla. Spread in tart crust.

Fruit:
Use 2-3 cups, any combination, of sliced fresh fruit. Amount of fruit will depend on the placement on the tart. Toss fruit with orange juice. Drain fruit before arranging on top of tart. Garnish with mint leaves. Chill.

Paper Bag Apple Pie

3-4 large baking apples
½ cup sugar
2 Tablespoons flour
½ teaspoon nutmeg
1 teaspoon cinnamon
1 unbaked 9-inch pie shell
2 Tablespoons lemon juice

Topping:
½ cup sugar
½ cup flour
½ cup butter or margarine

Preheat oven to 425 degrees. Pare, core, and quarter apples, then halve each quarter to make chunks. This should equal 7 cups of apples. Prepare filling by combining sugar, flour, nutmeg, and cinnamon. Sprinkle mixture over apples and toss to coat well. Spoon into pie shell and drizzle with lemon. For topping, combine sugar and flour then cut in butter. Sprinkle topping over apples. Slide pie into a heavy brown paper bag, fold open end twice, and fasten with paper clips. Place on large cookie sheet and bake for 1 hour. Split bag open and remove pie.
8 servings

A beautiful pie!

Elegant Apple Tart

1 stick butter
⅓ cup sugar
½ teaspoon vanilla
1 cup flour

Filling:
1 8-ounce package Neufchâtel
  cheese
¼ cup sugar
1 egg
1 teaspoon vanilla
1 Tablespoon flour

Topping:
5 large apples, peeled and
  thinly sliced, about 5-6 cups*
½ cup chopped pecans
½ cup sugar
1 teaspoon cinnamon

Preheat oven to 400 degrees. In a small bowl, cream butter, sugar, and vanilla. Add the flour. Gather quickly into a ball. This crust is like a cookie dough and should be handled gently. It breaks easily but can be patched together without any noticeable difference. Use floured hands to press gently into a 10-inch spring-form pan. Trim edges about ⅓-½ the way up the sides to form smooth edges for crust. Partially bake the crust at 400 degrees for 8 minutes. Remove crust and turn the oven up to 450 degrees.

Filling:
Combine all ingredients in food processor or mixer until very smooth. Pour into crust.

Topping:
Toss apples and pecans gently with sugar and cinnamon. To prevent the filling from being disturbed, layer apples carefully in an attractive pattern. Pour any remaining juice over the topping. Bake at 450 degrees for 10 minutes, then 400 degrees for 25 minutes. Let cool before removing the side of the spring-form pan.
*Use tart apples such as Granny Smith.
Makes 12 servings

This tart lives up to its name. Serve on a glass pedestal plate.

Apple Cream Pie

1½ cups peeled, thinly sliced
   Rome apples
¾ cup sugar
¼ teaspoon cinnamon
¼ teaspoon nutmeg
1 unbaked 9-inch pastry shell
⅛ teaspoon salt
2 3-ounce packages cream
   cheese, softened
2 eggs, beaten
½ cup whipping cream
2 teaspoons vanilla

Preheat oven to 450 degrees. Mix together apple slices, ¼ cup sugar, cinnamon, and nutmeg, and arrange in pastry shell. Bake for 15 minutes, then remove and reduce heat to 325 degrees. Whip remaining ½ cup sugar, salt, and cream cheese. Add eggs and beat until smooth. Combine cream and vanilla then add to sugar mixture. Pour over apples in pastry shell and bake 40-45 minutes. Serve warm or cold.
8 servings

Sour Cream Peach Pie

Filling:
2 Tablespoons flour
¼ cup sugar
1 teaspoon cinnamon
Pinch of salt
1 egg, beaten
½ teaspoon vanilla
½ teaspoon almond extract
1 cup sour cream
6 medium-sized ripe peaches,
   peeled and sliced
1 9-inch graham cracker crust

Topping:
⅓ cup sugar
⅓ cup flour
1 teaspoon cinnamon
4 Tablespoons butter, softened

Preheat oven to 400 degrees. Combine flour, sugar, cinnamon, salt, egg, vanilla, almond extract, and sour cream. Fold in peaches and coat each slice well. Pour into crust. Bake for 15 minutes, reduce heat to 350 degrees and continue to bake for at least 30 minutes. With a mixer, combine topping ingredients and crumble over the warm pie. Return to the oven and bake at 400 degrees for another 10 minutes. Cool to room temperature.

A truly different and delicious pie!

Desserts

Brandy Alexander Pie

Crust:
1½ cups Oreo cookie crumbs,
   about 14 cookies
3 Tablespoons melted butter

Filling:
½ cup cold milk
1 envelope unflavored gelatin
⅔ cup sugar
⅛ teaspoon salt
3 eggs, separated
¼ cup cognac
¼ cup creme de cocoa
1 pint whipping cream

Garnish:
Chocolate curls

To prepare crust, mix crumbs and butter with fork and press into a 9-inch pie plate. Chill. In a saucepan, sprinkle gelatin over cold milk. Add ⅓ cup sugar, salt, and slightly beaten egg yolks. Heat over low heat, stirring until gelatin dissolves and the mixture is slightly thickened. Do not boil. Remove from heat and add cognac and creme de cocoa. Allow the mixture to cool. Beat egg whites with remaining sugar until stiff and fold into the thickened mixture. Whip one cup of cream until stiff peaks form and blend with rest of filling. Turn into the crust and chill for several hours or overnight. Garnish with remaining sweetened whipped cream and chocolate curls.

Mama's Buttermilk Pie

1 stick butter
1 cup sugar
2 Tablespoons flour
Dash of salt
3 eggs
1 cup buttermilk
1 teaspoon vanilla
1 9-inch unbaked pie shell

Preheat oven to 350 degrees. In a large bowl, cream butter and sugar until light. Add flour and salt and mix well. Add eggs, one at a time, beating well after each addition until mixture is fluffy. Fold in buttermilk and vanilla. Pour into pie shell and bake for 50 minutes.

Choco-Chess Pie

1½ cups sugar
1 stick butter, melted
4 teaspoons cocoa
2 eggs
1 5-ounce can evaporated milk
1 Tablespoon Amaretto
1 teaspoon vanilla
1 9-inch unbaked pie shell

Preheat oven to 350 degrees. Combine sugar, butter, and cocoa and mix well. Add eggs, milk, Amaretto, and vanilla. Mix until smooth. Pour into pie shell and bake for 45 minutes. The pie will not look done after 45 minutes, but it will be. Let sit 1 hour before serving.
8 servings

A fast and good dessert.

Chocolate Pecan Pie

1 stick butter, softened
1 cup sugar
¼ cup cocoa
1 cup white Karo syrup
3 eggs
1 teaspoon vanilla
1 cup chopped pecans
1 unbaked 9⅝-inch pastry shell
Whipping cream

Preheat oven to 350 degrees. Cream butter and sugar. Add cocoa, then stir in Karo. Add eggs one at a time, beating on low after each addition. Stir in vanilla and pecans. Pour into pie shell and bake for 50-60 minutes. Serve with whipped cream, if desired.

For plain pecan pie, omit cocoa. A southern favorite. Perfect with tea or coffee.

Fudge Pecan Pie

1 recipe **Sugar Dough Pie Crust**
2 cups hot water
6 ounces baking chocolate
1½ cups whipping cream
3½ cups sugar
⅔ cup butter
1 cup flour
¼ teaspoon vanilla
1½ cups chopped pecans

Preheat oven to 375 degrees. Prepare two 9-inch pie shells, prick each shell several times, and partially bake for 5 minutes. In a saucepan, combine water and chocolate and stir until melted. Add cream, bring to a boil, remove from heat, and set aside. Meanwhile with a mixer, cream sugar and butter. Add flour and vanilla. Gradually add chocolate to creamed mixture and mix well. Pour into partially baked pie shells. Sprinkle with pecans and bake 45-50 minutes or until set. If the crust begins to brown too quickly, cover only the crust with aluminum foil. Remove and cool on racks. Serve with sweetened whipped cream, if desired.
12-16 servings

Wonderfully rich!

Peanut Butter Pie

1 8-ounce package cream cheese, softened
½ cup powdered sugar
½ cup peanut butter
½ cup milk
8 ounces Cool Whip
1 9-inch graham cracker crust
Salted peanuts

Beat the cream cheese, then add sugar and peanut butter and mix well. Add milk and beat until smooth. Fold in Cool Whip. Pour into crust. Garnish with coarsely-chopped salted peanuts, if desired. Freeze. To serve, let sit at room temperature for 15-20 minutes.
8-10 servings

Different. A light finish for a spicy meal.

Desserts

Sour Dough Pie Crust

2 *sticks unsalted butter, softened*
2½ *cups flour*
⅓ *cup sugar*
1 *egg*
2 *teaspoons vanilla*

In a food processor on high speed, combine butter, flour, and sugar. While processing, add egg and vanilla and mix until dough forms a ball. Remove dough and place in a plastic bag and chill 30 minutes. This dough will last several days in the refrigerator. To prepare pie crust, divide dough in half and roll out between wax paper.
Makes 2 single pie crusts

This is excellent for fruit pies and tarts. This sweet, cooked crust does not shrink.

Refrigerator Pastry Crust

3 *cups flour*
1 *teaspoon salt*
1 *teaspoon baking powder*
1 *cup shortening*

Combine flour, salt, and baking powder. Cut the shortening into the dry ingredients until the mixture is the size of small peas. Shape into a ball. Store in a ziplock bag and refrigerate. Use dough as needed. To make a single pie, measure out 1¼ cups dough. Add 2½ Tablespoons cold water and mix with a fork. Form into a ball and roll out on a floured board. The dough will make 3 single or 2 double pie crusts.

Praline Parfait Pie

1 *package Famous Chocolate
   Wafer Cookies*
¼ *cup butter, melted*
½ *gallon Pralines n Cream ice
   cream*
½ *cup caramel sauce*
½ *cup chopped pecans*
½ *pint whipping cream, whipped*
Chocolate shavings

Preheat oven to 350 degrees. Stand whole chocolate wafers around the sides of a spring-form pan. Roll the remaining chocolate wafers into fine crumbs. Mix with butter and press into bottom of spring-form pan, making crust about ¼-inch thick. Bake for 7 minutes. Cool. Slightly soften ice cream and spoon half in spring-form pan. Cover with caramel sauce, then sprinkle with pecans. Top with remaining ice cream and freeze. When ready to serve, top with whipped cream, if desired, and garnish with chocolate shavings.
10-12 servings

Serve with a spoon so you can eat every crumb!

Pralines 'n Cream Crêpes

Dessert Crêpes:
1½ cups sifted flour
2 cups warm milk
3 eggs
2 Tablespoons butter, melted
2 Tablespoons sugar
½ teaspoon salt

½ gallon Pralines 'n Cream Ice
    Cream
Rocky Road Praline Sauce

Whirl all crêpe ingredients in the blender. Store in refrigerator several hours. Spray a 6 or 7-inch pan with non-stick cooking spray. Heat pan until a drop of water sizzles. Pour a scant ¼ cup batter into the pan and swirl rapidly until the batter covers the bottom. Immediately pour off batter that does not adhere. Cook until browned, lift edge, and turn with spatula. Cook a few seconds on the other side and remove to a plate to cool. Reheat and spray pan as necessary before cooking each crêpe. Crêpes with a piece of wax paper between each, may be stored in refrigerator. These freeze well and are worth the effort. Spoon 3 Tablespoons ice cream on each crêpe. Fold over and place seam side down. This may be done ahead of time and frozen. To serve, top each crêpe with Rocky Road Praline Sauce.
20 servings

Mocha Ice Cream Cups

18-20 Oreo cookies, crushed
½ stick butter, melted

Filling:
1 quart Jamoca Almond Fudge
    ice cream, softened
¾ cup fudge sauce
½ pint whipping cream
2 Tablespoons Kahlua or
    Mexican vanilla

Garnish:
Almond slivers, toasted
Semi-sweet chocolate shavings

Line muffin tins with paper baking cups. Mix cookies and butter together and press lightly into bottom of muffin cups. Spoon in ice cream and top with 1 Tablespoon fudge sauce. Freeze. Whip cream and fold in Kahlua or Mexican vanilla. To serve, remove paper baking cups and top with whipped cream. Sprinkle with almond slivers and chocolate shavings. The toasted almonds on top add so much—they are a must!
12 servings

Desserts

Lemon-Orange Cups with Cardinal Raspberry Sauce

3 *navel oranges*
1½ *quarts Lemon Custard Ice*
   Cream*

Juice the oranges to make 6 attractive orange cups. Slice a thin sliver from the bottom of each orange so that they will sit on a steady base. Fill with ice cream and freeze. To serve, top with the sauce. Garnish with mint leaves and berries or a candied violet.
*May substitute any light-flavored ice cream.

Cardinal Raspberry Sauce

1 *10-ounce box frozen raspberries,*
   thawed
1 *teaspoon cornstarch*
1 *Tablespoon orange juice*
1 *Tablespoon Triple Sec*

Place raspberries in a blender and process until smooth. Put through a sieve to remove seeds. In a saucepan, combine the berries, cornstarch, and juice, and simmer over low heat until slightly thickened. When cool, add Triple Sec and mix well.
6 servings

Apricot Sherbet

1¼ *cups fresh lemon juice,*
   about 7 lemons
2 *cups sugar*
1 *17-ounce can apricots, drained*
   and puréed
1 *pint Half and Half*
Whole milk

Place lemon juice, sugar, apricots, and Half and Half in ice cream freezer. Add whole milk to fill line. Freeze.
Makes ½ gallon

Old South Mint Sherbet

2 *handfuls mint, about 1 cup*
4 *cups sugar*
4 *cups water*
1 *12-ounce can frozen orange*
   juice concentrate
¾ *cup lemon juice*
2¼ *cups water*
1 *pint whipping cream*
1 *pint Half and Half*
3 *drops green food coloring*

Wash mint thoroughly, chop fine, and set aside. To make syrup, mix sugar and water. Bring to a boil and allow to boil 5 minutes. Cool. In a large bowl, combine syrup, orange juice, lemon juice, and water. Add chopped mint and soak overnight. Strain mint from syrup. Whip cream until peaks form. Fold in Half and Half. Add food coloring, then stir cream into syrup mixture. Freeze.
Makes 1½ gallons

Rich and refreshing.

Summer Sorbets

Simple Syrup:
3 cups sugar
3 cups water

Combine sugar and water in a small saucepan and simmer until sugar is dissolved. Cool to room temperature. Refrigerate in a covered jar. This makes enough simple syrup for the three following sorbets.
Makes 3 cups

Pineapple Sorbet

1 small ripe Hawaiian
   pineapple*
¾ cup simple syrup
1 Tablespoon fresh lemon juice

Peel, core, and cube pineapple. Place cubes in food processor and process until very smooth and frothy. This yields 2 cups. Stir in simple syrup and lemon juice. Place in covered container and freeze overnight. Whip with electric mixer and refreeze.
*May use 1 20-ounce can crushed pineapple, undrained.
Makes 1 quart

Peaches or strawberries are a great alternative for pineapple.

Kiwi Sorbet

6 kiwi fruit
1 cup simple syrup
3 teaspoons fresh lemon juice

Peel kiwi. Purée in food processor. This yields 1½ cups. Stir in simple syrup and lemon juice. Place in covered container and freeze overnight. Whip with electric mixer and refreeze.
Makes 1 quart

Cantaloupe Sorbet

1 large cantaloupe*
1 cup simple syrup
1½ teaspoons fresh lemon juice

Peel, seed, and cube cantaloupe. Place cubes in food processor and purée. This yields 3 cups. Stir in simple syrup and lemon juice. Place in covered container and freeze overnight. Whip with electric mixer and refreeze.
*Any ripe melon may be substituted.
Makes 1 quart

Country Vanilla Ice Cream

4 eggs
2¼ cups sugar
1 cup milk
4 cups Half and Half
4 cups whipping cream
4½ teaspoons vanilla
½ teaspoon salt

Beat eggs and gradually add sugar. Continue to beat until mixture is very stiff. Add remaining ingredients and mix thoroughly. Pour into gallon ice cream freezer and freeze according to freezer directions.
12-16 servings

This is absolutely the best homemade vanilla ice cream. Enjoy!

Desserts

Ruston Peach Ice Cream

6 cups pureed peaches, about
    10-12 peaches
3 cups sugar
Juice of 2 lemons
1 12-ounce can evaporated milk,
    chilled
1½ cups whipping cream,
    whipped until stiff but not in
    peaks
Pinch of salt
Whole milk

Mix all ingredients except whole milk. Put in freezer and fill to "freeze" line with whole milk. Freeze. This makes 4-6 quarts, depending on size of freezer.

Amaretto Sabayon

4 large egg yolks
¾ cup Amaretto De Saronno
⅓ cup sugar
1 cup whipping cream
2 Tablespoons sugar

In the top of a double boiler, combine yolks, liqueur, and sugar. Whisk until well blended. Place over simmering water and whisk constantly until the mixture thickens and coats a metal spoon, about 20 minutes. Do not boil or mixture will curdle. Transfer to bowl and cool. Whip cream with 2 Tablespoons sugar until stiff peaks form. Fold into thoroughly cooled Sabayon. Serve with a platter of fresh seasonal fruits such as whole strawberries, sliced peaches, or raspberries.

A teaspoon of Sabayon in a cup of coffee is wonderful!

Chantilly Creme

½ pint whipping cream
1-2 Tablespoons powdered sugar
2 teaspoons almond extract
Fresh strawberries*

With an electric mixer whip cream, adding sugar slowly. While still whipping, add almond extract. Whip until soft peaks form. Serve over fresh strawberries.
*Raspberries may be substituted for strawberries.

Meringue Chantilly

3 egg whites
Pinch of salt
1 cup sugar
1 teaspoon vanilla
1 teaspoon vinegar
½ pint whipping cream
2 Tablespoons sugar
Grated baking chocolate

Preheat oven to 250 degrees. Beat egg whites and salt until stiff and very dry. Gradually add sugar and beat until stiff peaks form. Do not under beat. Add vanilla and vinegar. Spoon into a 10-inch glass pie pan which has been greased and lined with greased wax paper. Bake 1 hour and 20 minutes. When cool enough to handle, loosen with a sharp knife and invert on plate. Cool completely. Whip cream and gradually add sugar until stiff peaks form. Frost meringue and sprinkle with baking chocolate. Let mellow at least 4 hours in refrigerator before serving. This freezes well either before or after icing with whipped cream.
8 servings

This dessert is delicious served with fresh strawberries instead of chocolate.

Caramel Delight

2 14-ounce cans sweetened
  condensed milk
½ pint whipping cream
1 teaspoon Mexican vanilla
½ cup chopped pecans

In a saucepan, cover 2 cans of sweetened condensed milk with water. Bring to boil. Be sure cans remain covered with water. Cover and gently boil for 3 hours. Cool. Refrigerate for 2 hours or overnight. Whip cream with vanilla and set aside. Open both ends of can and slide out dessert. Slice thinly and top with whipped cream. Sprinkle with chopped pecans.
12 servings

Deliciously rich!

Boiled Custard

¾ cup sugar
Dash of salt
2 Tablespoons cornstarch
3 egg yolks
1 quart whole milk
1 teaspoon vanilla
Whipped cream
Whole nutmeg, grated

In a heavy saucepan, combine sugar, salt, and cornstarch. Mix well. Beat egg yolks and add to dry mixture. Slowly add milk and cook over medium heat, stirring constantly, until custard coats the spoon and is slightly thickened, about 8-10 minutes. Remove from heat and add vanilla. Serve warm or cold in stemmed glasses with a dollop of whipped cream and grated whole nutmeg over the top.
6-8 servings

For delicious banana pudding custard add an additional 2 Tablespoons cornstarch and bananas.

White Chocolate Cloud

2¼ cups whipping cream
1 envelope unflavored gelatin
6 ounces Nestle Premier White
   baking bar, grated
1 teaspoon vanilla
2 egg whites
¼ teaspoon salt
2 Tablespoons sugar

In a medium saucepan, place 1¼ cups whipping cream. Sprinkle gelatin on top and let stand for 5 minutes. Add baking bar. Cook over low heat, stirring constantly until chocolate and gelatin are melted and mixture is smooth. Transfer to a large bowl and chill for 10 minutes, stirring occasionally. In a small bowl, combine remaining 1 cup whipping cream and vanilla. Beat until stiff peaks form and set aside. In a small bowl, combine egg whites and salt and beat until soft peaks form. Gradually add sugar, beating until stiff peaks form. Fold whipped cream and egg whites into the first mixture. Chill several hours. Makes 1 quart

This is especially festive served in a stemmed compote and garnished with fresh mint and a strawberry or chocolate shavings. Another idea is to drizzle a rich chocolate sauce over the top, then garnish with mint and a strawberry.

Praline Cream Puffs

Cream Puffs:
½ cup butter or margarine
1 cup boiling water
1 cup sifted flour
¼ teaspoon salt
4 eggs

Fluffy Custard:
2 cups milk
1 3⅛-ounce package cook-style
   French Vanilla pudding
Dash of freshly grated nutmeg
½ pint whipping cream
2 Tablespoons sugar
1 teaspoon vanilla

Praline Topping:
1 Tablespoon butter or
   margarine
½ cup packed brown sugar
½ cup chopped pecans

Garnish:
½ pint whipping cream

Cream Puffs:
Preheat oven to 450 degrees. Melt butter in boiling water. Mix flour and salt and add at once. Stir vigorously. Cook, stirring constantly, until the mixture forms a cohesive ball. Remove from heat and cool slightly. Add eggs one at a time, beating after each addition, until mixture looses its slickness. Shape into 2-inch balls and drop onto greased cookie sheet. Bake 15 minutes. Without opening the oven door, reduce heat to 325 degrees and bake an additional 25 minutes. This allows cream puffs to dry out and become hollow inside. When cream puffs have cooled, cut the top off each. Fill the hollow with fluffy custard and replace the lid of the cream puff. Ice the top with sweetened whipped cream and sprinkle with praline topping.

Fluffy Custard:
Cook pudding according to package instructions and add nutmeg. Beat cream, sugar, and vanilla until stiff peaks form. Fold into pudding.

Praline Topping:
In a skillet over medium heat, stir butter and sugar until bubbly. Add pecans and cook for 2 minutes, stirring constantly. Remove from heat and pour onto foil. Cool. Crumble with fingers into small pieces.

This is an easy but time consuming process. Just wait until you taste these puffs. A dessert fit for royalty!

Festive Yule Log

2 pints whipping cream
1 package Famous Chocolate
   Wafer Cookies
2-3 Tablespoons sugar
2-3 Tablespoons Grand Marnier
2 blocks semi-sweet chocolate,
   shaved*

Whip cream until stiff peaks form. Drizzle in sugar and Grand Marnier. By hand, fold in chocolate. "Ice" each cookie and stack in log fashion. Tightly seal with plastic wrap, being careful not to mash the whipped cream. Freeze. Using a serrated knife, slice diagonally. To serve, place on a tray, and add more freshly shaved chocolate for garnish.
*For ease of handling, keep chocolate frozen.
8-10 servings

Perfect with a glass of champagne for an elegant dessert.

French Bread Pudding with Whiskey Sauce

1 cup milk
1 cup Half and Half
¼ cup butter
½ cup sugar
4 cups cubed stale French bread
1 cup raisins
3 eggs, beaten
½ teaspoon nutmeg
1 teaspoon vanilla
Pinch of salt
¼ cup shredded coconut,
   optional
½ cup chopped pecans, optional

Whiskey Sauce:
½ cup butter
1 5-ounce can evaporated milk
1 cup sugar
1 egg yolk, beaten
6 ounces whiskey

Preheat oven to 350 degrees. In a saucepan, scald milk and Half and Half. Add butter to milk and allow to melt. Stir in sugar. Pour over bread cubes and raisins and let stand for 15 minutes. Add eggs, nutmeg, vanilla, salt, coconut, and pecans. Pour into a well-greased 3-quart casserole and bake for 45 minutes. Serve warm with whiskey sauce.

Whiskey Sauce:
In a saucepan, combine butter, milk, sugar, and egg yolk. Cook, stirring constantly, over medium heat until thickened. Stir in whiskey and serve warm over bread pudding.
8 servings

Desserts

Oriental Oranges

8 large oranges
1½ cups sugar
1½ cups light corn syrup
3 drops red food coloring, optional
1½ cups water
¼ cup lemon juice
¼ cup Cointreau

Remove peel and white membrane from all oranges. With a small, sharp knife, remove all the white membrane from the peel of 4 oranges. Cut these orange peels into very thin julienne strips. Boil these strips in water until they are tender. Slice the oranges crosswise, ¼ to ½-inch thick. In a saucepan, combine sugar and corn syrup with a few drops of red food coloring and 1½ cups water. Bring to a boil, stirring until sugar is dissolved. Cook uncovered over medium heat for 10 minutes. Add julienne strips of peel and cook for 30 minutes until syrup is slightly thickened. Remove from heat and stir in lemon juice and Cointreau. Pour over orange slices. Cover and refrigerate for at least 8 hours. To serve, place oranges in glass bowl and spoon syrup over them, decorating each with some of the caramelized orange peel.

Strawberries on Pastry Shell

Pastry Shell:
2¼ cups flour
¼ cup sugar
2 sticks butter, cut into 16 pieces
1 egg
1 teaspoon vanilla
4 Tablespoons ice water

Cream Cheese Filling:
½ pint whipping cream
1 3-ounce package cream cheese, softened
½ cup sugar
1 Tablespoon fresh lemon juice

Glaze:
⅓ cup seedless raspberry preserves
2 Tablespoons Cointreau or Grand Marnier

2 pints strawberries, hulled and halved

Pastry Shell:
In a large bowl, combine flour with sugar. Cut in butter until mixture resembles cornmeal. Beat egg and vanilla to blend and stir into flour mixture. Mix in water, one Tablespoon at a time, just until dough holds together. Gather into a ball and form into a cylinder that is 1-inch in diameter. Wrap in plastic and refrigerate for one hour. Preheat oven to 400 degrees. Spray back of scallop shells with non-stick cooking spray. Cut dough into 12 pieces. Roll out each piece on a floured board ⅛-inch thick. Press firmly onto back of scallop shell, allowing for shrinkage of dough. Pierce dough with a fork. Bake at 350 degrees for 12 minutes or until brown. Immediately remove pastry from back of shell. Cool.

Filling:
Beat cream until soft peaks form and set aside. Using a wooden spoon, stir cream cheese, sugar, and lemon juice until smooth. Fold into whipped cream. Cover and chill until ready to use.

Glaze:
In a saucepan over low heat, melt preserves with liqueur, stirring constantly. Cool. To assemble the tarts, spoon filling in pastry, top with strawberries and brush with glaze.
12 servings

This recipe can easily be adapted to make two 8-inch pies.

Tiny Meringue Shells

4 egg whites
¼ teaspoon cream of tartar
1⅓ cups sugar

Preheat oven to 275 degrees. Beat egg whites until foamy. While continuing to beat, sprinkle with cream of tartar. When egg whites are stiff enough to hold a point, begin to gradually add sugar. Continue to beat until mixture is stiff and glossy and the sugar is well blended. Drop meringue on baking sheet that has been sprayed with cooking spray. Use a small teaspoon and make the shells about 1-inch in diameter. Make an indentation in each meringue with the back of a tiny "baby-feeding" spoon. Bake for 1 hour. Turn the oven off and leave the meringues in the oven to cool. These may be made a few days in advance and kept in an airtight container. Serve with a bowl of **Chocolate Mocha** or **Lemon Cream Filling** alongside a tray of meringues or fill them yourself at the last minute and pass them on a tray adorned with a flower.
Makes 8-9 dozen meringues

Light and luscious.

Chocolate Mocha Filling

1 4-ounce bar cooking type German Sweet Chocolate
3 Tablespoons water
2 teaspoons instant coffee powder
1 teaspoon vanilla
½ pint whipping cream
3 Tablespoons sugar

In a heavy saucepan over low heat, stir chocolate into water until it melts, stirring constantly so the chocolate will not burn. Add coffee and stir until dissolved. Cool mixture until it thickens, then add vanilla. Whip cream with sugar until stiff peaks form. Fold into chocolate. Before serving, stir well to make creamy consistency. Garnish with shaved chocolate, chopped pecans, or a fresh raspberry, if desired.
Makes 2½ cups

Lemon Cream Filling

4 egg yolks
½ cup sugar
3 Tablespoons lemon juice
1 Tablespoon grated lemon zest*
⅛ teaspoon salt
1 cup whipping cream
3 Tablespoons sugar
1 teaspoon vanilla

In a double boiler over medium heat, beat the egg yolks until smooth. Add sugar, lemon juice, lemon zest, and salt. Cook mixture until thickened. Cool. Whip cream with sugar and vanilla until stiff peaks form. Gently stir the whipped cream into the lemon mixture. Garnish with a tiny mint leaf or sliver of fresh lemon if desired.
*This takes about 3 lemons, removing only yellow rind and chopping in the food processor.
Makes 2 cups

Desserts

English Toffee Nut Sauce

1½ cups sugar
1 cup evaporated milk
½ stick margarine
¼ cup corn syrup
Dash of salt
1½ cups chopped Heath or Skor
    Bars

In a saucepan, combine sugar, milk, margarine, syrup, and salt. Bring to a boil over low heat, stirring constantly for one minute. Remove from heat and stir in toffee bars. Cool. Serve over ice cream. This is better made a day ahead. Keeps well in the refrigerator for several days.
Makes 3¼ cups

*To make an ice cream pie, place ice cream in a crumb crust. Top with **English Toffee Nut Sauce** and additional toffee bar shavings. Freeze until ready to serve.*

Out-Of-This-World Chocolate Sauce

¾ cup sugar
3 Tablespoons cocoa
Dash of salt
2 Tablespoons water
1 5-ounce can evaporated milk
2 Tablespoons butter
1 teaspoon vanilla

In a saucepan, combine sugar, cocoa, and salt. Stir in water to make a thick paste. Blend in milk. Cook over low heat, stirring constantly until thick, about 10 minutes. Remove from heat and add butter and vanilla.
Makes 1¼ cups

Serve hot or cold over ice cream or as a fondue for spearing banana chunks, pecan halves, maraschino cherries, or pound cake squares.

Rocky Road Praline Sauce

2 cups dark brown sugar,
    packed
½ cup light corn syrup
4 Tablespoons butter
¼ teaspoon salt
2 teaspoons vanilla
2 cups chopped pecans
1 cup Half and Half

In a saucepan, combine the brown sugar, corn syrup, butter, and vanilla and bring to the boiling point. Remove from the heat. Stir in pecans, mixing well, then stir in Half and Half until thoroughly blended. Store in jars in the refrigerator. This keeps for quite a long time. Serve over **Praline 'n Cream Crêpes** or ice cream. Great for gifts.
Makes 3½ cups

*For Praline Sheet Cake, bake a yellow sheet cake and cool. Spread **Rocky Road Praline Sauce** over the cake. Store in the refrigerator. Quick, easy, and delicious!*

Orange Sauce

1 8-ounce package cream cheese,
    softened
1 7-ounce jar Kraft
    Marshmallow Creme
¼ cup orange juice

Combine ingredients, mixing at medium speed on electric mixer until well blended. Chill. Serve with fruit or pound cake cubes.
Makes 2 cups

*For the **Children's Christmas Party** serve as a fondue for spearing maraschino cherries, pineapple chunks, apple slices, miniature marshmallows, bananas, and raisins.*

Lagniappé

LAGNIAPPÉ: ESPECIALLY FOR YOU

Lagniappé is a French expression which means "a little something extra." Often it is a small gift given as a token of gratitude to a customer, or it may be a "favor" given to a guest to take home from a party.

Louisianians love to cook and entertain. Sharing a recipe or a meal is one of our favorite ways to enjoy a friend's companionship. Friends travel widely and bring home as "lagniappé" favorite recipes and culinary delights from all parts of the world. Louisiana's abundance of fresh foods, as well as the talents and traditions of Louisiana cooks, combine to create a truly memorable cuisine.

The cooking style of North Louisiana is similar to the "home cooking" for which the South is famous, but with this "lagniappé" — a notable Indian influence. Creole and Cajun, two of Louisiana's most famous cooking styles created by our cousins in South Louisiana, are also prevalent in North Louisiana, again with some embellishments of our own. The Creole style of cooking originated with the descendants of French and Spanish settlers. The careful blending of sauces and slow cooking help to achieve the tenderness and delicate flavors characteristic of Creole cuisine. The Cajun cooking brought to Louisiana from Nova Scotia by the French uses the natural herbs found in our bayou areas to enhance the flavors of the bounty found here. The spicy, hot flavors blend well with our fresh produce, fish, and game. To both of these were added the "lagniappé" of African influences — okra to thicken the gumbo, for example.

Our "lagniappé" for you is this collection of excellent recipes and menus that we enjoyed as we prepared *Celebrations on the Bayou.* Just as we invited you to dine in our "Cotton Country," we also invite you to try these "little extras." Enjoy!

Creole Seafood Seasoning

3 Tablespoons onion powder
⅓ cup salt
¼ cup freshly ground black
  pepper
2 Tablespoons thyme
2 Tablespoons oregano
⅓ cup paprika
1 teaspoon cayenne

Mix all ingredients and store in jar.
Makes 1½ cups

May be used in place of any purchased Creole seasoning. Excellent sprinkled in gumbo or on fish for the grill or fryer. The best seasoning for all seafoods.

Basic Tart Shells

3 cups flour
1½ teaspoons salt
1 cup shortening
5-6 Tablespoons water

Combine flour and salt in bowl. Cut in shortening with a pastry blender until mixture resembles coarse meal. Sprinkle water evenly over dough and stir with a fork until all dry ingredients are moistened. Shape dough into a ball. Chill. On a lightly floured surface, roll dough to ⅛-inch thickness. Cut with a 2-inch scalloped cutter. Fit each pastry into miniature muffin pan and prick each tart shell with a fork. Bake in 400 degree oven for 10-12 minutes.
Makes about 8 dozen tart shells

So light they melt in your mouth.

Basic Pizza Dough

Thick Crust Ingredients:
1½ cups warm water, 105-115
  degrees
3 Tablespoons vegetable oil
1 Tablespoon sugar
1 Tablespoon salt
2 packages dry yeast
4½ cups flour

Thin Crust Ingredients:
1 cup warm water, 105-115
  degrees
2 Tablespoons vegetable oil
2 teaspoons sugar
2 teaspoons salt
1 package dry yeast
3 cups flour

In food processor, mix water, oil, sugar, and salt. Sprinkle yeast over this and mix slightly. Let sit for 5 minutes. Gradually add flour, mixing well. Turn onto floured board. Knead until smooth and elastic. Shape into ball and place dough into greased bowl making sure top of ball is greased. Cover and let rise for 1 hour. Pinch dough down and divide into halves. Put on lightly greased pizza pans. Let rise until doubled. Bake at 450 degrees for 5 minutes. Add sauce and toppings. Bake thick crust 15 minutes at 450 degrees. Bake thin crust 10-12 minutes at 450 degrees.
Makes 2 12-inch pizza crusts

Lagniappé

Spiced Peaches

2 29-ounce cans Extra Large
  Del Monte peach halves*
¾ cup cider vinegar
¾ cup sugar
1 stick cinnamon
½-1 teaspoon whole cloves
¼ cup finely diced green bell
  pepper
¼ cup finely chopped onion
½ cup Italian salad dressing

Reserve ½ of the syrup from the 2 cans of peaches. To this syrup, add the vinegar, sugar, cinnamon, and cloves. Boil for 5 minutes. Arrange the peaches in a flat casserole. Pour hot mixture over the peaches and let them stand in syrup overnight in the refrigerator. To prepare, drain and fill each peach center with a mixture of bell pepper and onion, about 1 teaspoon. Drizzle 1 Tablespoon of dressing over peach half. Serve on a lettuce leaf or as a garnish and accompaniment for ham.
*It is important to buy the large, better-quality peach halves.
Makes 14 peach halves.

These are especially nice on a luncheon buffet.

Hot Pepper Sauce

This recipe was from the files of Dr. Neil Buie who was famous throughout Northeast Louisiana for his Hot Pepper Sauce. These are his instructions.

Thoroughly cleaned 10-ounce Worcestershire bottles make ideal pepper sauce bottles for this recipe.

In the bottom of each bottle, put 2 cloves garlic, 1 whole clove, and ⅛ teaspoon salt. Pack the bottle with stemmed, washed, and thoroughly dried, green Tabasco peppers (adding a few red and yellow for color, if available). Fill bottle with boiling white vinegar. While still warm, but not hot, put 2 or 3 drops of olive oil on top of vinegar. Ready to use in 3 weeks.

This sauce adds an extra zip to greens and peas of all kinds.

Pico de Gallo "Mexican Hot Sauce"

2 large onions, coarsely chopped
3 small celery stalks, coarsely
  chopped
4 medium tomatoes, coarsely
  chopped
2 jalapeño peppers, seeded and
  chopped
2 Tablespoons chopped fresh
  cilantro*
1 Tablespoon olive oil
Juice of 1 lime
1 teaspoon garlic powder
1 teaspoon salt
1-2 teaspoons black pepper

Combine all ingredients and mix well. Refrigerate for at least two hours before serving. Serve with fajitas.
*If cilantro is not available, use parsley.
Makes about 5 cups

Corn Relish

2 quarts vinegar
2 cups sugar
2 Tablespoons dry mustard
1 Tablespoon tumeric
6 large green peppers, chopped
1-1½ hot peppers, chopped
3 large onions, chopped
½ large cabbage, chopped
¼ cup salt
9-10 ears corn, cut off cob,
    about 6-7 cups

In a large pot, combine vinegar, sugar, dry mustard, and tumeric, and bring to a boil. Add green peppers, hot peppers, onions, cabbage, and salt, and boil 5-10 minutes. Add corn and heat to thicken, about 20 minutes. Pack in hot sterilized jars, seal while hot.
Makes 6-7 pints

Crunchy and tart

Squash Pickles

10 small squash, sliced thinly
2 medium onions, sliced thinly
4 green bell peppers, sliced
    thinly
¼ cup salt
Ice
3 cups sugar
2 cups vinegar
2 teaspoons mustard seed
2 teaspoons celery seed

In a large pot, layer squash, onions, and bell peppers and sprinkle with salt. Cover with ice and water and let sit for one hour. Pour off water. In a saucepan, mix sugar, vinegar, mustard seeds, and celery seeds and bring to a boil. Pour over squash and bring back to a boil for one minute. Pack in sterilized jars and seal while hot.
Makes 8-10 pints

Zorba's Greek Olives

Marinade:
½ cup vegetable oil
½ cup olive oil
3 Tablespoons fresh lemon juice
2 Tablespoons red wine vinegar
2 teaspoons dried oregano,
    crumbled
Salt
Freshly ground black pepper

1 pound pitted black olives*
1 pound pitted green olives

Combine all ingredients for marinade and pour over olives. Cover and refrigerate at least one day before serving. Serve on a platter with sliced fresh tomatoes, green onions, and Feta cheese.
*Either Kalamata or ripe black olives absorb this marinade well.

Lagniappé

Mayonnaise

1 egg
1 Tablespoon oil, olive or
   vegetable
1 teaspoon Dijon mustard
1 teaspoon salt
1 teaspoon lemon juice
1 teaspoon wine vinegar
1 cup vegetable oil
¼ teaspoon cayenne

Place the first six ingredients in bowl of food processor fitted with steel blade. Process for a few seconds. With the machine running, drizzle oil slowly through the feed tube and process until thick, approximately 30 seconds. Stir in cayenne.
Makes 1 cup

Hollandaise Sauce

4 egg yolks
2 Tablespoons lemon juice
½ teaspoon salt*
Dash hot pepper sauce
½ cup unsalted butter, melted
   and bubbling

In the food processor with the metal blade in place, or using a blender, add the egg yolks, lemon juice, salt, and hot pepper sauce. Process for 3 seconds. While still processing, pour in the bubbling melted butter. It is essential that the butter be bubbling or the sauce will not thicken. If more than one recipe is needed, make two recipes. DO NOT DOUBLE RECIPE.
*If using salted butter, omit salt from the recipe.
Makes about ¾ cup

Perfect every time.

Tartar Sauce

2 10-ounce jars sweet pickles,
   drained and finely chopped
1 quart Hellman's mayonnaise
½ cup sour cream
½-1 onion, grated
⅛ teaspoon garlic salt
⅛ teaspoon celery salt
⅛ teaspoon cayenne

Combine all ingredients. Store in jar and chill well. This is best made 24 hours before serving.
Makes about 1½ quarts

Barn Sauce Marinade

1 pint vinegar
1 cup tomato juice
1 cup ketchup
⅓ cup sugar
3 Tablespoons salt
3 Tablespoons dry mustard
2 Tablespoons cayenne
1 Tablespoon Liquid Smoke
⅛ teaspoon garlic powder

Combine all ingredients and bring to a boil. Allow to cool. Store in refrigerator.
Makes 4 cups

Especially good for marinating a turkey breast. Marinate turkey 24 hours, then cook uncovered, basting frequently with sauce. To serve, slice thinly and serve cold. This also is wonderful for a buffet. Serve with homemade mayonnaise and rolls.

Tangy Pork Sauce

⅓ cup chili sauce
⅔ cup hot ketchup
½ cup white wine vinegar
2 Tablespoons Worcestershire sauce
2 Tablespoons candied ginger
1 teaspoon garlic powder
Pinch of cayenne
1 Tablespoon sharp mustard
Juice of 1 lemon
½ teaspoon salt
½ stick butter, melted
1 cup maple syrup

Combine all ingredients and simmer over low heat for 15 minutes. Refrigerate.
Makes 3 cups

Exceptional with grilled pork tenderloin or ribs.

Vermouth Mushroom Sauce

1 stick butter
1 pound mushrooms, washed and stemmed
2 cloves garlic, crushed
¼ teaspoon salt
Few drops of lemon juice
2 Tablespoons vermouth

In a saucepan, sauté butter, mushrooms, garlic, and salt. When ready to serve, heat sauce and add lemon juice and vermouth. Simmer for 1-2 minutes maximum. Serve at once.
4 servings

Serve over beef tenderloin or veal. Easily doubles.

Lagniappé

Garden-Fresh Tomato Sauce

3 Tablespoons olive oil
3 cups tomatoes, peeled and
   puréed
¼ cup chopped Italian parsley
2 Tablespoons fresh basil*
6 cloves garlic, minced
¼ teaspoon salt
⅛ teaspoon black pepper

In a large skillet, heat oil over moderate heat. Add remaining ingredients and simmer for 15-20 minutes. Cover and keep warm. Freezes well.
*If fresh basil is not available, use 1 teaspoon dried basil.
Makes about 3 cups

Makes a lighter sauce when tomatoes are at the peak of the season.

Classic Tomato Sauce

2 teaspoons olive oil
½ green bell pepper, chopped
1 large onion, chopped
2 cloves garlic, minced
3 Tablespoons chopped parsley
1 16-ounce can whole tomatoes,
   drained
1 6-ounce can tomato paste
1 teaspoon dried oregano
1 teaspoon dried basil
2 teaspoons sugar
½ teaspoon salt
¼ teaspoon black pepper

In a Dutch oven heat oil. Add green pepper, onion, garlic, and parsley, and sauté until tender. Set aside. Purée tomatoes and tomato paste in food processor or blender until smooth. Add to sautéed vegetables. Crush, by hand, dried basil and oregano. Add crushed herbs, sugar, salt, and pepper to tomato sauce. Bring to boil, reduce heat, and simmer for 1 hour or until sauce is reduced to 3½ cups. Makes sauce for 2 large pizzas.

Lagniappé

"A Little Something Extra!"

Summer Pasta Brunch
Cheese Straws

Garden Party Pasta
Spicy Tomato Aspic
Party Bread Sticks

Old South Mint Sherbet
Ornamental Chocolate Leaves

Menu for 8

Sunday Supper For Old Friends
Vegetable Chowder
Country Club Salad
Bayou DeSiard Cheese Logs

Apricot Sherbet
Almond Butter Cookies

Menu for 6

Celebration Dinner
Brie with Green Peppercorn Mustard
and Bremmer Crackers*

Crab Bisque

Tenderloin Perfect
Wild Rice*
Zucchini Boats with Spinach
Classic French Bread*

Chocolate Mousse Cake

With the Tenderloin Perfect
French Bordeaux

With the Chocolate Mousse Cake
Moet et Chandon Brut Champagne

Menu for 8

Acknowledgements

The Junior League of Monroe gratefully acknowledges those who have generously supported the creation of **Celebrations on the Bayou.** Our pride in sharing North Louisiana in photographs, menus, and recipes can only be equalled by your celebrating Louisiana with us.

Marketing

We wish to extend a very special thank you to the members of the Marketing Committee for their dedication, time, and expertise in making the tremendous success of this book possible.

Anna Lynn Oliver . . . . Co-Chairman
Vicki Williams . . . . Co-Chairman
Louise Altick . . . . Sustaining Advisor
Sylvia Loftin . . . . Sustaining Advisor

Lila Loftin	Sharon Pankey
Colleen Johnson	Linda Sheehan
Sara Greene	Pam Stratton
Posey Moller	Mandy Fritzer
Becky Mintz	Kathy Van Veckhoven

Special Thanks

We express our appreciation to those who have supported **Celebrations on the Bayou** by providing valuable assistance and professional expertise.

C'est Si Bon
Scott Change
Les Petite Fleurs
Bruce Fine
The Flower Shoppe
Beverly Fontenot
Marta Franklin
Fresh Affair
Angie Hargiss
Jean Huenefeld
Judy C. Martin, Inc.
The Pillars
The Trenton House
Upper Crust
Lane Wilson

Celebrated Homes

We give special thanks to those who have graciously opened their homes and gardens and allowed us to experience true Southern hospitality in Cotton Country style.

Dr. and Mrs. Ralph Asbury
Boscobel Plantation
Bayou DeSiard Country Club
Dr. and Mrs. Leonard Bunch
Mr. and Mrs. Victor David Cascio
Mr. and Mrs. David Cattar
Dr. and Mrs. Frank Cline
Mr. and Mrs. Robert Cudd
ELsong Gardens
Mr. and Mrs. Barry Erwin
Dr. and Mrs. Louis Gavioli
Mrs. Suzanne Brunaxxi Grant
Mr. and Mrs. Joseph Haddad
Mr. and Mrs. Walter Hastings

Dr. and Mrs. John Hull
Mr. and Mrs. Bishop Johnston
Mr. and Mrs. Ivy Jordan
Mr. and Mrs. William B. Mattison, Jr.
Mr. and Mrs. Edward Lyle Miller
Mr. and Mrs. Saul Mintz
Mr. and Mrs. Travis Oliver, III
Mr. and Mrs. Robert Phillips
Dr. and Mrs. James Potts
Dr. and Mrs. Mike Sampognaro
Mr. and Mrs. Nat Troy
Mr. and Mrs. Billy Van Veckhoven
Dr. and Mrs. Robert Wood

Table and Floral Design

We owe our deepest gratitude to those who provided their valuable expertise and enhanced the beauty of our book with their artistic talents displayed through their table settings and floral designs.

Gabriella Armstrong
Danna Bradford
Marie Cascio
Victor David Cascio
Ann Cline
Barbara F. Corry
Mary Erwin
Agnes Griffin
Vee Hollis
Carolyn Hull
Debbie Husted
Keith Joiner
Jeannine Jordan
Nancy Frey Killgore
Joy Marshall
Libby Miller

Martha Reed Miller
Jean Mintz
Rebo Montgomery
Denise Moore
Catherine Mulhearn
Don Nixon
Mary Reed
Warren Ringham
Pam Sampognaro
Norma Sherman
Carol Shlosman
Margie Shlosman
Gail Thompson
Leila Turpin
Mary Ann Van Veckhoven
Nancy Williams
Camille Wood

Contributors and Testers

We thank our members, their families, and friends who contributed and tested party ideas, menus, and recipes. They have given generously of their time and talents to assure the quality and excellence of **Celebrations on the Bayou.** It is our sincere hope that no one has been inadvertently omitted.

Stephanie Abell
Frederick Adams
Dianne Adkins
Joyce Albritton
Irene Alexander
Margaret Alger
Gene Allen
Nancy Allen
Sandy Allen
Sherry Allen
Jim Altick
Louise Altick
Lana Ambrose
Cheryl Amman
Jeannine Amman
Martha Amman
Mary Annice Amman
Janet Anderson
Michelle Anderson
Kristen Anderson
Yvonne Anderson
Diana Anders
Libby Anders
Ana Anzelmo
Charles Anzelmo
Gabriella Armstrong
Maria Armstrong
Mark Armstrong
Ralph Armstrong
Gracie Arnold
Diane Aron
Tony Arpino
Priscilla Asbury
Ralph Asbury
Loretta Ashbrook
Karen Atkins
Loree Auttonberry
Thomas Ayer
Virginia Ayer
Nancy Bailes
Herbert Baker
Marion Baker
Margaret Balfour
Nancy Bancroft
Speed Bancroft
Beverly Doles Banks
Harrison Banks
Hutton Banks
Allen C. Barham
Jane Barham

Melba Pipes Barham
David Barker
Margaret Barker
Carolyn Barnes
Margaret Barnes
Janice Bunch Barraza
John Michael Barraza
Lionel Barraza
Mike Barraza
M'Elise Barraza
Jennifer Barr
Lula Bates
Deidre Baxter
Sarah Baxter
Tiny Bayne
Charles Bell
Judy Bell
Marjorie Benson
Nicholas Berry
Doll Biedenharn
Frederick Biedenharn
Kathy Biedenharn
Murray Biedenharn
Anne Birdsong
Ashley Birmingham
Dixie Bishop
Jennifer Blackbourn
Carolyn Bolton
Bruce Bond
Amy Bonin
Becky Bonin
Brenda Hamilton Bonin
Henry Bonin
Keith Bonin
Margaret Bordelon
Mari Bordelon
Sonny Bordelon
David Bowen
Cindy Boyce
Renee Boyce
Nan Boydstun
Charlotte Bradford
Damon Bradford
Danna Bradford
Michelle Bradford
Stacey Bradford
Barham Bratton
Pam Bratton
Caroline Brazeel
Ann Breard

Charlotte Breard
Danny Breard
Dot Breard
Graves Breard
Judy Breard
Ken Breard
Kent Breard, III
Kent Breard, Jr.
Kent Breard, Sr.
Lillian O. Breard
Susan Breard
Will Breard
Jeannie Breckenridge
Merle Brennen
Lance Bright
Sharon Bright
Laurie Brinkhaus
Bill Brockman
Jan Brockman
Marsha Brockman
Ralph Brockman
Francis Broussard
Buddy Brown
Charlene Brown
David Brown
Gwyn Brown
Michele Brown
Rebecca Brown
Robert Brown
Sharon Brown
Wendy Brown
Mike Broyles
Renee Broyles
Irene Bruce
Sharon Bryant
Peggy Buffington
Bobbie R. Buie
Gail Bunch
Holly Bunch
L.W. Bunch
Donna Bundrick
Larry Bundrick
Irma Burger
David Burkett
Sharon Burkett
Holly Burns
Alice Cabrey
Dianne K. Cage
Sally Cagle
Todd Cagle

Bryan Caldwell
Emily Caldwell
Ramona Caldwell
M.A. Calloway
Nell Calloway
Arden Campbell
George Campbell
Linda Campbell
Lisa Campbell
Mennon Campbell
Patrick Campbell
Richard Campbell
Gus Campbell
Ed Cannon
Jay Cannon
Lea Cannon
Leah Cannon
Mike Cappell
Paulette Cappell
Eleanor Caraway
Stone Caraway
Cindy Carmer
Jack Carmer
Jon Carmer
Marilyn Carmer
Marion Carmer
Annette Williams Carroll
Cindy Carroll
Don Carroll
Emma Jane Carroll
Lisa Carter
Pat Cascio
Erin Casey
Holly Casey
Sean Casey
Joe Caskey
Brent Casteel
Christopher Casteel
Kelly Casteel
Jordan Centola
Laura Centola
Lyle Centola
Ann Chandler
Sue Chastain
Michele Chastant
Naomi Chin
Betty Clack
Don Clack
Betty Earle Clark
Dean Clark
Hays Clark
Jason Clark
Peggy Clay
Ann Cline
Dana Cline
Frank X. Cline
Frank X. Cline, III

Jo Cline
Susan Coates
Tami Cobb
Adrienne Cole
Ann Cole
Eva Colvin
Melanie Colvin
Janie Conrad
Ken Conrad
Vicki Coody
Ann Cooksey
John Cooksey
Linda Cooper
Sally Corbin
Krista Corrent
Barbara F. Corry
Emily Stone Council
Frances Cox
Gary Cox
Brad Crain
Missy Crain
Collie Crank
Jim Crank
Brian Crawford
Cori Crawford
Dorothy Crawford
Kate Crawford
Susan Crawford
Trent Crawford
Sara Cromwell
Ann Crowe
Jan Crozier
Zoe Crumpler
Delphine Crump
Emily Csendes
Marlene Csendes
Leigh-Susan Cunningham
Terri Cunningham
Frances C. Curry
Kevin Curry
Cindy Dahnert
Ann Daigle
Jennifer Ann Daigle
Laura Elise Daigle
Martha Dampier
Dottie Daniel
Sally H. Daniel
Simie Daniel
Warren A. Daniel, Jr.
Lynda Davis Dansby
Linda Davidson
Sandy Davidson
Ann Davis
Claire Davis
Glenda Davis
Leesa Davis
Lester Davis

Tony Davis
Patsy Deal
Amanda Dean
Gerald Dean
Gretchen Dean
Denny DeCelle
Leah DeCelle
Malcolm DeCelle
Sandy DeCelle
Carolyn DeGennaro
Claus Denholm
Gabby Denholm
Charlottie Dent
Katherine Dent
Kathy Amman Dent
Thurman Dickey
Paul von Diezelski
Terese von Diezelski
Caroline Dixon
Jean Dixon
Joe H. Dixon, Jr.
Katherine Dixon
Kay Dixon
Jennifer Doles
John Doles
Thelma Doles
Brenda Domangue
Don Domangue
Peggy Downey
Delores Downing
Robert Downs
Tommy Driemeir
Sandra Dufrene
Kathy Duke
Mary Dukes
Paul Dunn
Fredrika Durham
Lauren Dwyer
Debbie Edgerton
Ed Edgerton
Bill Edmondson
Brian Edmondson
Ellen Edmondson
Judy Morrow Edmondson
Abigail Edwards
Karen Embanato
Emily Ensminger
Barbara Estis
Brett Estis
Dennis Estis
Ginger Estis
Pat Ethridge
Debbie Ewing
Jason Ewing
David Ezernack
Gretchen Ezernack
Jeanette Farrar

Betty Farr
Douglas Farr
James Farr
Robert Farr
Kristi Farr
Nell Faulk
Judy Fellows
Evelyn Ferguson
Jean Fields
Betsy Files
Marion Files
Janet Fisher
Jan Fishman
Jimmy Flanagan
Kathleen Flanagan
Linda Lavender Ford
Peggy Ford
Percy Ford
April Foster
Kathy Wroten Foster
Lisa Fowlkes
Jeffrey Fritzer
Mandy Giffen Fritzer
Betty Frey
Dick Fuchs
Janie Fuchs
Bob Fudickar
Jane Fudickar
Riley Fudickar
Terri Fudickar
Erin Furr
Jim Furr
Jo Furr
O'Neal Furr
Derak Futch
Judy Futch
Ellen Galligan
Susan Garrett
Elizabeth T. Garrison
Florence T. Garrison
Mitch Garsee
Gordan Gates
Ida Gavioli
Laura Gavioli
Lindsey Gavioli
Louis Gavioli
Lynda Gavioli
Opal Gavioli
Robbie Gavioli
Robert Gavioli
Cora Gay
Claudia Gebhardt
Beth Geist
Jared Geist
Jean George
Rachel George
Susan George

Pam Gibbs
Sharon Gibbs
Tommy Gibbs
Jean Giffen
Danny Gilbert
David Gilbert
Wilma Glaze
Brodie Glenn
Cameron Glenn
Kyle Glenn
Walter Glenn
Snookie Godwin
Sara Golson
Catherine Goodin
Tim Goodin
Betsy Goza
Rhonda Grafton
Cathy Grammer
Walter Grammer
Alicia Grant
Gail Grant
Suzanne Grant
Tommy Grant
Betty O. Gray
Adam Greene
Austin Greene
Jarrod Greene
Jordan Greene
Randy Greene
Sara M. Greene
Julie Green
Jane Greer
Joan Gregg
Fran Gregory
Linda Griffin
Ormond Guenard
Mary Guerriero
Gayle Guidry
Jason Guidry
Josh Guidry
Mike Guidry
Ben Gulick
Frances Guthrie
Roz Haas
Dot Haddad
Joey Haddad
Judy Haddad
Lisa Haddad
Robin Hadden
Janet Haedicke
Stephen Haedicke
Betty Halley
Genie B. Hallmark
Cathy Hall
Randy Hall
Doyle Hamilton
Jean Hamilton

Wanda Hamilton
Marilyn Hammett
Ron Hammett
Adam Hanks
Carol Hanks
Jamie Hanks
Lisa Hanna
Ann Hargrove
Bob Hargrove
Linda Hargrove
Barbara Harkey
Melanie Harkins
Mamie Harrington
Renie Harrison
Rosemary Harrison
Ann Hart
Bob Hart
Cory Hart
Dean Hart
Dean Hart, Sr.
Dottie Hart
Linda Hart
Mike Hart
Michelle Harvey
Margaret Hastings
Sheila Hatten
Andrew Hayes
Karen Hayes
Mary Edith Hayes
Mary Helen Hayes
Al Hayward
Alex Hayward
Amanda Hayward
Sarah Hayward
Nancy Hearne
Holly Hearn
Amy Herlevic
Lisa Herlevic
Ricky Herlevic
Anna Herrington
Brittany Herrington
Frankie Herrington
Karen Herrington
Frank Hewitt
James Hewitt
Jimmy Hewitt
Kathy Hewitt
Ruby Nell Higgins
Denise Hill
Pat Hill
Stephen Hill
Lucille Hinkle
Sue Hinkle
Lynn Keller Hodge
Susan Hoffman
Bobbie Hogan
Cathy Hogan

Earl Hogan
Lisa Holland
Betty Holley
Harper Hollis
Marshall Hollis
Tom Hollis
Vee Hollis
John Holmes
Peggy Clay Holmes
Karol Files Hood
Keith Hopkins
Lloydelle Hopkins
Chris Horne
Bess Howell
Shelli Huffman
Carolyn Hull
Edmund Hull
John Hull
Rachel Hull
Joe Humble
Sylvia Humble
Lisa Hummel
Elise Hunt
Ed Hurley
Gayle Hurley
Peter Hurley
Stuart Hurley
Martha Stone Husmann
Billy Husted
Debbie Hamilton Husted
Holly Husted
Lindsey Husted
Carrick Inabnett
Nancy Inabnett
Hugh Inabnet
Pam Inabnet
Sharon Ingram
Marily Irby
Cathy Ivanov
Karen Jackson
Myrtis Jackson
Susan Jackson
Lee Jacks
Susan Jacks
Tim Jacks
Betty Jean James
Beverly James
Carroll James
Marie James
Beverly Jarrell
Dana Jefferson
Gretchen Jefferson
Dave Jeffrey
David Jeffrey
Martha Jeffrey
Kaye Jennings
Melissa Jennings

Wayne Jennings
Pamela Johananoff
Ann Johnson
Anna Johnson
Caroline Flannery Johnson
Carolyn Johnson
Charles A. Johnson
Charles T. Johnson
Colleen Cline Johnson
Conner Johnson
Dot Johnson
Ellen Johnson
Jason Johnson
Jason M. Johnson
Jessica Johnson
Lisa R. Johnson
Marsha Johnson
Matt Johnson
Mattie Johnson
Dix Johnston
Jan Johnston
Mary Ann Johnston
Clarice Johns
Denise Johns
Dorothy John
Sandra John
Ben Jones
Bobbie Jones
Connie Jones
Floyd Jones
Jane Jones
Marianne S. Jones
Mary Jones
Sara Jones
Susan Jones
Kaye Jordan
Gay Joyce
Nancy Joyner
Brit Katz
Kay Kellogg Katz
Ben S. Katz
Hope Keith
Betty Kelley
Sarah Kelley
Flo Kelly
Roy Kelly
Katie Kennedy
Janet Kicker
Thelma Kifer
Carol Kight
Kate Kincannon
Joan Sugar King
Margaret Ann King
Reggie Kitchens
Mildred Kitches
Marilyn Koepke
Paul Koepke

Elieen Kontrovitz
Mervin Kontrovitz
Hans J. Korridi
Bill Krutzer
Vicki Krutzer
Dottie Kulcke
Max Kulcke
Delores Kvaternik
Linsey Kvaternik
Leigh Ann La Borde
Sue La Borde
Dean Ladner
Alex Landrum
Allyson Landrum
Jim Landrum
Lindsey Landrum
Eleanor Larsen
Pat Lary
Bibb Latch
Judy Laudenheimer
Pam Laudenheimer
Sophie Laudenheimer
Margaret Lauve
Bobby Lawrence
Lisa Lawrence
Blake LeBlanc
Brad LeBlanc
Carol LeBlanc
Ron LeBlanc
Dee Ledbetter
John Ledbetter
Mac Ledbetter
Ann Ledoux
Kaye Lee
Ola Lee
Lauren Magdalen Lefebvre
Richard Lefebvre
Richard Lefebvre, Jr.
Sybil Lefebvre
Cynthia Leidy
Gail Lencicien
Kathy Leonard
Ramona Leon
Eric Lewis
Marilyn Lewis
Sally Liebetrau
Arthur Liles
Chi Chi Liles
Melanie Liles
Dinky Liner
Harry Liner
Kitty Liner
David Linzay
Natalie Lipscomb
Rita Lockett
Ann Lockhart
Billy Lockhart

Mary Alyce Loflin
Lila Loftin
Kathy Lofton
Cheryl Lolley
Abby Love
Carrie Love
Dickie Love
Kim Love
Susan Lowery
Debbie Luffey
John Luffey, Jr.
Lillian Luffey
Monte Luffey
Rosemary Luffey
Sue Hayes Lyon
Betty Mabray
Gayle Madison
Stuart Madison
Bonnie Mahaffey
Keith Majure
Cynthia Malone
Joe Malta
Vickie Manchester
Georgia Manning
Judy Manning
Melinda Manning
Woody Manning
Jean Newsome Maran
Beverly Mardis
Heather Maris
Ben Marhsall
Joy Marshall
Lois Martinez
Roy Martinez
Allan Martin
April Martin
Barbara Martin
Catherine Martin
Diane Martin
Hap Martin
Susan Marx
Dorothy Mason
Thelma Mason
Theresa Massey
Janet Masur
Kindra Mathieu
Pam Mathieu
Billy Mattison
Jo Mattison
Kristen McCaskill
Todd McCaskill
Lavaun McClain
Lauren McClain
Donna McClure
Debbie McClure
Donnie McClure
Rita McClure

John McCoy
Joy McCue
Barbara McDonald
Kay McDonald
Suzy McDowell
Annette McEnery
Lynda McGeehee
Marsha McGee
Carolyn McGough
Mildred McGowen
Helen McInnis
Sandy McKellar
Sue McKenzie
Beverly McKinney
Toddy McKinney
Gerald McLendon
Irene McLendon
Leesa McMillin
Greg McMullen
Pat McNaughten
Roy McNaughten
Jeannete Mehl
Peggy Meredith
Claudia Merrill
Grady Merriman
Mae Merriman
Pat Merriman
Matthew Mickel
Rudi Miksa
Susan Stone Miksa
Agnes C. Miller
Jan Miller
Libby Miller
Lyle Miller
Pam Miller
Patty Miller
Polly Milner
Sheila Milner
Andy Mintz
Becky Mintz
Brucie Mintz
Ellen Mintz
Melinda Mintz
Morris Mintz
Anita Mitchell
Dennis Mitchell
Ashley E. Moller
Daniel W. Moller
Posey D. Moller
Eugene Montgomery
Julie Montgomery
Kim Montgomery
Vada Montgomery
Betty Moore
Billie Sue Moore
Jane Moore
Janet Moore

Lamar Moore
Lynn Moore
Milton Moore
Robert Moore
Tonya Moore
Anne Morimonp
Dick Morrison
Margaret Morrison
Rita Morrison
Alice Morris
Ann Morris
Jay Morris
Jenny Downey Morris
Jean Moses
Susan Mott
Carol Mouk
Marnie Mouk
Burns Mulhearn
Catherine Mulhearn
Tommy Mulhearn
Joan Mullens
Beth Murphy
Gladys Murphy
Jean Myatt
Erma Myers
Lynn Nash
Lolly Neel
David Nelson
Jan Nelson
Lauchlan Nelson
Linda Nelson
Marie Nelson
Shelia Netherland
Barbara Newman
Geneva Newton
Gladys Newton
Gloria Newton
Mike Nolan
Amy B. Norris
Debbie Norris
Hillary Norris
James Norris
Janet Norris
Jim Norris
Joy Norris
Stephanie Norris
Steve Norris
Damian Ogg
Daniel Ogg
Anna Lynn Corrent Oliver
Blake Oliver
Jane Oliver
Karen Oliver
Mac Oliver
McVea Oliver, Jr.
Robert Oliver
Ben B. Orlando

John Orlando
Josie Orlando
Pat Orlando
Patti Orlando
Amy Ormes
Duane Ormes
Libby Ormes
Liz Ormes
Joni Osbon
Charlotte Owens
Stephanie Owens
Ann Padgett
Meg Page
Sharon Pankey
Ann Pardue
Carol Layton Parsons
George Pate
Maggie Pate
Meredith Pate
Nina Pate
Marion Patrick
Currie Patterson
Sally Patterson
Anne Patton
Jackie Peacock
Jane Pearce
Alarie Peeples
Mary Beth Pendly
Fran Perrer
Amy Perry
Carolyn Williams Perry
Cyndy Rivers Perry
Harvey Perry
Jamie F. Perry
John W. Perry, Jr.
Jonathan Perry
J.W. Perry
J.W. Perry, III
Kimberly Perry
Mary Frances Perry
Mary Kathryn Perry
Parnell Perry
Dawn Pesnell
Diane Peterson
Dollie Smith Petrus
Jamie Pettway
Harry H. Petty
Polly Petty
Gladney Peyton
Cathy Cook Phillips
Charles Fox Phillips
Cole Phillips
Jan Phillips
Joshua Phillips
Judith Fox Phillips
Linda Phillips
Steve Phillips

Todd Phillips
Ann Pipes
Ethel Pistorius
Elizabeth Poetker
Elsa Poetker
Joe Poetker
Cathy Pohl
Susan Poholsky
Amy Ponder
Billie Pool
Georgie Porter
Les Potter
Marilyn Potter
Georgiann Potts
Jim Potts
Marsha Powell
Martha Powell
Ron Powell
Ronna Powell
Ruth Powell
Ryan Powell
Bill Pratt
Lamar Price
Margaret Price
Lee Rainer
Barry Ramsey
Deborah Ramsey
Dot Ramsey
Jonathan Ramsey
Lauren Ramsey
Madura Rangaraj
Uma Rangaraj
Curtis Rape
Kathy Rasco
Richard Rawler
John Paul Rawson
David Raymond
Deborah Raymond
Sarah Raymond
Sheldon Ray
Selene Rea
Agnes Reighney
Merlin Reisir
Vee Reisir
Carolyn Rester
Kelley Reynolds
Suzanne Rice
Stephanie Richards
Kenneth Rich
Susan Riggin
Carolyn Riggius
LaDoris Riley
Terri Riser
Chelle Rivers
Lynn Rivers
Fee Roberts
Joe Roberts

Kevin Roberts
Lane Roberts
Rachel Roberts
Rebecca Roberts
Susan Roberts
Drake Robertson
Frederick Robinson
Janie Robinson
Jennifer Robinson
Linda Robinson
Susan Robinson
Vickie Robinson
Chris Roche
Ellen Roche
Erin Roche
Eva Roche
Ken Roche
Kenneth Roche
Trey Roche
Jimmy Rogers
Mollie Rogers
Rose Romeo
Dorothy Rorex
Bill Rose
Jo Margaret Rose
Ahsley Roth
Chip Roth
Chris Roth
Connie Roth
Elizabeth Roth
Matthew Roth
Edie Rusnak
Marge Rusnak
Steve Rusnak
Vince Rusnak
Bryan Russell
Erin Russell
Kate Russell
Lea Russell
Paula Russell
Mike Ryan
Pete Sadler
Laura Sain
June Saloman
Ed Salisbury
Nan Salisbury
Mae Salsbury
Robin Salsbury
Pam Sampognaro
Ann Sanders
Mack Sanders
Verna Sanders
Don Sandifer
Tony Sandifer
Van Sandifer
Bert Sandoval
Daniel Sartor, III

Daniel Sartor, Jr.
Georgie Sartor
Jane Sartor
Nancy Sartor
Tommy Sue Sartor
Bill Sawyer
Bradley Sawyer
Brenda Sawyer
Debbie Sawyer
Mike Sawyer
Robert Sawyer
Mary Scalia
Connie Scheanette
Kathy Schendle
Susan Schendle
Mathilde Schochet
Dorothy Schween
Jennifer Schween
John Schween
Laurie Schween
Stephen Schween
Sharon Scioneux
Margo Scott
Erin Scurria
Lillie Seay
Bob Seegers
Katie Seegers
Lee Seegers
Nell Seegers
Billie Shaw
Sherman Shaw
Vylnda Shaw
John Sheehan
J.J. Sheehan
Katie Sheehan
Linda M. Sheehan
Meg Sheehan
Tim Sheehan
Claire Shelby
Emily Seegers Shelby
Kaki Shelton
Gayle Shepard
George Shepard
John Shepard
Saundra Shepard
Sylvia Shepard
Amy Sherman
Norma Sherman
Rahn Sherman
Carol Shlosman
Harrison Shows
Heather Shows
Lauren Shows
Nelwyn Shows
Nancy Shutt
Tom Shutt
Johnny Sievers

Karen Sikes
Dustin Simeon
Josh Simpkins
George Singleton
Jessica Sinitiere
Shelly Slack
Bo Smith
Carol Smith
Cindy Smith
Curtis Smith
D.N. "Woodie" Smith
Flora Smith
Jessie Smith
Kay Smith
Lynn Smith
Marilyn Smith
Pete Smith
Preston Smith
Ruth Smith
Thelma Gunter Smith
Frank Snellings
George M. Snellings, III
Marie Louise Snellings
Mary Snellings
Susan Sparks
Bob Spatafora
Doris Spatafora
Leah Spatafora
Lisa Spatafora
Sarah Spatafora
Jean Speed
Doug Steed
Lynda Steed
Delores Stegall
Anna Beth Stephens
Susan Stephens
Henry Stevenson
Jimmy Stevenson
Martha Stevenson
Nell Stevenson
Paula Waggoner Stidham
Dean Stockstill
Debbie Stockstill
Betty Bass Stone
Kim Stone
Pam Stratton
Georgia Street
Mike Street
Bill Stubbs
Doris Suidy
Carroll Swander
Linda Swor
Dana Smith Taliaferro
Van Taliaferro
Barbara Tarver
Earl Lester Tarver
Josh Tarver

Justin Tarver
Susan Tarver
Jay Taylor
Jim Taylor
Marilyn Taylor
Sharon Taylor
Frances Terry
Janice Terry
Kay Terry
Lelia Terry
Ed Theus
Mary Theus
Brenda Thompson
Gail Thompson
Levins Thompson
Vera Thorn
Gayle Tinsley
George Tonore
Georgie Touchstone
Hugh Touchstone
Barbara Trascher
Carolyn Boyce Traweek
Kathy Traweek
Steen Trawick
Jennifer Trinca
Barbara Ann Tripi
Philip Tripi
Rosalie Tucker
Allison Tugwell
Carlean Tugwell
Abby Tullos
Anna Ruth Turner
Michelle Turner
Caroline Turpin
Jeff Turpin
Judy Turpin
Leila Turpin
Amy Twitchell
Annamarie Tyler
Dale Tyler
Steve Tyler
Lynn Tynes
Maxine Tyson
Gay Ulrich
Mark Ulrich
Ruth Ulrich
Martha Jane Upshaw
Kathy Van Veckhoven
Mary Ann Van Veckhoven
Damian Vanderpool
Lee Vanderpool
Mildred Vanderpool
Jennifer Vanderyst
Teddy Varino
Barbara Venable
Ruth Vogel
Melanie Vogt

Babs Voorhees
Jackie Voorhees
Burton Wade
Burton Wade, III
Burton Wade, Jr.
Josephine Wade
Kate Wade
Nancy Wade
Jere Waggoner
Beverly Wagoner
Chris Walker
Damon Walker
Daniel Walker
Eric Walker
Jennifer Walker
Linda Walter
Mike Walker
Myka Walker
Paula Walker
Bunny Wallace
David Waller
Marilyn M. Waller
Michael Waller
Wendy Waller
Amy Wallis
Katie Walsh
Kay Walsh
Stacey Walsh
Bill Warner
Cynthia Warner
Joshua Warner
Kate Warner
Virginia Warner
Barbara Watson

Kathy Weaner
Debbie Wear
Mac Wear
Bob Webb
Claire Webb
Davis Webb
Mike Webb
Nancy Webb
Robert Webb, Jr.
Mary Webster
Corrine Weems
Curtis Weems
Marilyn Weems
Donnie Weil
Louis Weil
Carlin Weirick
Elizabeth Wells
Kathy Wells
Richard Wells
Michelle Westney
Sharon West
Shirlane West
Debbie Miller Westbrook
Anice Wheeler
Joe Wheeler
Susan Wheeler
Clyde White
Pat White
Penny White
Robert White
Allison Wilkes
Herndon Wilkins
Bobbie Williamson
Barbara Williams

Clarke M. Williams, Sr.
Clarke M. Williams, Jr.
Dot Williams
Evelyn Williams
Judy Williams
Mary Kathryn Williams
Melba Williams
Molly Williams
Ruth Williams
Sam Williams
Trey Williams
Vicki Williams
Ann Wilson
Elizabeth Wilton
Madeline Windsor
Pat Wolff
Dodee Womach
Claudia Woods
Debbie Woods
Pat Woods
Wayne Woods
Pam Wood
Jo Ann Worley
Joe Worley
Judy Worthen
Jean Wyatt
Kathy Wyatt
Miriam Wyatt
Ginny Yatco
Rey Yatco
Cy Young
Norma Lee Young
Jean Zentner
Marion Zentner
Addie Zimmerman

Notes

Index

Index

Index

Index

Index

The Junior League of Monroe, Inc.
THANKS YOU FOR BUYING
CELEBRATIONS ON THE BAYOU
and
THE COTTON COUNTRY COLLECTION

Cotton/Bayou Publications
P. O. Box 7138
Monroe, Louisiana 71211-7138
(318) 322-3863

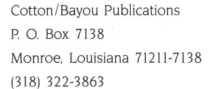 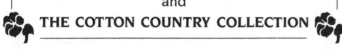

CELEBRATIONS _____ copies $19.95 each _____   Name _____

COTTON COUNTRY_____   14.95 each _____   Address _____

Louisiana residents add 4% tax   _____   City _____

Add shipping and handling   2.50 each _____   State _____ Zip _____

Add gift wrap   1.00 each _____   Telephone _____

                                TOTAL _____

Make check payable to: Gift from _____

_____Cotton/Bayou Publications or   Mail gift to _____

Please charge to: _____Master Card _____Visa   Address _____

Card Number_____   City _____

Expiration Date _____   State _____ Zip _____

Proceeds from the sales of these cookbooks are used to support the many community projects of the Junior Leage of Monroe, Inc.

The Junior League of Monroe, Inc.
THANKS YOU FOR BUYING
CELEBRATIONS ON THE BAYOU
and
THE COTTON COUNTRY COLLECTION

Cotton/Bayou Publications
P. O. Box 7138
Monroe, Louisiana 71211-7138
(318) 322-3863

CELEBRATIONS _____ copies $19.95 each _____   Name _____

COTTON COUNTRY_____   14.95 each _____   Address _____

Louisiana residents add 4% tax   _____   City _____

Add shipping and handling   2.50 each _____   State _____ Zip _____

Add gift wrap   1.00 each _____   Telephone _____

                                TOTAL _____

Make check payable to: Gift from _____

_____Cotton/Bayou Publications or   Mail gift to _____

Please charge to: _____Master Card _____Visa   Address _____

Card Number_____   City _____

Expiration Date _____   State _____ Zip _____

Proceeds from the sales of these cookbooks are used to support the many community projects of the Junior Leage of Monroe, Inc.